The

HUDSON MOHAWK GATEWAY

With contributions from Lois M. Feister, Diana S. Waite, and
Robert G. Waite

Photo Research by Peter Shaver
"Partners in Progress" by Jane Bennett Smart and Tom McGuire

Produced in cooperation with the Hudson-Mohawk
Industrial Gateway

Windsor Publications, Inc.
Northridge, California

The
HUDSON MOHAWK GATEWAY

An Illustrated History • By Thomas Phelan

TROY • WATERFORD • COHOES • GREEN ISLAND • WATERVLIET

Windsor Publications, Inc.
History Books Division

Publisher: John M. Phillips
Editorial Director: Teri Davis Greenberg
Design Director: Alex D'Anca

Staff for *The Hudson-Mohawk Gateway: An Illustrated History*
Senior Editor: Lynn Kronzek
Photo Editor: Nancy Evans
Assistant Editor: Gail Koffman
Text Editor: Marlene Zweig
Director, Corporate Biographies: Karen Story
Assistant Director, Corporate Biographies: Phyllis Gray
Editor, Corporate Biographies: Judith Hunter
Editorial Assistants: Kathy Brown, Patricia Cobb, Jerry Mosher, Lonnie Pham, Pat
Pittman, Deena Tucker
Designer: Chris McKibbin

First Edition

Library of Congress Cataloging in Publication Data:

Phelan, Thomas, 1925-
    The Hudson-Mohawk Gateway.

"Produced in cooperation with the Hudson-Mohawk Industrial Gateway."
    Bibliography: p. 188
    Includes index.
    1. Hudson River Valley (N.Y. and N.J.) — History, Local. 2. Hudson River Valley (N.Y.
and N.J.) — Description and travel. 3. Hudson River Valley (N.Y. and N.J.) — Industries. 4.
Mohawk River Valley (N.Y.) — History, Local. 5. Mohawk River Valley (N.Y.) — Descrip-
tion and travel. 6. Mohawk River Valley (N.Y.) — Industries. I. Feister, Lois M. II. Hudson-
Mohawk Industrial Gateway, inc. III. Title.
F127.H8P55   1985   974.7'3   85-9340
ISBN 0-89781-118-6

CONTENTS

PREFACE

A short distance below the confluence of the Mohawk with the Hudson River is the first dam on the Hudson, marking the headwater of navigation on this great waterway. Nearby, along both banks of the river, a harmonious grouping of communities developed toward the end of the eighteenth and into the nineteenth centuries. Troy occupies some seven miles of the east bank of the Hudson in this area. Opposite, dotting the west bank from north to south and bordered by the various fingers of the Mohawk's mouth, are the municipalities of Waterford village and town, Cohoes, Green Island, and Watervliet.

The themes of commerce and industry, labor and management, business and services prevail here. More recently, the establishment of this Gateway area as New York State's first Urban Cultural Park—*Riverspark*—has woven these adjacent communities of the Upper Hudson into a natural grouping, though each has maintained its political separateness, integrity, and special character. The region works together in spite of boundaries reinforced by location in three different counties. Thus, it seemed wise to advance these five cities' common cause by preparing a single local history which would focus to a considerable extent on the theme that draws them together: their industrial heritage.

The principal author has been fortunate in enlisting the cooperative service of three persons better equipped to write three of the ten chapters of this area history. Lois M. Feister, author of the first chapter, is a scientist working in the Archaeology section of the Historic Sites Bureau for New York's Office of Parks, Recreation and Historic Preservation. The sixth chapter is the work of Troy native Professor Robert G. Waite of Idaho State University's Department of History. Diana S. Waite is an early collaborator and author of the eighth chapter; she is currently the Executive Director of the Preservation League of New York State, and the author of several publications on architectural history. Research material was put together by Caroline A. King; Kathryn A. Larsen saved the principal author from his own hand by perfectly translating his abysmal handwriting onto a word processor. Great gratitude to all. Gratitude, too, to F. Jill Charboneau and Lynn C. Kronzek of Windsor Publications, editors in succession, for their patience, good advice, and editorial services. What you read here is a much shortened version of what was written. Hopefully, it is accurate and will serve the Gateway area well.

Thomas Phelan
Troy, New York
April, 1985

The Cohoes Falls on the Mohawk River, slightly idealized by the engraver, encumbered travelers in the seventeenth and eighteenth centuries but was an early tourist attraction nonetheless. Courtesy, New York State Library

*To my father who loved Troy
and taught me to see what
is here and to my mother
from whom I inherited the
discerning eyes*

Prehistoric caribou were hunted by the first inhabitants of New York State, known as Paleo-Indians, using spears with chipped stone projectile points. Courtesy, New York State Museum/The State Education Department

CHAPTER ONE

IN THE BEGINNING

W hen Henry Hudson sailed into the Hudson-Mohawk Gateway in 1609, he was greeted by people whose arrival predated his by many thousands of years. The native Americans who boarded his ship, the *Half Moon,* were probably Mahicans, members of the Algonkian-speaking family of Indians. The Iroquoian speakers, a separate linguistic group, dwelled in the woodlands farther west up the Mohawk River, with settlements reaching into northern and western New York. In 1609 all of the Gateway's native Indian tribes shared a common way of life at a time characterized by archaeologists as the Late Woodland period— about A.D. 1000 to 1600. They were agriculturists, living in villages, with intricate trading networks stretching far beyond the boundaries of the Hudson-Mohawk region.

The prehistoric Indians left no written records. Only by analyzing artifacts left buried in the earth have archaeologists discovered how the Indian cultures grew and developed in the Gateway area. Even to this day the story remains incomplete. However, recent excavations, along with scholarly research, have resulted in the reconstruction of a useful, though somewhat fragmented, history.

The first inhabitants of the Hudson and Mohawk valleys were Paleo-Indians. They probably arrived around 10,500 B.C., after the retreat of the last glacial ice sheet. Characterized as big game hunters, these Indians followed herds of large animals, such as caribou, and also foraged food from the land. Moving in small bands through vast conifer forests and grassy meadowlands, the Paleo-Indians kept this nomadic way of life until approximately 8000 B.C. Their chipped stone tools have been discovered in the immediate Gateway region.

Few people seem to have occupied the upper Hudson valley from roughly 8000 B.C. to 5000 B.C. During this interlude, known as the Early Archaic period, coniferous forests dominated the area. The environment, according to some prehistorians, did not support plants and animals needed by man, thus the sparse human population. By

5000 B.C., deciduous forests had grown and Indians, following the game, returned. Called "specialists in diversification," they were also gatherers who lived a semi-nomadic lifestyle. They traveled in small bands, setting up fishing stations near the rivers and establishing hunting base camps on the long, low terraces above the alluvial flats so characteristic of the upper Hudson valley.

In the upper Hudson region, archaeologists in recent years have found the remains of small Archaic Indian campsites, mostly dating from after 3000 B.C. The Thompson Collection, acquired by the State Museum in 1914, displays thousands of chipped stone tools from the Archaic period gathered principally from the areas around Lansingburgh, Waterford, and Green Island.

By about A.D. 1000, the Indians were living in semi-permanent villages. They continued to hunt and gather, but also began cultivating crops such as corn, squash, and beans. Agriculture made them a more sedentary group. Woodland sites have been discovered in the upper Hudson area as well. The first Early Woodland site to be unearthed in eastern New York State was recently discovered just south of Watervliet. Three early horticultural

Above: In 1609 English navigator Henry Hudson, sailing on behalf of the Dutch East India Company in his ninety-ton yacht, Half Moon, *traveled 160 miles up the river that now bears his name. From* The Empire State, *by Lossing*

Right: The bones of an Ice Age mastodon were discovered while excavating for an addition to Harmony Mills in 1866. This photograph recorded the important find and eventually the animal was reconstructed at the New York State Museum. Courtesy, Rensselaer County Historical Society

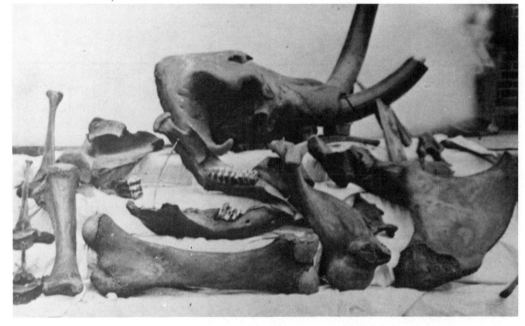

sites in Waterford have also been uncovered since 1976.

Over thousands of years, the early inhabitants of the Gateway region enjoyed the Hudson valley's many advantages. Living at the confluence of two great rivers—the Hudson and the Mohawk—afforded numerous benefits. The area had much the same appeal, in fact, for the Indians as for Europeans who arrived in the early seventeenth century.

Like the aboriginal tribes before them, Europeans soon discovered that the Hudson-Mohawk region held a unique position as a gateway for travel both north to south and east to west. However, from the earliest time, natural barriers blocked the free flow of river traffic. The rifts, or rapids, two miles north of Waterford impeded north to south travel by boat. And the Cohoes Falls obstructed east to west passage. Because travel in these directions was essential for trade and commerce, the Hudson-Mohawk Gateway was where traffic paused. Here men unloaded batteaux and canoes and piled their produce on wagons or on backs to be taken north to Stillwater or west around Cohoes Falls. Once past these barriers, the boats returned to the water.

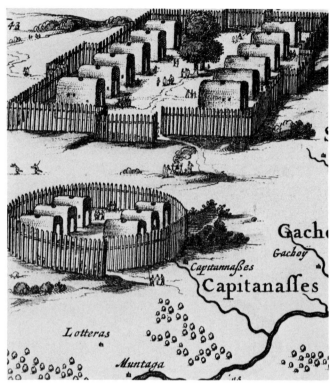

Above: This detail of a mid-seventeenth-century Dutch map of the Northeast shows what a Mahican Indian village may have looked like. Courtesy, New York State Library

Left: Both mammoth and mastodon were once present in New York State. Courtesy, New York State Museum/The State Education Department

Above: This hearth, from the Woodland stage of Indian occupation, was discovered at the Mechanicville Road site in 1979. Much evidence of prehistoric inhabitation of the Gateway area has been destroyed by over 300 years of development along the riverbanks where many of the Indian encampments and villages were located. Courtesy, Hartgen Archeological Associates

Right: Projectile points unearthed at the Mechanicville Road site in Waterford date from the Late Archaic to the Middle Woodland eras. Courtesy, Hartgen Archeological Associates

Henry Hudson's visit opened the Gateway region to Dutch traders. Establishing their early posts in the Albany area, these European entrepreneurs encouraged the Indians to come to them, which caused territorial disputes among local tribes. The Mahicans, with villages located largely on the east side of the Hudson, were historic rivals of the Mohawks, the nearest tribe of Iroquoian speakers to the west. The Dutch traders soon learned to stay clear of inter-tribal battles, and the Mohawks, with their far-reaching networks to the west and north, eventually took over the fur trade. However the Mahicans remained a local influence in trade and warfare well into the eighteenth century.

Before 1629, when the Dutch established a colonization plan for their New World territories, the Hudson-Mohawk Gateway was a busy area for trade. Beginning in 1630, the new Dutch landowner, or patroon, Kiliaen Van Rensselaer, had his agents purchase large tracts of land from the Indians. A map prepared about 1632 for the patroon demonstrated his claim over territory that stretched south from a Mahican village on Peebles Island to Beeren Island, south of Albany. This was land Van Rensselaer's agents thought most promising for settlement. That the patroon himself had little idea of the vastness of his new

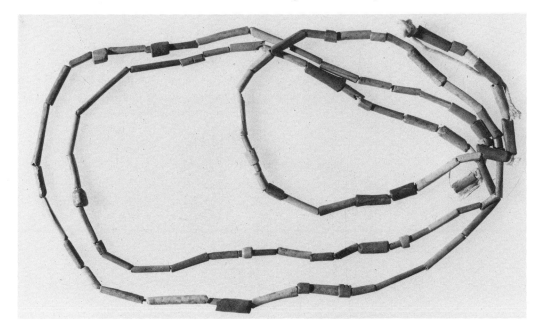

These bone beads (left) and glass and copper beads (below) were traded by the Indians and Dutch. From Prehistoric Archeology, *by Phil Lord, Jr., 1979. Courtesy, New York State Museum/The State Education Department*

holdings is shown by his July 20, 1632 request that someone pace off the area from Peebles Island to Cohoes Falls and south to Watervliet. However, he readily expressed his faith in the area's potential, writing, "the territory of the Mahicans ... has altogether over 1,200 morgens of cleared land ... being not only fat, clayey soil of itself, but yearly enriched by the overflow of high water. ..."

Lubbert Gijsbertsz, a 1634 arrival, may have been one of Troy's original European settlers, since the early name of the Troy area was Lubbertsland. However the first recorded European pioneer in the Hudson-Mohawk Gateway was a carpenter named Thomas Chambers. In 1646 Chambers entered into a five-year agreement with Van Rensselaer to lease land along the river between the Wynantskill and the Poestenkill, part of what is now South Troy. The lease also gave him first preference for constructing a mill on the land. Chambers left his farm in 1654 to become a prominent citizen in the Kingston area. His valuable land was then taken over by mill operator Jan Barentz Wemp.

By 1651 the patroon Van Rensselaer had purchased the Wynantskill area from the Indians and tried to build a mill there. He apparently succeeded by 1656, when waterpower on the creek was leased. Two years later Wynant Gerritse van der Poel entered into a partnership, and for thirty years operated a mill on the Wynantskill, which still bears his name.

At this time of early settlement and growing industry in the Troy area, an unusual visit by a sea creature made every Rensselaerswyck resident acutely aware of the rest of the Gateway region. After an especially severe spring flood, a whale somehow found its way up the Hudson and was grounded on an island near Cohoes Falls. This island, thus called Whale Island since 1646, became a hub of great excitement and curiosity. Despite the settlers' best efforts to boil out huge quantities of whale oil, the river was slick for three weeks. An observer described the incident: "As the fish lay rotting, the air was infected with its stench ... perceptible for two miles to leeward."

By the 1660s Van Rensselaer had leased most of the Gateway region to arriving settlers. Since every farmer was also a trader, attempts to intercept the routes to Albany provided ongoing drama and intrigue until the 1730s when Albany lost its legal monopoly on the fur trade. While acquiring title to the property from the patroon, however, the new occupants still had to satisfy the claims of the resident Indians.

In 1664 two well-known citizens joined forces in an ef-

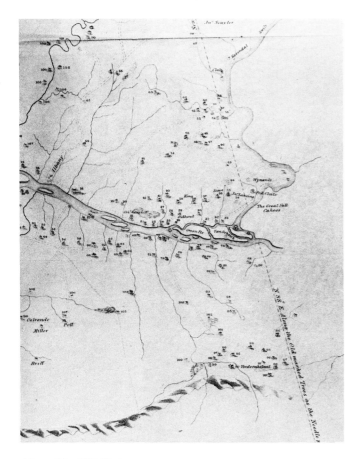

Above: The 1767 Bleeker map identified property owners and Van Rensselaer tenant farmers along the Hudson and Mohawk rivers. Van Schaick and Green Island still retain a similar configuration to what was shown. Courtesy, New York State Library

Facing page: Among the items traded between the Indians and Dutch in the seventeenth century were (from top to bottom) an Iroquois clay pipe, a Dutch pipe, a stone celt (axe), and an iron axe. From Prehistoric Archeology, *by Phil Lord, Jr., 1979. Courtesy, New York State Museum/The State Education Department*

fort to gain control of the Half Moon tract. Philip Pietersen Schuyler and Goosen Gerritsz Van Schaick purchased the area from Van Rensselaer, including two islands at the mouth of the Mohawk. In 1674 Schuyler deeded his portion to Van Schaick. But then in 1676 Schuyler purchased Green Island from the Indians. The original deed states that a nearby island was already sown with winter wheat; cultivation had begun even before the sale was completed. Meanwhile settlers were also coming to Troy. A 1663 account of an Indian scare mentions eighteen families there.

As early as 1660 patroon Van Rensselaer contemplated establishing a village at present-day Watervliet, then called the Stone Hook. Instead he leased the land to Bastiaen de Winter, who then set up a farm. After De Winter's death in 1678, Schuyler purchased the property to add to his own farm.

The patroon evidently maintained control of the Cohoes area until the 1690s, when he began to extend leases. But even then he reserved for himself a strip of land on the west side below the falls, no doubt recognizing its value for mill sites. Other settlers farmed areas outside the manor line, choosing the Boght and the Lansingburgh region, known then as Stone Arabia, which was acquired in 1670 by Robert Sanders. The farmland north of the Poestenkill and south of the Piscawenkill (now the heart of Troy) was also deeded throughout this period. By the early eighteenth century, most of this land was acquired by the Van der Heyden family who farmed and operated a ferry across the Hudson.

The power struggle between the French and the British for control of the North American continent which started at the end of the seventeenth century greatly increased the dangers of life on the frontier. Between 1686 and 1763 four wars erupted. During the peaceful interludes, sometimes lasting as long as thirty years, each side expanded its territory until warfare broke out anew. Both the French and the British enlisted the aid of Indian groups, and sudden raids kept the northern frontier in turmoil.

During these years of warfare, the Hudson-Mohawk Gateway region served as a corridor for the transport of military supplies and troops. Albany became a center of military activity. Crews of twenty-five men moved large batteaux carrying supplies from Albany through the Hudson-Mohawk Gateway to points around the falls and rapids. Beginning about 1690 small forts were erected to protect this vital route. One was located at Half Moon

Above: General James Abercrombie led his British troops to horrible defeat against the French garrison at Ticonderoga during the French and Indian War. From Dictionary of American Portraits, by Cirker, 1967

Right: This was a map of the Hudson-Mohawk Gateway at the time of the American Revolution. The Van Rensselaer family owned much of the land south of the confluence of the Hudson and Mohawk rivers. Vanderheyden farm occupied the area of present-day Troy. Courtesy, New York State Library

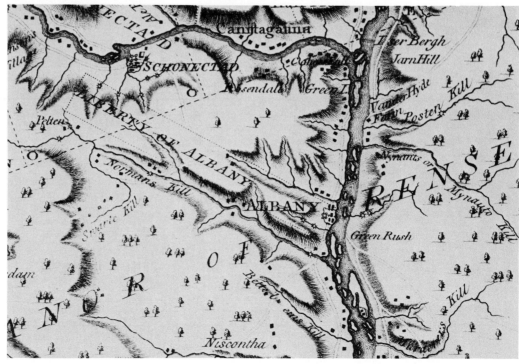

Facing page, top right: Indian commissioner William Johnson was well liked by the Iroquois. In 1755 he led an expedition of British soldiers and Iroquois warriors to victory over the French at Lake George and earned the title of Baronet of the British Empire in New York. From Dictionary of American Portraits, *by Cirker, 1967*

Above: Major General Horatio Gates replaced General Philip Schuyler as commander of the Northern Department of the Continental army. From Dictionary of American Portraits, *by Cirker, 1967*

near the ferry operating just north of Waterford. A military road ran north from Albany along the Hudson, across the islands at the mouth of the Mohawk to Half Moon, and north to Saratoga. These islands—stepping stones as they were—provided fords across the mouth of the Mohawk. Thus during the eighteenth century, Green, Van Schaick, and Peebles islands became centers of military encampments, while Waterford duly received its name.

Between the wars, British settlements expanded north and west of Albany. The Van Schaick house on Van Schaick Island was built in the 1730s during the longest interlude of peace, and other farms were reestablished in the Gateway region. Meanwhile the French were extending their influence southward from Canada. In the 1730s they established Fort St. Frederic at Crown Point in the Champlain valley. This daring French expansion into what the British regarded as their territory eventually led to another outbreak of hostilities. During the two wars

that followed, Fort St. Frederic posed a serious threat to settlers in New England and in the Gateway area. One historian calculated that from 1744 to 1748 as many as twenty-seven raids were launched southward from Fort St. Frederic into British frontier areas. Settlers in the Gateway region were particularly terrified in 1745 when Saratoga was destroyed. Farmers on the east side of the Hudson and north of Albany deserted their farms.

The last of the French and Indian Wars broke out in 1755. During this final conflict large provincial and British armies, under the command of such leaders as William Johnson, James Abercrombie, and Jeffery Amherst, marched through the Hudson-Mohawk Gateway. Finally in 1759, Fort St. Frederic and Quebec fell to the British, bringing peace to the area. The French were defeated and the British added Canada to their burgeoning empire.

Settlers once again pushed into the lands north of Albany, no longer fearful of French and Indian raids. True settlement of Gateway areas away from the rivers and creeks then began in earnest. One early resident of present-day Menands observed: "The settlers ... set up sawmills on every stream, for the purposes of turning to account the fine timber which they cleared in great quantities off the new lands."

The islands at the mouth of the Mohawk once again became the scene of military encampments and the movement of military supplies in the War for Independence. By 1777 they were strategic points to be defended against the British advance led by General John Burgoyne in his southward march from Canada to Saratoga and Albany. First General Philip Schuyler and General Horatio Gates, in succession, established command headquarters at the old Van Schaick house; their troops camped around the house. Under the direction of Polish engineer Thaddeus Kosciusko, the American army fortified Peebles Island facing north toward Saratoga, protecting the ford across the Mohawk on the road towards Albany. General Burgoyne noted: "Mr. Gates ... is now strongly posted near the mouth of the Mohawk River, with an army superior to mine." Because Burgoyne was halted at Saratoga, the fortifications were never used in battle.

By 1790 the Hudson-Mohawk Gateway region faced a new era. The population of the area would soon be swelled by new arrivals, the mill creeks utilized in more efficient ways for power, and the barriers on the north-south and east-west transportation corridors eliminated—all contributing to a busy, booming nineteenth century expansion of business and commerce.

*This was the first boat through
Lock Two of the Waterford flight
of the Barge Canal in 1915.
Courtesy, Gene Baxter*

CHAPTER TWO

WATER: THE KEY TO POWER AND GROWTH

L ike most flourishing areas of the young republic, the Hudson-Mohawk Gateway owed its settlement and early growth largely to water. In the early years, water afforded transportation for settlers and goods as well as power for industry. Even today, the abundant water supplies of the Gateway area have continued to serve a multiplicity of needs for businesses and factories, homes, and public institutions.

The Gateway area has been blessed by nature, and enhanced by engineering genius, with generous water resources. It is, first of all, the place where two great rivers meet. The Mohawk rises near the center of New York State and flows east. At Little Falls and "the Noses," the river breaks through mountain barriers into a deep, rocky ravine. Less than a mile from its island-studded mouth at Cohoes, it flows over a perpendicular precipice some seventy feet high and nearly a quarter-mile wide, forming one of the greatest and most powerful waterfalls of the Northeast. About ten miles north of Albany, the Mohawk merges into the mighty Hudson.

The Hudson rises in Tear-of-the-Clouds, a lake nestled among the highest peaks of the Adirondacks, more than 4,000 feet above sea level. Starting as a small stream, the river descends rapidly through narrow gorges, collecting the output of lakes and streams along the way. At the dam between Troy and Green Island, approximately 160 miles from the sea, the roaring river falls into a tidal estuary. From Troy to its mouth, the Hudson is broad, deep, and somewhat sluggish.

The Gateway area has always existed first and foremost as the headwater of navigation on the Hudson. Early Lansingburgh had a landing for sloops as large as ninety tons, but the wharf was functional only during springtime, when the water was running high. A news item appearing in the Lansingburgh *American Spy* on March 8, 1793 suggested that only if dams were erected to the south would there be "sufficient depth of water up to this town to navigate vessels of 40 to 50 tons burden," presumably

Right: The confluence of the Mohawk and Hudson rivers is depicted in this 1843 map. Courtesy, New York State Library

Far right: A typical homestead of the 1760s in the Gateway area was the Douw Fonda house in Cohoes, shown here as it appeared in the late nineteenth century. Courtesy, New York State Library

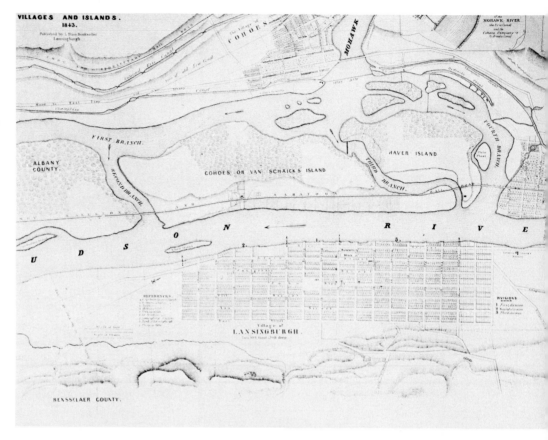

most of the year round. The first dam constructed between Troy and Green Island in 1823 did precisely that; it opened Lansingburgh to sloop navigation in seasons other than spring. Earlier, its cross-river neighbor, Waterford, also offered a sloop dock, but it was submerged when the dam was built.

Troy had no need of dams. Elkanah Watson, in his brief description of what was soon to become Troy, stated unequivocally, "This place is situated precisely at the head of navigation on the Hudson." Watson noted that, even in these early times, "several bold and enterprising adventurers have settled here; a number of capacious warehouses and several dwellings are already erected. It is favorably situated in reference to the important trade of Vermont and Massachusetts."

Lansingburgh had its origins in 1763 when Abraham Jacob Lansing purchased the Stone Arabia patent. He had the land surveyed and a portion of it laid out in building lots. The map was filed in the Albany County Clerk's office on May 11, 1771. A steady stream of immigrants, mainly from New England, began pouring into the settlement. In a short time, a thriving community had sprung up at the head of sloop navigation. Nieuw Stadt, or New

City, was the popular name given the village to distinguish it from Oude Stadt, or Old City, the name by which Albany was first known. Lansingburgh received its first charter on April 5, 1790, and seven men were appointed to act as trustees for one year.

To the south of Lansingburgh, Dirck Van der Heyden purchased, in 1707, the property which became the center of the original city of Troy. The patroon of Rensselaerwyck confirmed this transaction on December 15, 1720. The annual rent was three bushels and three pecks of wheat and three fat hens or capons. By 1786 Dirck's land had been divided into three farms. The owners were Jacob I., Jacob D., and Matthias Van der Heyden.

The Van der Heydens strongly opposed all suggestions that a community be established on any portion of their land. However, with Old City prospering to the south and New City growing by leaps and bounds to the north, the Van der Heydens soon realized that they were passing up an opportunity that might prove more profitable than farming. Jacob I. sold a lot to Benjamin Thurber of Providence, Rhode Island, who had earlier located in Lansingburgh. Thurber set himself up as a merchant and trader at the foot of Hoosick Street under the sign of a bunch of

grapes.

The next applicant was Captain Stephen Ashley of Salisbury, Connecticut, who bought the old residence of Matthias Van der Heyden at the corner of Division and River streets. Ashley opened the house as an inn which became popularly known as Ashley's Tavern. Under the terms of his lease, he also took control of the ferry that operated from the foot of Ferry Street. His monopoly over the only public crossing of the river in the vicinity—Ashley's Ferry—brought him increasing prosperity and influence.

Jacob D. Van der Heyden, the owner of the middle farm and the last holdout of the three, finally succumbed to the influence of friends who advised him to apportion his land in city lots. Subsequently the middle farm was surveyed, and lots for homes and sites for shops were established. This planned area, with squares and rectilinear blocks modeled after Philadelphia, became the very center of Troy.

Jacob D. called the projected village Vanderheyden, but the earlier names of Ashley's Ferry and Ferry Hook continued in popular usage. Benjamin Covell was the first to bargain for a land parcel, selecting lot number five on the

west side of River Street. Dr. Samuel Gale, a physician from Guilford, Connecticut, built a two-story structure on the west side of River Street north of Covell's store. And so the settlers came.

The majority of the new arrivals, being New England Yankees, felt uncomfortable with the Dutch place names that dominated the area. Thus, on January 5, 1789, they met at Ashley's Tavern to rename the village of Vanderheyden. They selected Troy. The new name was not a surprising choice in a young nation modeled after Greek democracy and captivated by classical styles of architecture. The Van der Heydens, however, were not happy with the name change. In fact Jacob D. went as far as to write "Vanderheyden, alias Troy" on all his deeds and leases for many years afterward. But the settlers were clearly satisfied. When the city was incorporated in 1816, the motto attached to the seal read, "Ilium fuit; Troja est." "Ilium is dead; Troy lives." Meanwhile, the first village charter was passed in 1791, and another in 1798.

Waterford, to the north of Troy, had its beginnings in the ancient tract of Half Moon. Named for its shape, it also evoked memories of the ship on which Henry Hudson had first explored the Gateway region. As early as 1664, Philip Pieterse Schuyler and Goosen Gerritse van Schaick received permission to purchase the Half Moon tract. At the time, Half Moon included Half Moon Precinct, Half Moon Point, Half Moon-on-the Hudson, and Half Moon Village. It was Half Moon Point that was destined to become Waterford. A map representing Half Moon Point in 1784 showed two log cabins, two wood houses, and two taverns: the Eagle, haven of the rebels, and the Lion, meeting place of the Tories. Half Moon Point was purchased by the founders of the village in 1784.

Waterford was charter-incorporated by the New York State Legislature on March 25, 1794. Only one of a few villages in the state operating under such a special charter, it is also the oldest incorporated village in the state. At first part of Albany County, it became the southeast anchor of Saratoga County when that county was established in 1791.

Waterford's charter provided for seven trustees, all equal. Fire was a subject of primary concern to the citizens. Freeholders were compelled to equip themselves with fire buckets and tools to extinquish blazes, and fifteen citizens were appointed to care for all fire-fighting tools and instruments. The town of Waterford was formed from Half Moon in 1816.

Waterfordians, of course, were river-oriented. Realizing that the great Cohoes Falls nearby interrupted river trade on the Mohawk, they built a 244-foot pier extending out into the confluence of the Hudson and Mohawk rivers for the landing of goods to be carried overland around the falls. This early engineering achievement was submerged by the construction of the Troy-Green Island Dam in 1823.

In 1795 the first bridge across the Mohawk was erected between Waterford and neighboring Cohoes. In describing the bridge, Count Rochefoucauld Liancourt wrote: "It is constructed of timber and rests on stone pillars about 25 or 30 feet distant from each other. The masonry is not remarkable for solidity or neatness; but the carpenter's work is exceedingly well done." With its weak piers, the bridge, located west of the present railroad bridge, was soon damaged by ice. On April 4, 1806, the Cohoes Bridge Company was incorporated to rebuild it. Stock was sold, higher tolls were charged, and a second bridge was erected, opening the area to further development.

The falls, however, were the true key to Cohoes' growth. In 1811 the Cohoes Manufacturing Company was incorporated. With wise forethought, the founders purchased sixty acres of river bank, along with rights to the water. After building a wing dam the new company turned to manufacturing screws. Development slowed for lack of capital, however, and in 1815 the screw factory burned. Two brothers from New York City then bought a large share of stock in the company and built a cotton factory. Despite their efforts development again came to a standstill. Then construction began on the Erie and Champlain canals, and everything changed. The waterways brought attention and people to Cohoes and renewed life and vitality in the entire area. The southern section of modern Cohoes, the place where the two canals merged on their way to Albany, became a lively, bustling junction frequented by merchants, travelers, traders, and seamen.

The first successful design for the systematic and complete utilization of the Cohoes Falls' waterpower was developed by Canvass White of Waterford, one of the chief engineers of the Erie Canal. White got financial backing from the patroon Stephen van Rensselaer, and from the firm of Peter Remsen and Company of New York City. With others, they incorporated in 1826 as the Cohoes Company. The Cohoes Company acquired all water rights a half-mile above and below the falls. It also gained permission to dam the Mohawk above the falls, construct a system of power canals, and lease and sell waterpower as well as land.

The dam was built in 1831 and, although destroyed by ice the following winter, it was soon replaced. The first power canal was completed in 1834, and the company began selling land privileges in 1836. Thus the Cohoes Company's activities grew, and at the same time, so did the surrounding community. In 1848 Cohoes was formally established as a village. Just twenty years later, it became a city.

Slightly to the south of Cohoes, the town of Watervliet was formed in 1788. It included the entire west district of the sprawling manor of Rensselaerswyck, exclusive of Albany. In the nineteenth century Watervliet was the most populous town in the state. The village of Gibbonsville in the town of Watervliet, opposite Congress and Ferry streets in Troy, was incorporated in 1823. It stood at the beginning of what was to become the present city of Watervliet. To the south arose two other settlements known as Washington and Port Schuyler.

On June 18, 1812, Congress declared war against Great Britain. The United States Army Ordnance Department was little more than a month old, and Decius Wadsworth,

Above: Although a major obstacle to the early transportation network of the Gateway, the harnessing of the Cohoes Falls of the Mohawk River in the 1830s led to the development of Cohoes as a major textile manufacturing center. Photo by Robert Chase

its commanding officer, set out to select suitable sites for military arsenals. It was decided to establish one arsenal somewhere in upstate New York so that material could be easily shipped either north or west to meet an anticipated British attack via Lake Champlain and/or from the Niagara frontier. Colonel Wadsworth discovered an appropriate location in what was soon to be the incorporated village of Gibbonsville.

After purchasing a twelve-acre tract of land from James Gibbons, the Ordnance Department was ready to build. At first, the new establishment was known vaguely as the arsenal "at Gibbonsville" or "near Troy," but by 1817, people began to call it the "Arsenal at Watervliet."

Some years later, in 1836, the hamlets of Gibbonsville, Washington, and Port Schuyler were incorporated as the village of West Troy. Some residents, however, preferred the name Watervliet, a word of Dutch origin meaning "floodtide" or "rolling water." In 1897 West Troy was incorporated as a city and its name changed to Watervliet.

Green Island, the southernmost island in the mouth of the Mohawk River, chose not to join West Troy and was incorporated as an independent village in 1853. This event coincided with another major benchmark in Green Island's history: the arrival of the car works of Eaton, Gilbert and Company in the same year.

As the Gateway area began to grow and prosper, the need arose to provide easy access between the municipalities developing on opposite banks of the rivers. Ferry boats were the earliest means of linking such neighboring communities. As early as 1786, a stagecoach line, running between New City and Old City, Lansingburgh and Albany, stopped at Ashley's Tavern and took a ferry across the Hudson.

The ferry boats used in the eighteenth century were large, flat-bottomed scows, propelled by poles. At the dawn of the nineteenth century, the vessels were attached to ropes stretched across the river and driven "by force of the current from one landing to the other." Still later, horses were employed to turn paddle wheels extending below the deck. The first steam-propelled boat was introduced in 1826.

One of the earliest ferries, eventually known as the upper ferry, connected Troy with what was to become Watervliet. In 1798 Mahlon Taylor, a Poestenkill Gorge manufacturer, started a lower ferry. It left from the foot of Washington Street in Troy and connected with the west bank at an area soon to be occupied by the Watervliet Arsenal. Two ferry lines linking Troy and Green Island were established in 1823 and 1854, respectively. The 1854 ferry sustained a major disaster in its first year of operation. On Friday morning, October 13, 1854, as the vessel was crossing to Green Island from Troy, the steamer *Alice* passed. The swell raised in the steamer's wake caused passengers in the rear of the ferry to stand up to avoid getting wet. This action, plus the crowding of the ferry and the inexperience of its captain, caused the vessel to capsize, drowning eleven of the seventeen passengers.

Another ferry, operated by Harmon Leversie, was said to have been in use as early as 1685, connecting what was to become Lansingburgh and Waterford. First known as the Half Moon Ferry, it later was called the Upper Lansing Ferry. It continued to operate until 1805, a year after

Above: The waterfalls of the Poestenkill look untouched in this late-nineteenth-century view, but above and below the gorge the stream was channeled to provide power for several mills. Courtesy, Rensselaer County Historical Society

Left: The Troy-Watervliet Bridge was constructed in 1970. Upon completion of the new bridge, the Congress Street Bridge to the north was removed. Photo by Gene Baxter

the Union Bridge was constructed.

Bridges eventually replaced the ferry boats. They became dramatic silhouettes in an area so punctuated by great rivers and numerous streams. The first important bridge in the Gateway area linked Waterford and Cohoes. The second, the Union Bridge, connected Lansingburgh and Waterford. Constructed in 1804 by the Union Bridge Company, it employed the Burr Arch Truss, a wooden bridge system named after its inventor, Theodore Burr. This was the first bridge to span the Hudson north of New York City. It burned in 1909 and was replaced by the current bridge which was constructed on top of some of the original 105-year-old piers.

A wooden railroad bridge, 1,600 feet in length, built by the Rensselaer and Saratoga Railroad in 1835, crossed the Hudson River between Troy and Green Island. At the Troy end it had a draw of sixty feet to allow boats to pass through. This bridge, ignited by a spark from a passing engine, burned on May 10, 1862. The fire, fanned by a strong wind from the west and north, spread to engulf seventy-five acres in the heart of Troy's business section. It was replaced first by a wooden bridge, and then by a steel one, the western section being completed in 1876 and the eastern section in 1884. The steel bridge was constructed on 1834 piers, but, on March 15, 1977, one of the piers gave way during high water. The bridge collapsed, leading to the construction of the current Green Island Bridge which opened in 1981.

Bridges abound in the Gateway area. The Lansingburgh-Cohoes Bridge, also known as the 112th Street Bridge, was completed in 1923, replacing two earlier bridges on the same site. The Troy-Menands Bridge was dedicated in 1933, and the current Troy-Watervliet Bridge, which opened in 1971, replaced two earlier Congress Street Bridges, built in 1874 and 1917, respectively. One of the most recent bridges in the area, the Collar City Bridge, is a high-level span connecting Troy and Green Island and leading by a limited access highway, under construction at present, from Hoosick Street in Troy to the Northway, Interstate Route 87.

Waterfalls are among the natural wonders and resources of the Gateway region. Along the Hudson, cascades of water as high as 225 feet fall from the upper level to the alluvial plane below. The roar and majesty of the Cohoes Falls on the Mohawk have inspired awe in onlookers from the earliest times to the present.

Besides drawing visitors, the area's waterfalls were also destined to attract industry to the Gateway region. First,

though, a way had to be found to go around the falls, which in the case of the Cohoes Falls presented a natural obstruction to the westward movement of travelers and goods. Getting around the falls was the challenge; the opening of the Erie Canal met this challenge successfully.

In 1810 Jonas Platt, an avid supporter of a canal that would cut through the barriers of the Appalachian Chain to the Midwest, enlisted the support of DeWitt Clinton, then mayor of New York City. Although Clinton had previously demonstrated little interest in a canal, he soon emerged as the driving force toward its construction. This advocacy helped to catapult him to the governorship of what would soon be dubbed "the Empire State."

The Erie Canal was one of the longest locked canals ever built, running 363 miles through an unfriendly, untamed wilderness marked by hilly terrain and turbulent streams. The builders had to accommodate a water-level difference of 568 feet between its two terminals at Albany and Buffalo. It presented a mammoth engineering challenge.

On April 15, 1817, the New York State Legislature passed the Canal Law, creating a fund to build the canal. Ground was broken on July 4 that year, at Rome, New York, and the canal was constructed east and west from the center of the state. The portion that ran through the Gateway area was ready in 1823, and the entire, completed canal opened on October 26, 1825.

During the opening day ceremonies, Governor Clinton's barge had barely passed by the Watervliet "cut" when merchants from Troy locked the barge, *Trojan Trader,* into the waterway. The vessel laden with Trojan goods was the first barge bound west for Rochester. No time for celebrations for the enterprising Trojans!

The original Erie Canal was forty feet wide and four feet deep, accommodating horse- or mule-towed boats of about thirty tons capacity. It had eighty-three locks, each of which was ninety feet long and fifteen feet wide. The Champlain Canal, constructed at the same time, had identical dimensions. The two canals met at the junction in Cohoes and traveled through Watervliet to the basin north of the center of Albany.

In the folklore of the Erie and Champlain canals, the Watervliet "cut" into the Hudson opposite Troy developed a rowdy and lawless reputation. At one point it hosted twenty-nine saloons bearing suggestive names like "Black Rag" and "Tub of Blood," and it is said to have witnessed "a hundred fights a day, and a body a week in the canal." Today's settlement of Maplewood was the loca-

These barges were waiting for the early spring opening of the Erie division of the New York State Barge Canal at Waterford circa 1920. The United Shirt & Collar Company and Lansingburgh are in the background. Use of the Barge Canal for recreational purposes has increased recently; pleasure boats can travel from New York City through Waterford west to the Great Lakes or north to the St. Lawrence River. Courtesy, Gene Baxter

Canal boats are tied up in the Hudson River at West Troy waiting for the Erie Canal to open in the spring. Courtesy, Rensselaer County Historical Society

tion of one of the four weighlocks which determined passage fees for barges. The toll post was a flat-roofed, columned building now commemorated with a historical marker.

The canal was such a success that it soon needed to be widened and deepened. Enlargement began in 1836 and was completed only in 1862, making the Erie seventy feet wide and seven feet deep to handle boats of 240 tons' capacity. Tonnage climbed rapidly, peaking at 6,673,730 tons in 1872. But the railroads chipped away at the canal's monopoly. At mid-century seven independent railroads stretching across New York State were united as the New York Central Railroad. Much faster than barges traveling through the canal, the trains quickly stole canal passengers and began to make inroads into canal freight. The first significant decline in canal tonnage occurred during the 1870s, coinciding with a tripling of rail freight. The New York-to-Buffalo run which took ten days by canal took only eleven hours by rail in 1875.

Eager to rescue the canal from its precipitous decline, the New York State Legislature approved the Barge Canal Referendum Bill in 1903, and construction of a new barge

canal system began in 1905. Completed in 1918, the updated waterway used river and lake channels wherever possible and connected these by man-made aqueducts. During this period the so-called Waterford flight of locks was built, raising boats from the Hudson River, around Cohoes Falls, to the Mohawk River above the falls. Five proximate locks lifted boats 170 feet, making them the highest set of lift locks in the world.

Canvas White had developed a satisfactory hydraulic (Portland) cement for "waterproofing" the Erie Canal. In the process, he built stronger retaining walls and tighter locks and aqueducts. Despite this and other improvements throughout the nineteenth and into the twentieth century, tonnage continually declined on the Erie Canal until today; the waterway is now host mainly to recreational boats. At this writing the canal has become a financial burden and its future is in doubt. However, for well over a century, the Erie and Champlain canals made the Gateway a booming commercial area and, with the advent of the railroads, one of the greatest crossroads of commerce in nineteenth-century America.

Water, besides spurring the Gateway's commercial

growth, was also the key to its industrial development. Up to the time when a usable steam engine was available in America in 1806—and well beyond—running, falling water was the main energy source for industry. Power canal systems were constructed to take advantage of this natural energy resource.

The first and greatest power canal system was built in Cohoes. Canvass White designed the original system but died before it got underway. His brother, Hugh, directed the building of the dam and the first channels. More or less parallel canals were designed to bring water to successive levels, culminating in the return of the water to the river below the falls. By 1880 seven levels had been built. The fall between levels provided power for factories constructed between the channels.

Troy also had a successful power canal system. Benjamin Marshall created a reservoir in 1840 by damming the Poestenkill immediately above the falls at the eastern end of the gorge. An intake was then constructed on the north side of the reservoir not far behind the dam, and a 600-foot tunnel was cut through the rock of Mount Ida to bring water to a succession of mills built on the hillside, one of which was Marshall's cotton mill. In later years, a turbine connected to an electric generator at the lower end of the system added a new form of power to the mechanically generated power above.

This particular system meant power in the Gateway area until 1962, when Marshall's creation finally went off line. Water had been used to operate a mill at the mouth of the Poestenkill gorge at least as early as 1667, marking a 300-year history of waterpower in that locale. It is interesting to note that a new hydroelectric power system has been recently built, using some of the 1840 system.

Water, which originally caused the Gateway to develop,

Right: The Waterford sidecut of the old Champlain Canal was photographed at the time of the opening of the Barge Canal. This set of locks is a reminder of the significance of the Gateway as a major crossroads for commerce in the nineteenth century. Photo by George Michon. Courtesy, Paul E. Grattan

Below: A weigh lock for determining tolls on the Erie Canal was located just above where the sidecut entered the Hudson River opposite Troy, in present-day Maplewood. Courtesy, Rensselaer County Historical Society

is still a vital area asset. In recent years, Rensselaer Polytechnic Institute has tried to focus local attention on the rivers as a valuable regional asset. The Hudson River Celebration features creative and inexpensive boats which cross the river from near the Cluett Peabody Factory and return to the Troy side near the new City Hall. The *Nightingale,* a small cruise boat owned by Michelle Brown of Troy, offers tours and dinner passages, using the area's waterways for education and recreation. Troy's new Riverfront Park, with its ethnic festivals, represents another attempt to reconnect people with the river and with their past—and hopefully their future.

Electric street railways connected all of the Gateway communities until before World War II.

CHAPTER THREE

CREATING A TRANSPORTATION NETWORK

The Hudson-Mohawk Gateway is an area traversed and crisscrossed by numerous waterways. From the earliest times, the inhabitants used boats to transport themselves and their products from one locale to another. The Indians plied the rivers and streams in their canoes. The early settlers used scows and sailing vessels. By the end of the eighteenth century the sloop was the mainstay of travel and commerce in the Gateway region. And commercial sloops, as well as schooners, could still be seen sailing the Hudson at least fifty years after the first steamboat was introduced.

Colonial Lansingburgh and Waterford had sloop docks. Troy was an even more important port. As early as 1788 the sixty-ton schooner *Flora* carried wheat and other cargo from Vanderheyden to New York "and to different points along the New England coast." By 1830 eighty sloops were conducting commerce between Troy and New York City.

Travel by sloop, however, was slow and tiring. In Troy's *One Hundred Years*, historian Arthur J. Wiese says some interesting things about sloop travel in the 1820s:

A voyage to New York from Troy in a sloop, although pleasurable and inexpensive, was sometimes long and tedious. Contrary winds and calm weather not infrequently lengthened the time beyond a week .... Fourteen hours were considered to be the time of a short passage to the city. A sloop making a voyage down and back in four days was exceedingly fortunate .... Sailing with a "white-ash breeze," when there was no wind, implied the use of long, white-ash oars or sweeps, as they were usually called, to advance the progress of the vessel. Fourteen miles a day was the distance commonly accomplished by rowing and floating with the tide. Kedging was a more tiresome and slower way of moving a sloop in calm weather. A boat carrying a line from the sloop having been rowed to

Right: Matton shipyard of Cohoes was originally located in Waterford along the old Champlain Canal. The last three wooden canal boats built there are ready for launching in this circa 1915 photo. Photo by George Michon. Courtesy, Paul E. Grattan

an island in advance of it, where a small anchor called a kedge having been sunk into the ground, the vessel was hauled forward by means of the line fastened to the kedges. Ten to fourteen passengers were the number which could be accommodated conveniently with berths on a sloop.

Travel by sloop could indeed be wearisome. It is no wonder, then, that the advent of the steamboat was welcomed with such enthusiasm. As early as 1798 Robert R. Livingston was promised a steamboat monopoly over New York's waterways, provided he could produce a vessel of the required size and speed within one year. He did

not, but the time limit was extended. Livingston then met Robert Fulton, an artist turned engineer and inventor, and they became collaborators. Their steam-propelled invention marked the beginning of a new era in American navigation. On August 22, 1807, Fulton left New York City aboard the *North River Steamboat of Clermont,* which became famous as simply the *Clermont.* The initial trip to Albany and back won Fulton and Livingston a twenty-year monopoly over steamboat operation on New York State waters. On September 4 the *Clermont* formally entered commercial service and ran to Albany in 28 hours, 45 minutes. The much slower sloops could not compete. After being rebuilt and enlarged, the *Clermont*

Facing page, top: The City of Troy steamboat is seen docked at the Citizens' Steamboat Company in Troy in the late nineteenth century. This steamboat made daily trips between Troy and New York City from 1876 to 1907. An excursion ticket in 1898 was $2.50. Courtesy, Frances D. Broderick

Right: This certificate was for ten shares of stock in the Troy Steamboat Company in 1825, the year the company was chartered. Courtesy, Rensselaer County Historical Society

continued to operate on the Hudson until 1814. In the meantime, Livingston and Fulton added other steamboats to their fleet, including the *Firefly* in 1812 which traveled between Troy and Albany.

In 1824 the United States Supreme Court declared Livingston and Fulton's monopoly unconstitutional: steam on the Hudson was open to all. Troy immediately began to make the move from sailpower to steam. The Troy Steamboat Company was chartered in 1825. Its first steamboat, the *Chief Justice Marshall,* was named for the Supreme Court judge who had opened the river to competition. This 314-ton ship plied the Hudson from March 31, 1825, until April 22, 1830, when her boiler burst shortly after departing from Newburgh. Eight persons died, and five were seriously injured.

During this early period of steamboat travel, the Troy Public Shipyard launched three experimental steamers: the *Star,* the *Helen,* and the *Diamond.* The *Star* initially set sail in 1827. She was designed by William Annesley, a naval architect who was then living in Troy. Annesley designed his boats with crisscrossing layers of wood, much like modern plywood. The lamination strengthened the boat so that it did not require structural members. The hull had a channel extending through the middle from front to back, and the paddle was housed in this channel. A band of planking around the hull above the waterline served to tighten and strengthen that part of the ship.

The next experimental steamboat was built by Henry Burden, an inventor and iron manufacturer from South Troy. Burden designed an early steam catamaran, the *Helen,* named for his wife and sometimes referred to as the "Cigar Boat." The vessel had two wrought-iron cylindrical pontoons or hulls, 300 feet in length and eight feet in diameter. A deck was built on top of the twin hulls, and a large center paddle wheel was inserted with the steam engine located on deck.

Burden theorized that his "floating island" would draw only four feet of water and travel at twenty-five miles per hour. But he did not understand the surface tension problem caused by so much exposed hull. On July 7, 1834, in a race from New York City to Albany, the *Helen* arrived two hours after her competitor, a conventional steamboat. Worse yet, on August 2, the *Helen,* "with a full head of steam, ran on the Castleton dam," breaking up in the process.

Burden at first planned to rebuild the *Helen,* but he eventually gave up the notion. Nonetheless, he did construct the *Diamond* with a more conventional hull and sidewheels. Launched in 1837, this ship ran on the Albany-to-New York City route for eleven years. She was distinguished by the truss system of latticework Burden used to strengthen the shallow hull. The lattices formed diamonds, giving the ship its name. Although they strengthened the shallow hull, the small diamond openings on

Left: By the mid-nineteenth century steamboats had become invaluable for carrying people between cities on the Hudson River. In this 1845 lithograph, based on a drawing by E. Whitefield, the Empire of Troy *and the* Troy *steamboats cross paths with the city of Troy in the background. Courtesy, Rensselaer County Historical Society*

Below: The Troy waterfront was photographed circa 1910 from the Congress Street Bridge. The rear of the businesses on River Street were outfitted with cargo doors and lifts to receive goods from the river; the Alhambra Garden restaurant (left of center) was a convenient waiting place for steamboat passengers. Courtesy, Rensselaer County Historical Society

both sides of the ship impeded the movement of passengers and goods. No other Hudson River steamboat employed this truss system.

But there was yet to be a 100-year history of steamboats out of Troy. The *Troy* and the *Empire* were built by the Troy Steamboat Company in 1840 and 1843, respectively. These ships started out as "day boats," that is, vessels making the trips between Troy and New York City during daylight rather than nighttime hours. Night boats soon followed.

While the *Troy* and the *Empire* continued as day boats, the *Albany* and the *Swallow,* of the Peoples' Line, ran between Troy, Albany, and New York City at night. Lighthouses had not yet been built along the Hudson to warn navigators of treacherous shoals. Thus, on the night of April 7, 1845, the *Swallow,* not long out of Troy, struck a rocky islet off Athens during a snow squall. Her hull broke open, the stern sank back into the river, and fifteen lives were lost. It was one of the worst steamboat disasters in Troy's history.

The *Troy* and the *Empire* continued to operate until the early 1850s, but after 1848, they ran as night vessels. In 1854 the Troy Night Line was established, and every night for nearly three decades it ran steamboats along the

Hudson.

In 1872 the Citizens' Steamboat Company was organized, launching the *City of Troy* in 1876 and the *Saratoga* in 1877. These beautiful, stately vessels took over the Troy-to-New York City run. In 1906 the *Saratoga* was rammed by another steamboat off Cougers Island, carrying away the port boiler. She later sank. The following year the *City of Troy* caught fire on the way up the river, put in at Dobbs Ferry, and burned to the water's edge.

In 1909 the Hudson Navigation Company launched the *Trojan* and the *Rensselaer* which did the night run out of Troy until the eve of World War II. It was in 1937 that the last of the night-line steamers, the *Trojan* and the *Berkshire,* made their final runs. The age of steam on the Hudson out of Troy had ended.

At the same time that Gateway residents were developing better and faster methods of traveling over water, they were also creating finer and more efficient modes of journeying over land. Before the coming of the railroads, stagecoach lines carried settlers between neighboring villages and hamlets. An early stage connected Lansingburgh and Albany, crossing the river at Ashley's Ferry. There also were coaches serving Schenectady, Saratoga Springs,

and even more distant places like Boston and Montreal. The coming of the railroad, however, rendered the stagecoach obsolete.

A group of Troy businessmen proposed to build a railroad from Troy to Ballston Spa. In 1832 the Rensselaer and Saratoga Railroad (the R&S), was chartered and granted an exclusive franchise to construct railroad bridges between the two points. The citizens of Albany at first failed to recognize the threat implicit in this exclusive Trojan franchise. As a result, they spent nearly thirty years in court seeking permission to build a railroad bridge at Albany, crossing the Hudson at their city, rather than at Troy.

The R&S line was surveyed and built, and a railroad bridge constructed between Troy and Green Island. On October 6, 1835, the first train arrived at the western end of the bridge. The locomotive was detached, and the cars drawn across the bridge by horse—assuring that the wooden structure would not be set afire by a spark from an engine. The line passed through Green Island, and across bridges connecting the islands at the mouth of the Mohawk, to Waterford. This part of the line to Waterford was maintained until 1982 when it was abandoned and the track taken up.

At the Ballston Springs terminus of the railroad, passengers bound for Saratoga had to take a stage or wait for a Schenectady and Saratoga Railroad train to take them to their destination. However, about 1840, Troy merchants purchased a large number of shares thus outwitting Albany interests—and bringing the Schenectady and Saratoga under R&S control. So the R&S, chartered to go only as far as Ballston Springs, was extended to Saratoga Springs, a city fast becoming an important resort.

In 1836 the Schenectady and Troy Railroad was chartered, opening up the route to the west. The first train passed over the line in 1842. The railroad employed a novel means of getting its cars from Cohoes to the Green Island side of the R&S railroad bridge. All passengers were loaded in a single car, the car was given a push, and was then propelled by gravity downhill to the Green Island Bridge. From there it was towed by horses to the Troy side of the river. An account in the *Buffalo Gazette* had this to say about the line's importance in its heyday:

The Trojans are proverbial for their enterprise and public spirit. Everything which they take hold of "goes ahead." For two or three years past, they have been endeavoring to compete with Albany for the Western travel to New

Right: The W.H. Frear, *named after the wealthy Trojan dry goods merchant, was a connecting boat between Albany and Troy. Courtesy, Rensselaer County Historical Society*

Middle: The night boat Trojan *is seen docked at Congress Street in Troy a few years before its last run in 1937. Courtesy, Rensselaer County Historical Society*

Bottom: By the 1830s Troy had several large hotels such as the Troy House on the corner of First and River streets. Stagecoaches stopped at the hotels which provided overnight accommodations for the passengers. Courtesy, Rensselaer County Historical Society

Facing page, top: This is a broadside for the stagecoach line running between Troy and Saratoga in 1834. This particular line was short-lived because a year later the Rensselaer & Saratoga Railroad began operation. Courtesy, Rensselaer County Historical Society

Bottom: The Rensselaer & Saratoga Railroad ran this newspaper ad in 1836. Courtesy, Rensselaer County Historical Society

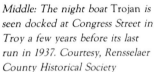

TROY, BALLSTON
AND
SARATOGA,

DAILY LINE OF
COACHES.

This line will commence running on the first day of July, leaving each place at half past 8 A. M. every day. Passengers wishing to travel from Saratoga to Lebanon Springs, will find this line not only the most expeditious but cheapest.

Passengers for Pittsfield, Northampton and Hartford by taking this line will dine at Troy, lodge at Pittsfield, and arrive at Hartford early the next day. The road is now put in the best order, and all that is now wanting is that liberality which the establishment merits.

☞ Seats taken at G. W. Wilcox's, York House, Saratoga, and at all the Principal Houses in Troy.

L. V. & J. B. REED, Proprietors.

J. S. KEELER, Agent, Troy.
S. DEXTER, Agent, Saratoga.

TROY, JUNE 25, 1834.

N. B. On the arrival of the ERIE or CHAMPLAIN, Parties can be accommodated with coaches to Saratoga or Ballston the same evening.

TROY, BALLSTON AND SARATOGA RAIL-ROAD.

UNTIL further notice the Cars will leave Troy,
At 9 3-4 o'clock, A. M.
2 do. P. M.
3 1-2 do. do.
Passengers going north of the Springs, should take the 9 3-4 o'clock train from Troy. Immediately after the arrival of the train at Saratoga, stages leave for Fort Edward, Glen's Falls and Sandy Hill. From Fort Edward they are conveyed in the fast packet boat *Red Bird* to Whitehall. Also, a daily line of stages from Saratoga to Lake George.

From Whitehall, the packet boat *Red Bird* will convey passengers to Fort Edward, and from thence to Saratoga by stages, where rail road cars will be in readiness for Troy, Schenectady and Albany by steam power.

JOS. S. DUTTON, Superintendent.
H. GREEN, Agent, Albany—office at Exchange Coffee House, opposite Eagle Tavern.
sept 1 A. REED, Agent, Whitehall.

TROY AND ALBANY.

York and the East. For this purpose, a railroad has been constructed to Schenectady which intercepts the Great Western Line at that point, and upon the river, a line of most splendid steamers has been put. . . . The railroad is one of the best constructed in the United States . . . This with the gentlemanly attention of those in charge of the cars—which by the way are superb . . . renders it a trip of pleasantness and comfort.

The Trojans had always been eager to provide uninterrupted train service between Troy and Boston. Their dream was realized with the construction of the Hoosac Tunnel. That five-mile underground passage, the longest railroad tunnel in the United States, was one of the great engineering feats of the nineteenth century. A start on the tunnel was made between 1855 and 1858, but the enormous undertaking was not completed until 1875. Not long afterward train travel between Troy and Boston took as little as five hours.

Troy's location at the terminus of four major railroads made it necessary to have an adequate railroad station. In 1853 the rail companies joined together to form the Troy Union Railroad Company. This fledgling firm then purchased a block on Sixth Avenue as the site for the proposed depot.

The Troy station, completed in 1854, was a huge brick structure, 400 feet long, that encompassed the entire city block. Its barreled roof was supported at each end by a great oak arch. Five hundred state legislators and dignitaries, most of whom had come to Troy by train, attended the opening banquet in the Union Depot on February 22, 1854.

With its bridge across the Hudson and its enormous depot, Troy became a prominent railroad center. In this new era of budding self-confidence, engines were finally permitted to cross the wooden bridge connecting Troy and Green Island. That proved to be a tragic misjudgment. On May 10, 1862, sparks from a passing locomotive ignited the bridge, creating a fire which destroyed much of central Troy, including the railway station. The edifice was rebuilt, this time with a roof supported by iron arches and without the high central tower that had distinguished the original building. Its life span was less than forty years, however; the Trojans then decided to construct a new Union Depot. It was a handsome red brick building with neo-classic elements and underground passages to each track. This third and last station was razed in 1958-59 after railroading in Troy had almost completely disap-

The Troy and Lansingburgh horse railway, the first in the Gateway, began operation in 1861. By the 1880s, 100 horsecars carrying five million people annually connected area communities. Courtesy, Rensselaer County Historical Society

peared.

In 1862 the Rensselaer and Saratoga (R&S), Troy's first line, carried 556,000 passengers, 310,000 tons of freight. Less than a decade later in 1871, the R&S and its lines were leased to the Delaware and Hudson Railroad, creating one of the larger—and still independent—railroads in the country. A year later, construction was completed on the R&S locomotive repair shops in Green Island. The Green Island shops continued building and refurbishing freight cars until the late 1930s when this work was transferred to the Colonie yards, near Watervliet. The round house of the Green Island shops was thought to be one of the earliest such structures still standing in the United

States. Unfortunately, it was recently razed by the present owner, who continues to use the locomotive and car shops for his business.

The only railroading to remain in the Gateway area are Conrail's freight line over the old Troy and Greenbush line and the freight line of the D & H passing through Watervliet, Cohoes, and Waterford. Unhappily, no passenger train stops or even passes through the Gateway region today. There is, however, an outside chance that railroading could enjoy a renewed burst of life in the area. At this writing, officials from Quebec, Vermont, and New York have commissioned a study for a high-speed train connecting Montreal and New York City, possibly passing through the Gateway.

In the mid-1800s, while steam on rails was successfully providing transportation over long distances, rails also began to be used for short-distance travel within and between cities. The vehicles originally used for short-haul traffic were drawn by horses, while later models relied on electricity. Improved transportation facilitated the growth of cities, the concentration of central business districts, and the beginning of suburbs. With the arrival of the horse car, the worker, who had always walked to and

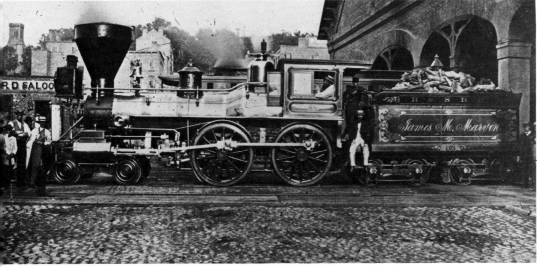

Above: Troy's last Union Depot is seen here circa 1915. When it closed in the late 1950s there was an unsuccessful attempt to convert it into a new city hall. Courtesy, Rensselaer County Historical Society

Left: The James M. Marvin locomotive of the Rensselaer & Saratoga Railroad was built in 1867 by the Schenectady Locomotive Works. This view was taken at the Fulton Street end of Union Depot in Troy as the train prepares for a northern trip. Courtesy, Rensselaer County Historical Society

The Fifth Avenue Bus Company, running between downtown Troy and Lansingburgh, provided an alternative to streetcars. Courtesy, Gene Baxter

from the factory, could live farther away from it. Residents no longer were constrained by the location of the neighborhood store and could travel quite easily to the center of town to do their shopping.

The earliest form of public intra-urban transportation was the omnibus, a horse-drawn wagon which picked up passengers and deposited them at, or nearer to, their destination. Cohoes enjoyed an early omnibus as did Troy.

The first horse railway in the Gateway joined Lansingburgh and Troy. The line opened in 1861 and was extended north through Lansingburgh to the Waterford Bridge the following year. In its first year of operation, the line made eighty trips daily, a tribute to its popularity. The railway became known as the "Red Line" because of the color its cars were painted.

The "White Line" from Troy to Cohoes opened in 1863, followed by a route connecting Troy and Albia. The steep climb up Congress Street along this track often made it necessary for passengers to get off and push.

A "Blue Line" linked Lansingburgh and Cohoes in 1880, and Waterford and Cohoes were joined by a "Green Line" in 1884. By 1885 the local street railways had 468 horses, car barns, and stables, and carried more than five million passengers per year.

One of the persistent problems posed by horse railways was the collection and disposal of manure. Another was the great "Epozooic" of 1872 in which thousands of horses died of equine encephilitis. During that period, men replaced horses to keep the street railways running. These problems spurred the search for an alternative to horse-

power. The first acceptable solution was an underground cable to which a car could be attached and detached by a gripper. The cost of installation, however, was usually prohibitive.

Finally, the electrically motorized car provided a solution. Thomas Davenport of Vermont produced a model railroad using a battery-powered rotary engine, first exhibited at the Rensselaer Institute in 1835. In 1885 Leo Daft, an Englishman, designed a small truck, placed on the roof of the car, which "trolled" on an overhead wire, and was attached by another wire to the motor inside the streetcar.

Frank Sprague, a former assistant to Thomas Edison, built the first successful electric street railway in Richmond, Virginia in 1888. In less than two years, Sprague's system was operating in Troy. In 1896 a transfer ticket program was adopted: patrons could transfer and ride to any point served by the line—for five cents.

In 1900 the street railway system of the Gateway area and Albany combined to form the United Traction Company. Shortly before this, the area witnessed the rapid growth of interurbans. The interurbans employed cars, each equipped with its own electric motor, to carry passengers from one city to another. Henry Averill opened the Troy and New England Railway, which connected Troy to Averill Park in 1895. The United Traction Company ran its first interurban to Schenectady in 1903. These electric cars were inexpensive to run and thus provided enormous competition for the steam railways. The giant railroads counterattacked by buying the street rail-

In the early twentieth century Franklin Square was an important center for Troy's business and transportation. Here the streetcar lines on Fourth and River streets intersected and, with the railroad tracks, crossed the Green Island Bridge. Courtesy, Rensselaer County Historical Society

ways. The United Traction Company, the last holdout in this area, was purchased by the Delaware and Hudson Railroad in 1905.

This purchase was not a happy development for area residents. By 1921 the Troy *Record,* while opposing an impending fare increase, went on to criticize the company's inferior service as follows:

Trojans always can count on the Traction Company doing everything in its power to unpopularize itself and make life disagreeable for those who from necessity are compelled to ride on its ill-smelling, flat-wheeled cars. The courteous grants of six and seven cent fares were followed by no appreciable addition in service in spite of promises, implied and actual.

Buses provided the first serious competition for the trolleys. After a long court battle, the first bus company was created in Troy in 1915 "so long as the routes were well removed from the trolley routes." As time passed, United Traction trolleys inevitably gave way to United Traction buses.

Meanwhile, strikes by motormen and conductors were a volatile part of the trolley scene. A motormen's strike occurred in 1900, another in 1901 over new schedules, and yet another over wages in 1905. Most of these strikes were short, and the motormen usually won their demands.

Trolley service was totally disrupted, however, by the great strike of 1921 when both motormen and conductors walked off their jobs for almost a year. The issues included an impending fare raise, possible discontinuation of the transfer system, and the reduction of motormen's wages from sixty to forty-five cents per hour. The Gateway area was accustomed to labor disputes, but this was the first strike to inconvenience a broad spectrum of people on a day-to-day basis over a long period of time. The strike finally ended, but its effects were deep and long-lasting. Both the union and the area lost. Merchants were hurt; recovery was sluggish. For the trolleys, it was the end of an era.

Trolleys continued to run in the Gateway until the 1930s. The last streetcar made its final run on February 4, 1932. Then trolleys disappeared into history—relics of a retreating past. A new epoch was dawning in the Gateway and in America as a whole: the age of the automobile. The invention of the internal combustion engine revolutionized travel and transportation. As increasing numbers of cars gave greater speed and mobility to more and more Americans, life was never again to be quite the same as it had been before. But public transportation is still important. Shortly after the failure of the United Traction Company in 1967, the Capital District Transportation Authority (CDTA) took over public transportation within the Gateway area.

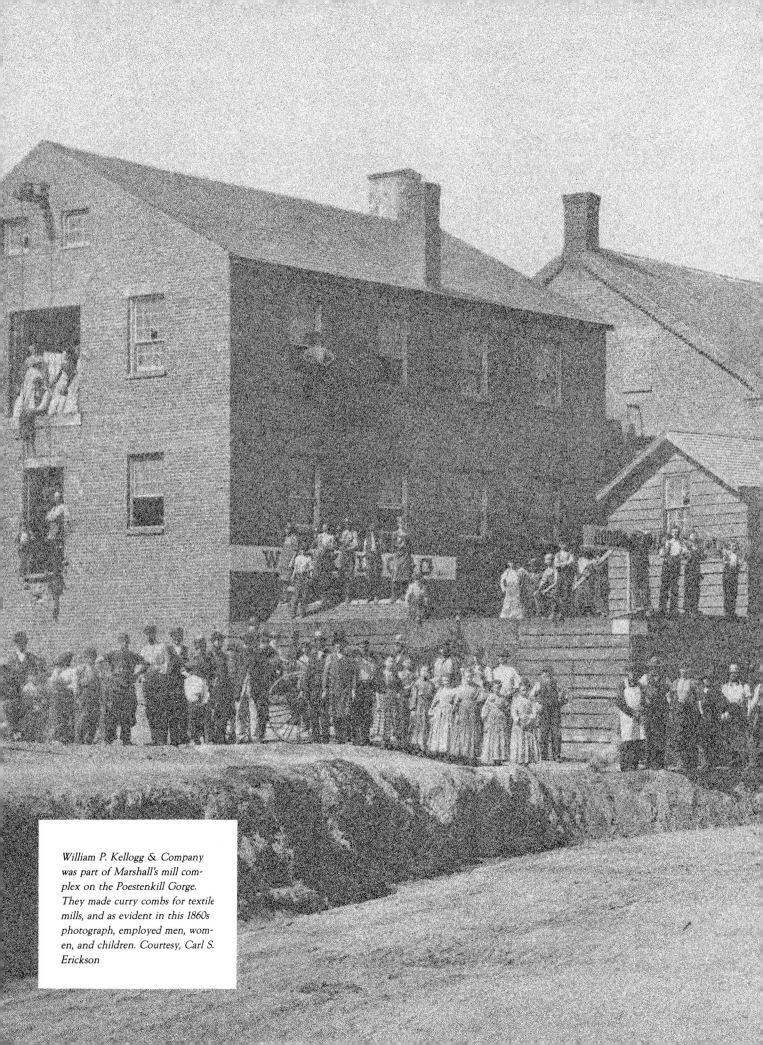

William P. Kellogg & Company was part of Marshall's mill complex on the Poestenkill Gorge. They made curry combs for textile mills, and as evident in this 1860s photograph, employed men, women, and children. Courtesy, Carl S. Erickson

CHAPTER FOUR

A BIRTHPLACE OF AMERICA'S INDUSTRIAL REVOLUTION

Change and innovation were characteristic of the Industrial Revolution. And, in a responsive social climate where each new invention inspired a dozen more, the process was accelerated, building on its own momentum. It is difficult to ascribe definitive dates to what is called the Industrial Revolution. However, a dramatic increase in inventions could be cited as an indication of the beginning of the period. If that is the case, then industrial history took a radical turn in Britain in the mid-1700s. In the United States rapid industrial growth began when Americans started borrowing freely from European technology and building on it. Imported ideas were quickly complemented by native ingenuity to launch America into its own Industrial Revolution.

The new nation's first Secretary of the Treasury, Alexander Hamilton, envisioned his country as a great industrial power. In 1791 he penned a "Report on Manufactures," a landmark document, which called for stimulating inventions, easing the movement of cash payments around the country, and encouraging the import and prohibiting the export of raw materials needed in manufacturing. Hamilton's statement aimed at making the United States independent in the manufacturing realm. It was not so much the cause of industrialization as an indicator of a process ready to begin.

Already in 1790 a young Englishman, Samuel Slater, arrived in Rhode Island to confer with Moses Brown, the owner of a spinning mill in Pawtucket. Slater agreed to reproduce British machinery in a new plant that Brown would finance. In 1793 Eli Whitney, who was working as a private tutor on an estate in Georgia, invented the cotton gin to remove seeds from the plant's fibers. The Industrial Revolution, announced by Hamilton, was underway.

The Gateway area possessed all the basic ingredients for becoming a great industrial center. It had abundant water-

Right: One of the earliest photographs of Troy was taken in 1860 by James Irving looking east on Congress Street which was the main thoroughfare between the Hudson River and the east. In seven blocks it accommodated over fifty businesses including clothiers, confectioners, hatters, four hotels, and an oyster dealer. The Tibbits mansion is at the head of Congress and on the hill is the short-lived Troy University which closed in 1862. Courtesy, Carl S. Erickson

Far right: A group of iron workers pose with their tools and castings outside Marshall Foundry in Troy circa 1870. Courtesy, Rensselaer County Historical Society

The Griswold wire works complex, along the Poestenkill Gorge, was photographed in the late nineteenth century. This mill and the others on the hillside were powered by Marshall's 600-foot tunnel which harnessed the power of the Poestenkill Falls. Courtesy, Rensselaer County Historical Society

power, excellent transportation, and ample raw materials, available locally or easily brought in by ship. The work force grew as New Englanders moved west and immigrants came up river from New York City. Successive waves of manufactures, strong inventive spirit, and wide mercantile interests allowed the Gateway to claim the title as one of the birthplaces of America's Industrial Revolution.

The Poestenkill Gorge developed rapidly in the nineteenth century. As early as 1667, there is mention of a mill at the mouth of the gorge in Troy. The mill appears again on a map dated 1720. By 1792 Mahlon Taylor, a New Jersey millwright, had purchased the site of the old mill, rebuilt the dam, and was constructing a sawmill, a flour mill, and the first paper mill established in northeastern New York.

Upstream at the foot of the falls, another flour mill was

being operated by Isaac Merritt by 1818. There also was a cotton factory, as well as a mill which produced augers and screws. The last plant on this location was the Griswold wire works, established in 1879, and dissolved in 1911.

Further development of the gorge took place in 1840 when the cotton manufacturer, Benjamin Marshall, undertook construction of the still existing underground/overground power canal system. Marshall moved up the hill and built a factory that specialized in making fine cotton goods. These fabrics were sent downriver near Hudson where they were printed into calicoes. Other industrialists subsequently erected factories near Marshall's mill, leasing land and purchasing waterpower from him. In 1846 the Tompkins machine works began turning out knitting machinery. Charles Kellogg built a factory at mid-century for the production of curry combs and other hardware. By the 1860s, the mills on the north slope of the gorge were manufacturing a wide variety of goods—from cotton cloth to rivets. Paper was an especially important product.

The original paper mill developed by Mahlon Taylor was purchased on December 29, 1792, by new owners, who bought the plant for 400 pounds sterling. To supply the factory with raw materials, they advertised in area newspapers that they would pay "three pence per pound for white, blue brown and check rags, and a proportionate price for other kinds." By the end of the eighteenth century, a second paper mill was built in Troy on the Wynantskill. It became known as A.&W. Orr in 1837, when Alexander Orr joined his brother, William, in the business of printing fine wallpapers. The brothers were said to have introduced the first cylindrical printing machine. With this new equipment, they could produce 1,000 nine-yard-long rolls of wallpaper in three colors each day. The Orrs also claimed to have been the first to manufacture mercantile printing paper with wood fibers in it. Meanwhile, R.T. Smart erected the Gold Leaf Mill and the Troy City Paper-Mill on the Wynantskill. There he made "an excellent quality of straw wrapping paper."

An important paper company that operated up to 1962 on the north slope of the Poestenkill Gorge in Troy was the one founded in 1846 by William H. Manning, Gardner Howland, and Alvin Williams. From the beginning the founders of the Mount Ida Mill manufactured manila paper. In 1855 the firm was reorganized and became known as Manning and Peckham. This company, now part of Hammermill Paper Company, has operated on Green Island since 1962.

Another early paper mill, the Enterprise Paper Company, was founded in Waterford some time after 1829. Today the firm is still in business and is known as the Mohawk Paper Company.

During this period, Troy became an important center of iron- and metal-related industries. Its growth was assisted by the fact that the Gateway area was surrounded on three sides by rich iron ore deposits. Limestone for flux in the smelting process was quarried in the Hudson

valley, and vast tracts of nearby forestland supplied raw material for the charcoal industry. Coal, which eventually replaced charcoal as fuel in the conversion process, was brought to the area from eastern Pennsylvania.

The Wynantskill stream in south Troy was the first site of the area's iron industry. In 1807, on the north side of the lower falls of that stream, John Brinckerhoff and Company of Albany built a mill to convert bar iron into hoop iron and nail rods. In 1849 this firm, then owned by Erastus Corning, built the first steam-powered rolling mill in the area, a plant which still stands today to the west of the Troy approach to the Menands Bridge.

In 1809 the Troy Iron and Nail Factory opened on the south side of the Wynantskill's upper falls. Scottish-born and trained engineer Henry Burden was to bring the firm to prominence. Having been named superintendent in 1822, this ambitious immigrant subsequently purchased the plant himself. Burden's inventive genius was responsible for the creation of many innovative machines such as the rotary concentric squeezer that mechanized the manufacture of wrought iron. The invention which brought Henry Burden his greatest success and wealth, however, was a machine for making horseshoes. He improved the original 1835 invention twice so that, by 1857, it could produce these items in a single movement and at the rate of one each second.

In its early days, Burden's factory employed five small waterwheels; yet, as production increased, the need for a

The Burden Iron Works was a major supplier of horseshoes to the Union army during the Civil War. Later improvements in horseshoe machines enabled the company to produce several million annually. Courtesy, Rensselaer County Historical Society

Left: Henry Burden's great overshot waterwheel was photographed circa 1900, a few years after its abandonment. It powered Burden's horseshoe factory on the Wynantskill from 1851 to 1896. Courtesy, Rensselaer County Historical Society

Julius Hanks, the Gateway's first bell founder, distributed this business card with an illustration of his foundry in the 1820s. The foundry was located at what now is the intersection of Fifth Avenue and Fulton Street. Courtesy, Rensselaer County Historical Society

larger prime mover became evident. Construction of a great wheel commenced in 1838 and continued for thirteen years. The result was distinguished by its huge size—sixty feet in diameter and twenty-two feet wide—and its detailed design. Burden's enormous creation became known as "the Niagara of Waterwheels," the overall largest waterwheel in the world, never surpassed by any other in either capacity or massiveness.

Iron goods manufactured in the Gateway were by no means exclusive to Troy. In 1832 David Wilkinson established an iron foundry in Cohoes. Under the direction of H.D. Fuller and Robert Safely, a new factory was built in 1867 to produce heavy castings and a wide variety of industrial machinery. George and Thomas Brooks rented a portion of the new Fuller and Safely factory and, using ten presses, manufactured wrought-iron nuts. Nevertheless it was Daniel Simmons who first produced axes, the iron product for which Cohoes became famous. By 1847, Simmons employed 200 men who turned out 600 axes a day. Thirty years later, after new owners had taken over Simmons' factory, production more than doubled.

In 1854 Jonas Simmons built a rolling mill in Cohoes. The firm produced shafting, axe poles, bar and band iron, and trestle work for buildings and bridges. The company employed 200 hands and consumed 1,200 tons of iron ore a year.

The Hudson-Mohawk Gateway was also renowned for

the quality of its bells and high-precision engineering instruments. The first bell manufacturer in the area was Julius Hanks who brought a foundry from Connecticut to Gibbonsville and then to Troy in 1825. Hanks was "prepared to execute any orders ... (for) church bells, with improved cast iron yokes, also town clocks, copper and brass castings, (and) surveyors' instruments of the most improved construction." Julius' brother bought out the firm in 1830, but continued to make similar products. They were "prepared to furnish church bells from 100 to 3,000 pounds."

The greatest name in Gateway bells was undoubtedly that of Andrew Meneely. At seventeen he was apprenticed to Julius Hanks and even married one of Hanks' daughters. In 1826 he founded his own firm in Gibbonsville. Meneely is credited with the invention of the "conical rotary yoke," later catalogued as "the most desirable and perfect rotary yoke in the world." His firm remained a family-held, single-product business for well over a century, casting some of the most important bells, pads, and chains used in this country and abroad.

Like the Meneely Bell Company, the W. & L.E. Gurley Company made products that were celebrated for their high quality. The firm's owners, William and Leland Gurley, became world-famous makers of high-precision instruments. Their products were widely distributed nationally and abroad, causing Troy historian Arthur J. Weise to comment that the company was an "enterprising firm (that) makes annually more engineering and surveying instruments than any other three mathematical and philosophical instrument manufactures in the United States, and widely distributes them in all parts of the world."

The Gateway area, especially Troy, along with Albany, was the premier stove-manufacturing center of the United States during the nineteenth century. In 1821 Charles and Nathaniel Starbuck and Ephraim Gurley were the first to regularly manufacture heating stoves in the region. By 1853, seven Trojan foundries employed 670 men to cast 75,000 stoves, collectively valued at one million dollars.

Above: This carillon was made by Meneely & Company in Watervliet in the early 1930s. Courtesy, Rensselaer County Historical Society

Left: These men were casting a bell at the Meneely Bell Foundry in the late 1930s. Courtesy, Rensselaer County Historical Society

Left: W. & L.E. Gurley Company, located at Fifth Avenue and Fulton Street, is seen here in the early twentieth century. The company, now under the name of Teledyne-Gurley, still operates in this building. Courtesy, Rensselaer County Historical Society

Below: The Empire Stove Works, located at Second and Ida streets in Troy, is shown circa 1880. In addition to cooking and heating stoves, train car wheels were manufactured in the foundry. Their four-story machine shop on the Poestenkill is now occupied by Lindy's hardware store. Courtesy, Rensselaer County Historical Society

In his *History of Rensselaer County*, Nathaniel Bartlett Sylvester says, "There is seldom an improvement in a stove that cannot be traced to the inventive skill of a Troy manufacturer." Indeed, patents for various components were granted to a number of local inventors. Cooking, for example, was a fireplace chore made difficult by bending and the unevenness of the heat. Benjamin Franklin had invented a cooking stove which was available in Troy as early as 1814, but it was Philo P. Stewart, an adopted Trojan, who created and patented the "Large Oven and Air-Tight Cooking Stove" which became the most popular in the nation. Stewart's invention was first manufactured by Starbuck and Company, and later by Fuller and Warren. Filling orders for Stewart's stove caused a mammoth production boom in the Hudson Mohawk Gateway.

High quality cloth was also produced in the Gateway, and Cohoes, while respected for its iron goods, was renowned for cotton textiles. The firm that contributed most to this fame was the Harmony Mills Company, incorporated by Peter Harmony and twenty-one others in 1836. One year later, the company erected its first mill, a four-story brick building capped with a slate roof, measuring 165 feet long and fifty feet wide. An adjacent picking

Left: Workers assemble kitchen ranges at Fuller & Warren Company's Clinton Stove Works in South Troy in the early twentieth century. Courtesy, The Times Record

Facing page, far right: This advertisement for P.P. Stewart's famous cooking stove, manufactured at Fuller & Warren Company, ran in the 1860 Troy city directory. Courtesy, Rensselaer County Historical Society

room and repair shop extended the plant's length to 213 feet. In addition, three double brick structures were built to house the superintendent and the workers. The mill began operation with 5,000 spindles. Within thirteen years there were 7,000.

In 1850 Garner and Wild bought Harmony Mills. Only two years later, the new firm built Harmony Mill #1 with a capacity of 30,000 spindles and a labor force of 750 operators. This plant was so successful that Mill #2 was completed in 1857.

In 1855 the Mohawk Mill, of which Joshua Bailey was president, was reported to be the largest knitting factory in America. It employed 600 workers and introduced a new laundry machine that could wash 1,200 pairs of drawers a day.

Troy was also known for producing high-quality cotton textiles. It was, however, the invention of the detachable collar that really launched the Trojans into their curious, yet rapidly growing, position in the industry.

The new-fangled collar was apparently invented by Hannah Montague who tired of washing her husband's voluminous shirts. It is said that the fastidious Orlando Montague changed shirts two or three times a day. Some

time in the late 1820s, Hannah cut the collars off Orlando's shirts and insisted that he keep his shirt on while she washed the collar. Retired preacher Ebenezer Brown was intrigued by Hannah's idea. With a true entrepreneurial spirit, he hired women to make "freestanding" shirt collars. He sold them in his dry goods store and peddled them door to door.

Orlando Montague and Austin Granger organized the process in 1834, opening the first firm to manufacture linen collars and "shirt bosoms," also called dickeys or shams. A year later, Independence Starks got into the business and soon added a laundry to his manufacturing operation.

Troy's textile industry gained further momentum with the invention of the detachable linen cuff in 1845 and the introduction of sewing machines in 1852. The firm of Bennett and Edison was the first to operate these machines by steampower. Trojan women had by this time become so skilled at this new employment that, when other cities tried to launch into this rapidly growing industry, they failed because of the less experienced nature of their labor force. It was not long before a single woman could stitch forty to eighty dozen collars a day, while an-

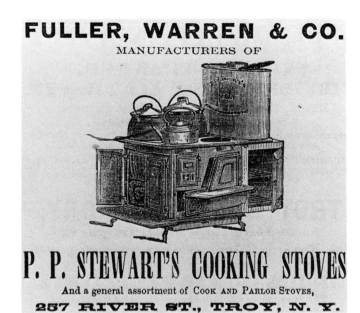

*Abram Haney of Morrison &
Morrison in Troy was issued a
patent for this coal-burning stove
in 1849. Courtesy, Rensselaer
County Historical Society*

other could sew thirty to forty dozen cuffs, bringing total sales of some five million dollars annually.

During this period, for the first time in history, women in large numbers left their homes to join the conventional work force. At the factories, females labored long hours—a fourteen-hour day was not uncommon—doing tedious work for low pay. Women thus became an integral part of the Industrial Revolution and later a voice in rising demands for shorter hours, better wages, and more humane working conditions.

Troy was also known for making distinguished coaches and carriages. Orsamus Eaton opened a factory in 1820, and Charles Veazie set up his factory several years later. By 1830 the two coach builders together employed about sixty men and turned out 150 carriages annually at a sale value of $50,000. As early as 1831, the Troy *Budget* remarked that "Eaton and Veazie have rendered Trojan carriages almost as noted as the wooden horse of old Troy." Stagecoaches made in Troy were renowned throughout the country. From Georgia to Ohio, the nation's stage lines clamored for coaches "of the best Troy manufacture."

In 1831 Eaton took on a partner, Uri Gilbert, who had earlier been apprenticed to him. Charles Veazie went out of business in 1836. Soon the only coach maker in the Gateway area, Eaton, Gilbert and Company, focused on manufacturing railroad passenger cars. Every order filled won the coach builders greater acclaim. In 1850 the firm employed 150 workers to build omnibuses, thirty-one passenger cars and 150 freight cars. After a disastrous fire

Right: Starbuck Iron Works was located on Center Island south of the Rensselaer & Saratoga Railroad Bridge (Green Island Bridge). Starbuck specialized in the manufacture of columns, window caps, plows, and bark mills. The foundry complex featured a row of worker housing to the right of the main building. Courtesy, Rensselaer County Historical Society

Below: This is an advertisement for the Pembroke collar, made by George P. Ide & Co. of Troy in the early twentieth century. Courtesy, Rensselaer County Historical Society

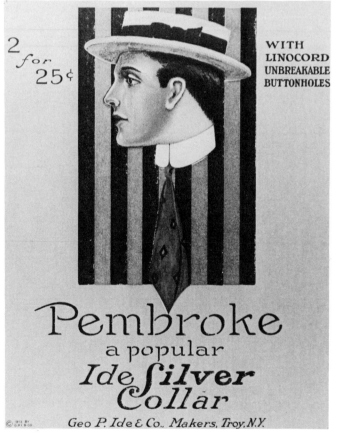

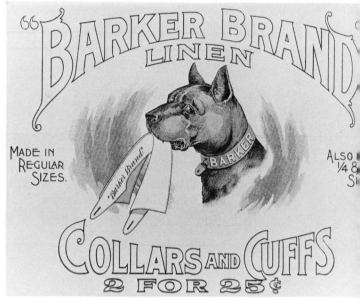

Above: William Barker & Co. used this ad in the early 1900s. Founded in Troy, the company built a modern factory in Watervliet in 1898 south of the Congress Street Bridge. They had salesrooms in New York City, Chicago, and Boston. Courtesy, Rensselaer County Historical Society

leveled the factory in 1852, the business moved to Green Island where it grew to huge proportions. Various Gateway artists worked for Eaton, Gilbert as muralists.

In 1817 William Powers of Lansingburgh, a former teacher, began to manufacture floor cloths, the forerunner of linoleum. The business was small, but, with his wife Deborah as an active partner, he found himself "realizing a handsome profit." Powers plowed this profit back into the business by building a large factory in 1828. The following year a vat of heated varnish caught fire. Powers was badly burned in the resulting blaze and died within a few hours.

Deborah, undaunted, carried on the business. When her son Nathaniel joined her as a partner in 1847, the firm was incorporated as D. Powers and Sons.

There is no doubt that Deborah Powers provided the force and drive that made the floor cloth business a huge success. She soon opened a factory in Newburgh and a warehouse in New York City. She, herself, sailed a sloop up and down the Hudson in pursuit of business.

It was a bold breed of men and women who initiated the Gateway's industrial boom. And, simultaneously, equally inventive and enterprising residents arose to become the area's leaders and business tycoons. Active in civic and community affairs, these dynamic entrepreneurs left their mark on the Gateway. Some arrived with financial means; others came equipped only with ideas and energy. All were characterized by limitless drive and burning ambition—and achieved extraordinary success.

One such man was George Tibbits who, at age twenty-

Above: Eaton, Gilbert & Company, located at what is now Sixth Avenue and Broadway, ran this ad in the city directory in 1850. In addition to making stagecoaches, they built passenger and freight cars. Courtesy, Rensselaer County Historical Society

Right: Gilbert & Bush Co. of Green Island manufactured this parlor car circa 1880. Courtesy, Rensselaer County Historical Society

Below right: Richard P. Hart was involved in many area businesses including banks, real estate, and railroads. From History of Rensselaer County, by Nathaniel Sylvester, 1880

Above: "Mount Ida," the Gothic Revival mansion of the Warren family on a promontory overlooking Troy, was purchased by the city in 1903 and became Prospect Park. The house was used as a museum until the 1930s. Courtesy, Rensselaer County Historical Society

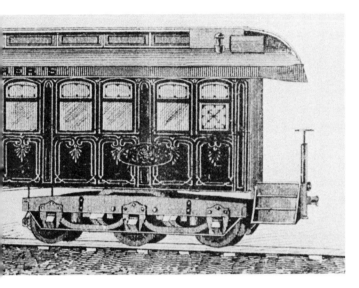

one, set up a mercantile business in Lansingburgh, which he later moved to Troy. The young merchant was so prosperous that he was soon able to retire and build himself a house on the slopes of Mount Ida.

George Tibbits then devoted himself to civic and political affairs. Eminently successful in politics, he was elected to office at the local, state, and national levels. Also active in banking, he became a charter founder of Troy's first commercial institution and also displayed a special flair for transportation as a director of numerous Trojan railroad, steamboat, and turnpike companies. Active well past seventy, Tibbits was one of the dynamos of his—or any age.

Another outstanding civic and business leader was Richard P. Hart, who started his career in Troy as a clerk in his uncles' store. He soon set up his own business and made his fortune supplying military needs during the War of 1812. Hart was the prototypical business tycoon. He was involved in banks, roads, steamboats, real estate, and utilities, and was a founding member of almost every railroad that originated in Troy. Hart also was a trustee on the original board of Emma Willard's Female Seminary and served the Rensselaer Institute in the same capacity.

Around the turn of the century, Eliakim Warren, a member of one of New England's oldest families, arrived in Troy aboard his ship, the *Three Brothers*, named in honor of his three sons. Thus was established in Troy a dynasty that for well over 100 years contributed leadership and capital to the city's development. Eliakim's sons and grandsons helped establish turnpikes, steamboats, and railroads. Four became presidents of Troy's financial institutions. And three Warrens—a son, a grandson, and a

great grandson of Eliakim—served as mayors of Troy.

At the tender age of twelve, Russell Sage began working in his brother's store in Troy. By the time he was twenty-one, he was owner of a thriving wholesale grocery business. Sage was eventually drawn into politics, and was elected to Congress; however, it was as a businessman and a wily investor in America's railroads that he realized his greatest success.

By 1863 Sage had outgrown both politics and Troy. He moved to New York City and proceeded to amass one of America's first great fortunes. After his death, his widow financed the building of the modern Rensselaer Polytechnic Institute, built the current Emma Willard School, and established the old campus as a college named for her husband.

It was during this exciting period of industrial beginnings that Troy became the home of the man who was to give America its symbolic representation as "Uncle Sam." In the early 1790s, two brothers, Samuel and Ebenezer Wilson, left New Hampshire and migrated west to Troy. There they began manufacturing bricks made from the blue clay of Mount Ida.

During the War of 1812, Samuel Wilson became a meat packer and supplier of beef and pork to the United States Army stationed outside of Greenbush. One tale has it that Elbert Anderson, a contractor who furnished beef to the army, visited Troy to inspect Wilson's operation. The barrels in which the meat was shipped were marked "US-EA." A workman asked what the letters meant and was told facetiously, that they obviously stood for Uncle Sam's and Elbert Anderson's initials. "Uncle Sam" was Samuel Wilson's nickname. The joke caught on and spread among workers and soldiers, who laughed and bantered about packing and eating Uncle Sam's meat. Another version says that soldiers misread the letters as "Uncle Sam" instead of United States.

One way or the other, the story first appeared in print in 1830 in the New York *Gazette* when it reported Elbert Anderson's death. The times were beginning to be prosperous, and the new nation was full of hope. An appropriate symbol was needed, and Uncle Sam captured the public imagination. The actual tall, lean, bearded figure, dressed in red, white, and blue, evolved in later years as the work of political cartoonists, especially Thomas Nast. In 1961 a resolution of Congress finally and officially acknowledged Samuel Wilson's role in the creation of the symbol. The original Uncle Sam was one of the Gateway's many gifts to the nation.

Major General Joseph B. Carr and staff of the New York National Guard led a parade on Second Street in Troy in the 1880s. During this time Carr served as secretary of state under governors Alonzo Cornell and Grover Cleveland. Courtesy, Rensselaer County Historical Society

CHAPTER FIVE

THE CIVIL WAR AND INDUSTRY

O ne does not think of the Civil War resulting in the triumph of industrial capitalism, yet this may have been its principal outcome. Although the war freed black Americans from the bonds of slavery, it certainly did not fulfill a promise of equality. It did, however, thoroughly liberate industrial capitalism, spurring mechanized production, expanding productivity, and increasing national income. American wages subsequently became the highest on earth. It is no wonder, then, that the Hudson-Mohawk Gateway, already mature as an industrial center, supported the war enthusiastically.

The 2nd Regiment of New York State Volunteers was organized in the spring of 1861. Some 900 strong, its soldiers came from the Gateway area and beyond. After gathering at Rensselaer Park in Lansingburgh, the volunteers marched to the courthouse in Troy. The 2nd Regiment received its flag, boarded barges at the steamboat dock, and six days later became the first volunteer unit to encamp in Virginia. As part of the Army of the Potomac, the 2nd Regiment fought valiantly at Fredericksburg and Chancellorsville. When the soldiers' two-year enlistments ended in 1863, only 300 were alive and well enough to return to the Gateway and receive hometown welcomes.

The 22nd Regiment, which had been organized at Albany in the spring of 1861 and included Company A composed of men from Waterford and Cohoes, returned in 1863. Out of 825 men, only 500 came home. About the same time, survivors of the 34th, including a Company A with men from West Troy, returned. The Gateway area was sacrificing some of its best young men to the Union cause.

In 1862 the 125th Regiment set off from Troy with George Willard in command. These men fought in twenty-one battles and confronted General Lee's troops at Gettysburg. That same year, 900 volunteers from Rensselaer and Washington counties arrived in Virginia. As members of the 169th Regiment, they fought against Lee at Richmond, participated in the siege of Fort Sumter, and

Right: The Troy City Artillery at Washington (Monument Square) probably was preparing for Abraham Lincoln's visit in February 1861. Soon afterward the artillery became Company F of the 2nd Regiment of New York State Volunteers. Courtesy, Rensselaer County Historical Society

Below: The return of the 2nd Regiment to Troy from service in the Civil War was celebrated on May 14, 1863. An arch was erected on Second Street and speeches were made at Washington (now Monument) Square. Courtesy, Rensselaer County Historical Society

formed part of General Grant's left flank in the battles of Cold Harbor and Petersburg. When Lee surrendered on March 12, 1865, the 169th returned home with fewer than 120 of its original 900 men.

Troy also contributed several high-ranking officers to the war effort. John Ellis Wool, for example, had distinguished himself during the Mexican War by leading a force of 3,000 men some 900 miles from San Antonio to Saltillo. Although already seventy-seven years of age at the outbreak of the Civil War, he was given a command and promoted to the rank of major general. Many of Wool's military accoutrements, including a great sword

awarded him for his services in the Mexican War, are on display at the Rensselaer County Historical Society.

Joseph Bradford Carr set off from Troy in the Civil War as commanding officer of the 2nd Regiment. When his horse was shot out from under him at the Bristol Station, he mounted the horse of an orderly, and at the head of his men, charged the enemy. Known as the "Hero of Bristoe," Carr was later brevetted a major general.

William Badger Tibbits was another Trojan soldier who marched off in 1861 as a captain in the 2nd Regiment and was soon promoted to major. At the head of a cavalry unit, he fought in most of the battles waged in Virginia. When he left the army after the war, Tibbits was raised to the rank of full brigadier and brevet major general.

Alonzo Alden, a descendant of John Alden of the *Mayflower*, entered the army as a private. While convalescing at home in Troy from a bout with typhoid fever, he was appointed a major in the newly formed 169th, and soon assumed command of the unit. Wounded at Suffolk, Virginia, Alden was shot in the head at Cold Harbor while planting the regimental colors upon the parapet. At Fort Fisher, he was thrown some thirty feet, buried by falling debris from a wrecked magazine, and left mangled and apparently dead. His obituary was published, but despite partial paralysis of his right side, Alden recovered and even rejoined his regiment. Shortly after 1865 he was appointed full brigadier general in the New York State National Guard.

Above: Colonel Joseph Bradford Carr was the commanding officer of the 2nd Regiment of the New York State Volunteers during the Civil War. Courtesy, Rensselaer County Historical Society

Left: The Soldiers and Sailors Monument was erected in Washington Square in Troy in 1890-91 to honor Rensselaer County soldiers and sailors who served in the Civil War. Courtesy, Rensselaer County Historical Society

Besides supplying men, the Gateway made another major contribution to the war effort: the building of the *Monitor.* This vessel, a milestone in naval annals and in the history of warfare, was made possible by a combination of ingenuity, money, and determination. While the Confederacy was assembling an ironclad ship in Virginia, Cornelius Bushnell of New Haven, Connecticut won a contract to build such a vessel, the *Galena,* for the Union navy.

Bushnell then met with two Gateway iron manufacturers: John F. Winslow and John A. Griswold of Troy. The three men initially discussed the building of Bushnell's ship, but ended up looking at a model of the *Monitor,* designed by Swedish-born engineer and inventor, Captain John Ericsson. Winslow became the spokes-

man for all of the principals in an effort to obtain a Navy contract to build the *Monitor.*

On October 4, 1861, the contract for "a floating battery" was signed. Ericsson rushed to New York City to prepare the plans, Winslow and Griswold to Troy to gear up their iron works, and Bushnell to New Haven to build the ironclad *Galena* for which he had earlier won a contract. The agreement read that they would produce the vessel in 100 days.

Exactly 101 working days later the completed vessel slid off the ways in Brooklyn. The Navy accepted and manned the *Monitor* on February 20, 1862. In March the former U.S. Navy steam frigate *Merrimack,* rechristened the *Virginia* by the Confederacy, was wreaking havoc in Hampton Roads. Towed to Virginia waters, the *Monitor*

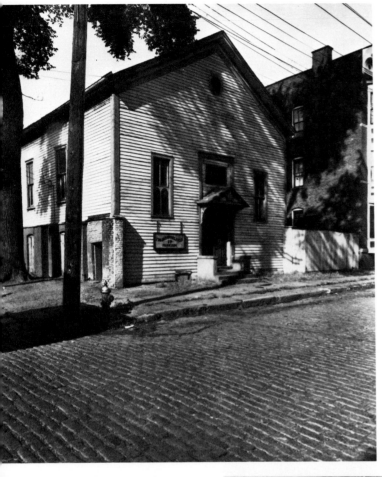

arrived in time to confront the Confederate ironclad on March 8, 1862. Although the ensuing battle is usually considered a stalemate, the *Virginia* never again ventured out to harass Union ships.

During this same period, opposition to the draft arose in the Northeast and exploded in Troy in the riots of July 1863. Though not as serious as similar draft riots in New York City, they were nevertheless the most serious civil outbreaks to date in that city. The white working class, especially Irish immigrants, opposed the inequity of a law that allowed men to escape conscription by hiring a substitute or paying the government $300. They considered it grossly unfair that rich men could use their money to buy poor men's blood. Opponents of the draft also harbored strong feelings of resentment against members of the black community, viewing them as a major cause of the war.

So, on July 15, 400 workers assembled at Burden's works in South Troy and marched north through the city. As other sympathizers joined them along the way, the mood became more and more hostile. Some marchers brandished clubs. Merchants and manufacturers prudently closed their shops. At Mount Olympus the mob turned south and swarmed into the Troy *Daily Times* building on River Street, pillaging and destroying machinery and generally venting its anger on the paper which had supported the draft in its editorials.

Above: Liberty Street Presbyterian Church was located on the north side of Liberty Street between Third and Fourth streets in Troy. As early as the 1830s it served the black community and narrowly escaped being burned by an anti-black mob during the draft riots of 1863. Courtesy, Rensselaer County Historical Society

Right: This plaque appears on the Soldiers and Sailors Monument in Monument Square in Troy. It depicts the famous battle between the Monitor (right side) and the Virginia (Merrimac), and a quotation from Troy's General Wool thanking the iron-maker Griswold for his efforts in building the ship. Courtesy, Rensselaer County Historical Society

Proclamation !

In view of the present state of affairs in the City, Breaches of the Peace having occurred, by which the peace and quiet of our citizens is greatly disturbed, I do hereby call upon all peaceably disposed citizens to enroll themselves, at my office, as Special Policemen or Militia. And I do further order that all disorderly assemblages of people and processions do immediately disperse and repair to their several homes and occupations.

W. L. VAN ALSTYNE, MAYOR.

Troy, July 16, 1863.

The mayor of Troy issued this broadside in 1863 in an attempt to put an end to the draft riots. Courtesy, Rensselaer County Historical Society

The enraged multitude then proceeded to unleash its wrath on black residents, stoning any blacks it happened upon, and headed toward the black Liberty Street Presbyterian Church intent on detroying it. A white clergyman, the Reverend Peter Havermans, persuaded them to spare the building. The draft was suspended, but that evening the rioters entered and ravaged the house of Martin I. Townsend, a vocal supporter of the war effort. To restore order, the mayor called up four military companies, and a loaded six-pound howitzer was trained on the rioters. The crowd disbursed. When the draft was resumed in September, two regiments of infantry and one of artillery arrived in Troy to preserve the peace.

Across the Hudson in West Troy, the Watervliet Arsenal started gearing up for the war as early as 1859. As its contribution to the Union cause, the arsenal produced ammunition, making as many as 33,000 bullets a day. Gas lighting was installed so that employees could work around the clock. At that time, the arsenal employed 2,000 workers, one-quarter of whom were children—girls as well as boys.

For a time, the mobilization effort induced by the war offered prosperity to mill owners and upward mobility to mill workers. On the other hand, the era was also marred by two depressions and great labor unrest. Also threatening Gateway industry was growing competition from western industries which had the advantage of cheaper labor, more available natural resources, and locations closer to expanding markets. At home, the immigrant labor

population exerted further pressure on local institutions as the newcomers began feeling their strength and started organizing to control the workplace, as well as the area's political apparatus.

As early as 1842 there was a brief strike in Cohoes by Harmony Mills Company workers who were protesting a 20 percent wage reduction. In 1849 Ogden Mill employees struck against a 15 percent pay cut, but they returned three weeks later when the company threatened to bring in workers from the outside. During the depression of 1857 woolen plants shut down altogether while cotton mills went on part-time schedules. Harmony later reinstated full employment, but reduced wages by 25 percent. The following winter the unemployed and the underpaid sought relief in a soup house and a bread line. By late February the workers began to fear that the owners were trying to nationalize lower wages. Female employees threatened to strike unless the 25 percent wage reduction was eliminated. The next morning, wages were increased by 10 percent, but production speedups were initiated as well; thus, 800 women went on strike for three weeks, returning only when a 12.5 percent increase was offered.

Labor activity in Troy was not as intense during this pre-Civil War period. In 1857 workers from twenty-three stove foundries formed the International Iron Molders Local #2. When in mid-March 1859 the foundries opened at the previous fall's wages, molders from the Clinton and Washington foundries walked out. This stimulated workmen to join the union. After a few weeks the owners made a concession far more important than increased wages: they gave their employees power to regulate the work force. By 1860 the Troy local, numbering 400 men, was the largest in the country. This same union was disbanded during the Civil War on a conspiracy charge of forming a secret and unfair combination. But it soon was revived and regained its former membership strength within two years.

By the mid-1850s commercial laundry had become a relatively large-scale industry in Troy with a complex division of labor that included washing, starching, and ironing. Six hundred women, mainly unskilled Irish immigrants, labored strenuously on eleven- to fourteen-hour daily shifts. They were confined to small shops with temperatures hitting ninety degrees in winter and unimaginable heights in summer. Many of the laborers also contracted consumption. Despite these grueling conditions, laundry work was nevertheless more prestigious than one alternative, domestic service.

RALLY FOR CASH!

GREAT
MEETING
AT
LANSINGBURGH,
🕿 TO-NIGHT. 🕿

The Journeymen and Workmen employed in
the BRUSH FACTORIES of Lansingburgh are
requested to attend a Public Meeting to be held

This, Saturday Evening, April 23d,
AT MORRIS HALL, Luke Read's Hotel,

To adopt such measures as may be deemed necessary to abolish the present system
of Store-Pay, and establish a Cash system in its place.

Good Speakers will be in attendance.   The Meeting will commence at
half-past 7 o'clock.   Come one! Come all!   Now is the time or never.

W. BARTLETT,
J. McDONALD,   } Committee.
THOS. CURRAN, Jr.,
E. PLUCKROSE,

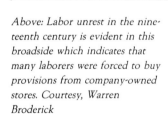

Above: Labor unrest in the nineteenth century is evident in this broadside which indicates that many laborers were forced to buy provisions from company-owned stores. Courtesy, Warren Broderick

Right: This was the collar dampening department at Cluett-Peabody in the early 1920s. Courtesy, Rensselaer County Historical Society

well as a cooperative laundry. Neither survived for very long.

A regional trades assembly was formed in 1864, at first with fourteen, and later twenty, unions participating. That year, 2,000 workers marched in a labor solidarity parade and 5,000 attended the picnic that followed. Profits were used to form a working men's free reading room and library, a cooperative grocery, a working men's clothing store, a debating society, and a labor newspaper, the *Saturday Evening Herald*.

Meanwhile, the Wool Spinners Association #1 of Cohoes set up a committee to work for the election of an Albany molder as a state assemblyman. The following year a "Working Men's Eight Hour League" was established in Troy to lobby for legislation for an eight-hour work day. Labor leader William Sylvis told the 1866 New York State Trades Assembly Convention: "Troy is the banner city of Americans upon the trades union sentiment, and everything concerning the welfare of working men," with "excellence . . . in the thoroughness of its organization" and "second to none in rendering . . . substantial aid."

The union movement by then had gathered so much strength that iron foundry owners from various industrial cities met in Albany to consider ways to eliminate the molders' union. This gathering led to the creation of a national trade association. Of the thirty-three companies that joined the organization, fourteen were from Troy, and Trojan Charles Eddy was elected president. The molders demanded equal wages among area foundries to be set at the highest prevailing salary level. They also sought a 25 percent wage increase, salary by the day rather than piece work, application for jobs to the shop committee rather than the foreman, and the ratio of one apprentice to ten molders. Foundry owners countered by posting notices which outlawed shop committees and emphasized management control over apprentices. More than 700 molders were locked out, and Sylvis instructed other locals to duplicate Troy's demands. He vowed to

In a time of growing union activity, the laundries were fertile ground for organizing. The ironers did band together to form the Collar Laundry Union. Kate Mullaney, the organization's president, was said to head the "only bona fide female union in the country." She won wage increases up to $10-$12 a week while other women were earning only $7, and men $13.50. She also lent financial support to Trojan molders and offered to send laundry union members to New York City to help organize women there.

But if unions were gaining strength through organization, so was management. A three-month strike of the Laundry Workers Union in 1869, for example, forged a bond between collar manufacturers and laundry owners. The former refused to send their collars and cuffs to unionized laundries and began recruiting and training new hands. They also convinced collar manufacturers in other cities to join their boycott. Meanwhile, the laundry owners offered a wage increase—provided workers quit the union. Most employees refused and instead set up a cooperative collar and cuff manufacturing company, as

start a cooperative foundry as well. The owners responded that molders could keep their jobs if apprentices could be employed when molders were unavailable. The molders accepted this proposal, but because there was no wage equalization, they stayed out. Finally, the owners capitulated, and the molders established the first of three successful cooperative foundries.

The owners' need to economize became more urgent in the early 1870s, owing to the combined forces of western competition and a severe depression. Daniel Walkowitz in his book *Worker City, Company Town* notes that the options available to owners were: lower wages, further mechanization, intensification of labor, dilution of well-paid skills, increased working hours, and the assertion of discipline. Cohoes, a company town, periodically enforced wage reductions and speedups. However, management's paternalistic approach stabilized the textile industry of the era, largely at the expense of adolescent, female workers who become dependent on their company.

In Troy the immigrant Irish labor force was beginning to show that numerical strength can sway elections. Control of the police force and the 1871 inauguration of Thomas B. Carroll, Troy's first Irish mayor, were both signs of rising ethnic voting power. In 1865 the Troy police force had been legislated out of existence by the establishment of a Capital Police District, embracing Albany, the Gateway area, and surrounding towns. This body lasted only five years. By 1871 the locally controlled Irish police force was inevitably sympathetic to its kin in their struggles with management.

Strikes and disruptions also affected Troy's iron and steel industry during this period. Late in 1874 workers at the Bessemer steel plant were told that their wages would henceforth be based not on hours but on tonnage. Although they accepted without protest, the iron workers were not so docile. When a 22 percent wage decrease was announced, blast furnace "puddlers" went out on strike with the "heaters" soon following their lead. Both the iron and steel mills were forced to close. Iron factory owners recruited scabs from New York City and Philadelphia, and private police, or "specials," were hired to guard the non-union workers during the reign of terror that followed. The local police force was, of course, unsympathetic to the scabs and, after a long seige, drove them out of Troy.

In the fall of 1877 there was talk of Gateway companies moving to non-union cities in the West. At the same time, the stove foundries were negotiating contracts to use prison labor in lieu of local workers. Another reign of terror followed, complete with ambushes and shootings.

The 1880s were marked by the emergence of strong national employee organizations like the Knights of Labor. Gateway workers joined out of fear for their job future. The Knights' attempt to submerge local trade union identity led to a revolt which resulted in the creation of the American Federation of Labor. Edward Murphy, then mayor of Troy, met with delegates in the spring of 1882 to establish a Workingmen's Trades Assembly. This group changed its name several times, always trying to distinguish itself from the Knights of Labor. As these competing Trojan labor organizations frustrated union solidarity during the 1880s, only one union retained its prominence, the molders.

On November 1, 1882, iron manufacturers asked the molders to approve a 30 percent wage cut because of declining prices and fewer orders. The union refused, and the foundries shut down. Six weeks later the owners offered to reopen with a 15 percent reduction. Their offer was again rejected. When most of the foundries finally opened at old rates, the Malleable Iron Company posted broadsides stating that workers must give two weeks' notice before quitting or forfeit the equivalent pay. Because the molders rejected this new rule, Malleable locked them out and shut down. The firm opened one week later with scab molders, and the lockout lasted sixteen months. Violence ensued. Local Republicans pushed a new Troy police bill through the state legislature, but Democratic Mayor Murphy managed to neutralize its effect. The Republican police commissioners then elected one-half of an alternate police force and asked the governor to impeach Murphy. The governor refused; however, Murphy had already made up his mind: he declined to seek reelection. Having served as mayor for seven years, he was eyeing a seat in the U.S. Senate, a position he subsequently won.

In the meantime, veteran Trojan police officers locked themselves in their stations, awaiting a court decision about the legal status of personnel changes within the department. While the old police were self-imprisoned, their replacements rushed to defend scabs against the assaults of union workers. The court finally ruled that the new officers were legally in power, leaving the workers without law enforcement allies. Assaults and shootings then became a daily occurrence.

By this time, stove manufacturers had started to exit Troy. Although the union finally agreed to a 20 percent wage reduction, high labor costs, expanding western mar-

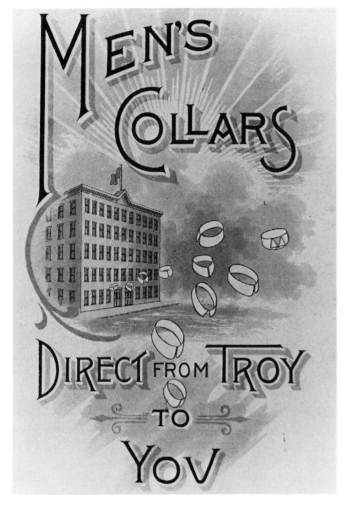

kets, and relatively poor access to raw materials caused the area's entire iron and steel industry to stagnate.

However, during the 1880s there was growing worker self-confidence in Cohoes. The French Canadians, who had arrived earlier and competed with Irish workers for jobs, had adapted so well to their new surroundings that one of their members, Samuel Sault, emerged as a labor leader. There also was considerable labor activity among women. On February 1, 1880, female weavers struck at Harmony Mill #1. The following day the walkout turned into a general strike with some 5,000 men, women, and children walking off the job. The women weavers had demanded a 10 percent pay increase, a longer lunch break, and an end to docking wages for imperfectly woven cloth. Children, a large part of the work force at that time, paraded through the streets, raggedly dressed, carrying banners which read: "Pity Our Hard Fate" and "No Time to Play in God's Sunshine."

After only nine days the strike ended successfully for

Above left: This was a typical advertisement for Troy collars. Most of the collar factories located in Troy had branch factories or outlets in larger U.S. cities. Courtesy, Rensselaer County Historical Society

Above right: This advertisement for collars made by Corliss, Coom & Co. was circulated circa 1915. The company began in Troy in 1838 and moved to Van Schaick Island in 1905. It remained in business until World War II. Courtesy, Rensselaer County Historical Society

Right: Bessemer steel works in South Troy is seen here in the late nineteenth century. Modern steel manufacturing in the United States was pioneered in a modified version of this building with the introduction of the Bessemer process in 1865. Courtesy, Rensselaer County Historical Society

Facing page: These women were ironing collars on Troy manufactured ironing machines at Cluett-Peabody in the early 1920s. Courtesy, Rensselaer County Historical Society

the workers, but also won them the enmity of management. Petty firings followed, ultimately causing mule spinners, then weavers, and finally section heads to strike. Management responded by giving the spinners thirty days' notice to vacate their tenements. In addition, no food was served in the company-owned boarding houses. Strikers were docked two weeks' pay for refusing to give notice. A detachment of police patrolled the mills and non-union French Canadian workers were recruited. A seasoned union man, J.P. McDonald, arrived from New Jersey to direct the strike and urged workers to ease their demand that overseers be dismissed. When workers went to court to sue for back pay, management finally received a joint committee of spinners and weavers. They came to an agreement whereby no trade union would be recognized by management, though mill operators would not interfere with the unions or blacklist workers. The workers regained their no-notice wages, but two impertinent weavers were not rehired.

In 1881 Harmony reduced wages by 10 percent, resulting in a four-month strike. After just two months destitution was so prevalent that the workers offered to compromise. Management responded by importing Swedish strike breakers. Although the company tried to intimidate non-striking relatives still working in the mills, the workers remained united and mostly non-violent. But hunger and poverty led to the dissolution of neighbor-hood solidarity and after four months, the strikers returned to work, having accepted the wage reduction.

During the second half of the nineteenth century, the Gateway's iron and steel industries experienced serious declines. However, metal-related manufacturing enjoyed a brief, renewed injection of vigor after 1860 when the men who built the *Monitor* brought about yet another industrial coup. In 1862 Alexander L. Holley, who became a partner with John F. Winslow and John A. Griswold, visited England and investigated Henry Bessemer's process for transforming pig iron into steel. Returning to Troy, he convinced Winslow and Griswold to join him in purchasing the American rights to this new steel-making process. The three men erected a plant on the banks of the Hudson in Troy, just north of the Menands Bridge. Here, the first Bessemer conversion of iron into steel on this side of the Atlantic took place on February 16, 1865. The works were enlarged several times and other Bessemer plants were built. In the early years of the twentieth century, however, the movement of the steel industry to the coal regions caused the last plant to go out of business.

While steel was declining, the textile industry was expanding. The second half of the nineteenth century was the great age of cotton in Cohoes. The Harmony Mills complex grew by leaps and bounds as higher speed turbines replaced lumbering waterwheels. In 1864 Harmony acquired the Strong Mill and installed a turbine there.

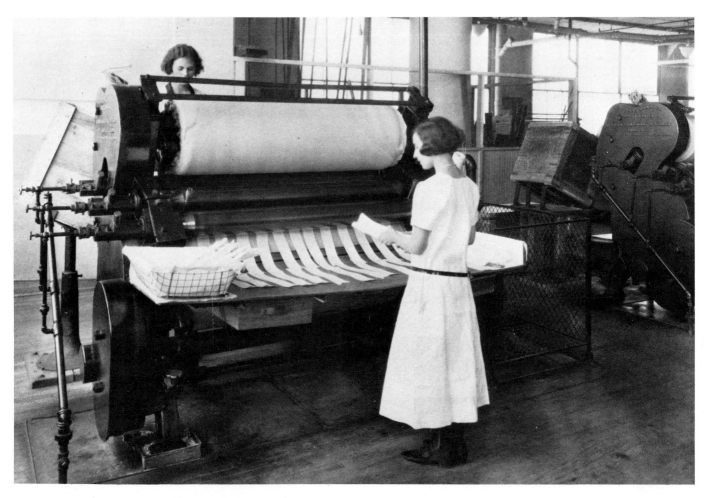

During 1866 Harmony Mill #2 was enlarged, with a Mansard roof on the top floor and turbines placed in the old wheel pit. The Mohawk Mill was purchased and French Canadian immigrant workers hired. The Harmony Company then announced that it was going to build the largest cotton mill in America, Mill #3. Ground was broken, and 700 feet of the 1,200-foot length mill were completed in that same year, 1866. The remaining 500 feet were added five to six years later.

Harmony Mills, in the late 1860s, employed 3,000 workers, ran 220,000 spindles, and in one year produced more than twenty-three million yards of cotton cloth. One hundred new tenements were constructed by John Land, the builder of Harmony Mill #3, who was so rushed that he substituted wood when he ran out of brick.

Child labor, particularly the employment of youngsters under ten, became an issue in Massachusetts in 1869. Cohoes children, however, continued to work as pickers, contributing to the inexorable growth of the Harmony complex. Then the depression of 1873 brought all indus-

trial growth to a sudden halt. Although the cotton textile industry was not so badly hit, from that time on, the mills were plagued by intermittent strikes. Skilled workers started moving out—to other plants in the area as well as to factories in the South whose competition would, before long, reduce northeast operations to a mere shadow of their nineteenth-century prosperity.

Overall, the era was a curious one. After 1850 the Gateway's once prosperous iron and steel industry began a steady decline. The area's textile industry peaked in Cohoes during the same period. However, the nation's industry, like its population, was inexorably moving to the West, and to some extent, the South. There was an urgent need for the consolidation of industry on a larger scale than was possible in the smaller Gateway cities. Continuing labor-management conflicts also exacted a toll from workers and employers alike. In the midst of apparent prosperity, then, the stage was set for a gradual downturn that would soon result in the eclipse of the Gateway as an important industrial center.

Rensselaer County's first court-house and jail, at the southeast corner of Congress and Second streets, is depicted in this late-nineteenth-century print. From History of the City of Troy, *by A.J. Weise, 1876*

CHAPTER *SIX*

GOVERNMENTS OF THE PEOPLE

Since the first communities were established in the Hudson-Mohawk Gateway area in the late 1700s, the political life of this area has reflected its growth and changing character. New England merchants and professionals, mostly young and ambitious, were the first to settle here permanently. These optimistic, transposed New Englanders expected this part of the Empire State to prosper, and this confidence was reflected in their politics.

The era of the New England mayors lasted well into the nineteenth century when, as Troy's industrial works attracted a large number of immigrants, political life changed. Increasingly, machine politics—a well-organized system of patronage and support—came to dominate. Challenges to the machine system came shortly after the First World War, and new leadership appeared in the Gateway area. Only in the last two decades has political and economic revival returned as each community again looks to the future.

After the Revolutionary War, a steady wave of merchants from New England came into the Gateway area. Already on January 1, 1771, the residents of Lansingburgh, which was known as New City, agreed to the "Proposals," a document which regulated political life. To the New England businessmen this seemed to guarantee stability, and it attracted additional immigrants. "Whereas . . . a considerable number of houses are already erected and occupied by merchants, mechanics, and others," the April 5, 1790 legislative act read, Lansingburgh was incorporated as a village. It was governed by trustees, mostly merchants who, with a vision of the village's promising future, dominated political life.

The entire area benefitted from Lansingburgh's growing economic importance and political organization. The settlement of Waterford was laid out in May 1783, on the former site of Half Moon Point. A charter granted by the state legislature on March 25, 1794 authorized freeholders and residents to make those rules and regulations necessary to maintain "the common streets and highways" as well as to prepare for "the extinguishing of fires." One of

Democrat William Marcy was elected governor of New York in 1832 and reelected in 1834 and 1836. From Dictionary of American Portraits, *by Cirker, 1967*

strated their community spirit, their democratic ideals, and their dislike of the original Dutch name.

Troy grew rapidly and an act of the legislature incorporated it as a village on February 6, 1798. Within two years Troy's population reached the 1,801 mark, and a local newspaper boasted that "a population so rapid has, we believe, but seldom been witnessed in the United States." And several years later an English visitor described Troy as "a well built town," and he predicted that it would "rival Albany" as an important center of trade.

With its growing population, Troy's political organization continued to evolve. In 1801 and 1803 the trustees gained additional rights for governing from the legislature. Political life became more intense and an English observer maintained that after arriving here he "soon perceived people divided into two parties, the Federalists and the Democrats, and that both were equally violent in their political altercations." By 1815, Troy's population had risen to 4,200, and a year later on April 12, the legislature incorporated the "City of Troy."

Troy's incorporation further defined the local governing body's responsibilities to the electorate. The Board of Magistrates was charged with organizing relief for the poor, who did not have the right to vote, and with establishing an almshouse. The mayor, who until 1840 was appointed by the governor, issued permits for the sale of alcoholic beverages and licensed butchers. The Common Council maintained the streets, bridges, and wharves. Officials were also responsible for keeping the peace and sending "disorderly persons or paupers" out of town. In addition, the city government had the responsibility to raise taxes for street lights and the operation of a night watch. On January 30, 1816, residents voted "with great unanimity" to generate funds for a local school through a new tax.

Until the 1870s the mayors of Troy retained strong connections to the merchant and professional class which had settled this area. The first mayor, Colonel Albert Pawling, operated a successful business in Lansingburgh and Troy before entering politics. The Troy Common Council later noted that Pawling "served his fellow citizens with a marked devotion, usefulness and acceptance."

Most of those who followed Pawling were guided by much the same commitment; most were transplanted New Englanders who had gained success and recognition from their commercial ventures. They reflected their constituency and its aspiring ambitions. Some of Troy's early political leaders ascended to higher office. William Marcy,

only a few villages operating under a special charter, Waterford is the oldest incorporated village in New York State.

Already in the 1780s some merchants from Lansingburgh, recognizing the limitations of ship travel that far north on the Hudson, moved southward onto land owned by three Dutch farmers. In 1786, after years of bargaining, the settlers bought building lots from the farmers, and at a meeting held on January 5, 1789, the merchants adopted the name "Troy" for their settlement. This action demon-

for example, served as a United States Senator and became governor of New York State in 1833. An ally of Martin Van Buren, Marcy coined the expression "to the victor belong the spoils."

Throughout these years the Gateway area prospered and a strong sense of community emerged. As a correspondent from the *New York Commercial Advertiser* wrote on September 18, 1835:

There is something in the character of the people. No matter where they come from, or what have been their previous habits, the moment they become residents of this place, they are Trojans. They not only look well to their own individual interests, but imbibe the same spirit of enterprise which they find prevailing and unite as one man in sustaining the interests and advancing prosperity of Troy. They know and feel that their interests are identified with those of the city, and in whatever way the latter is benefitted, they readily perceive their own general advantage.

A strong spirit of enterprise and commitment was found in other Gateway communities. Until the early 1800s, only a handful of farmers had settled at Cohoes. After the establishment of the Cohoes Manufacturing Company in 1811, the community grew moderately. By the 1840s, sentiment emerged for a more formal and better

organized local government. As the *Cohoes Advertiser* wrote in 1843:

Now for a village charter—for the water works—three or four good engines—clean streets—and a law limiting the number of dogs in each family to two, a law prohibiting swine running at large and we are a made community.

Cohoes received a charter from the Court of Sessions on June 5, 1848. In the 1860s, discussion about the incorporation of Cohoes opened again. Opponents, according to the local paper, feared that government, as in Troy, would "fall into the hands of a political rabble, and that the better class of citizens would have little or no voice in the management of affairs." Proponents insisted that local economic life would benefit and a strong sense of local pride would emerge, and this, in fact, occurred after Cohoes became an incorporated city in 1870.

The local government of the Gateway communities also established fire departments, police forces, schools, and maintained a reliable water supply. From the beginning, fire protection was a major consideration and responsibility. Already in June 1796, Troy established its first fire department and two years later, fire wardens, who controlled the firemen and directed the fire fighting, were appointed. In addition, the communities required homeowners to keep two buckets on hand at all times. When-

Fires have always plagued the Gateway. Here, in 1868, the well-known Cannon Place in Troy sustained its first of three fires. Courtesy, Rensselaer County Historical Society

Right: The great fire of 1862 in Troy started when sparks from a locomotive ignited the wooden Green Island Bridge. The fire spread into the city and much of downtown was destroyed. From History of the City of Troy, *by A.J. Weise, 1876*

Facing page: The Arba Read steam fire engine, acquired by the Arba Read fire company in Troy in 1860, was housed in the station at the northwest corner of Third and State streets. Courtesy, Rensselaer County Historical Society

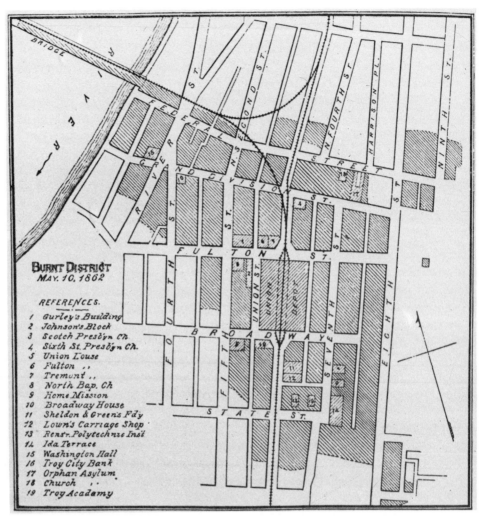

BURNT DISTRICT
MAY. 10. 1862

REFERENCES.
1 Gurley's Building
2 Johnson's Block
3 Scotch Presb'yn Ch.
4 Sixth St. Presb'yn Ch.
5 Union House
6 Fulton „
7 Tremont „
8 North Bap. Ch.
9 Home Mission
10 Broadway House
11 Sheldon & Green's Fdy
12 Lown's Carriage Shop
13 Rensr. Polytechnic Inst
14 Ida Terrace
15 Washington Hall
16 Troy City Bank
17 Orphan Asylum
18 Church „
19 Troy Academy

ever a fire broke out they were to run to the scene with the buckets and aid the fire wardens.

These measures were essential. A serious fire which struck Troy on December 8, 1797, prompted local authorities to purchase an engine. Another disastrous fire hit Troy in June 1820, destroying more than $370,000 in property. Even though Troy continued to update its equipment and personnel, a fire which started on May 10, 1862, destroyed more than 500 buildings and caused more than three million dollars in damage. Afterwards, Troy's fire department continued to improve and an early historian, Arthur Weise, called it "unexcelled in the United States."

Other Gateway communities faced similar problems. Fearing comparable property damage, measures were taken. Green Island relied on the Troy Fire Department until the 1850s, and Cohoes established a fire deparment in 1847. Unfortunately, the city's old Excelsior No. 1 en-

gine proved inadequate for the several major blazes that occurred that same year. Cohoes purchased some additional equipment and organized two fire brigades.

Besides providing fire protection, local governments were charged with maintaining public order. Already in 1786, Troy established a nightwatch of four men who patrolled the streets, checking for fires and controlling unruly behavior. In 1816, this protection cost the city $764.81. A ward system—a neighborhood based police— was introduced in 1833. But four years later a riot involving several hundred young Irish, who were responding to a hung effigy of St. Patrick, hit the city. When the police could not control the disturbance the mayor called out the Citizen's Corps.

In an effort to tighten control over the police, the Common Council in 1838 began appointing all watchmen on an annual basis. Several other measures helped increase police efficiency, and these reforms were put to a

severe test in 1863. On July 15, a public meeting opposing the conscription of soldiers into the Union Army sparked what a local newspaper described as "a rebellious demonstration."

The state government attempted local police reform when on April 22, 1865, "An Act to Establish a Capital Police District and to Provide for the Government thereof" was passed. The law provided for a new district which included Albany, Watervliet, West Troy, Green Island, Cohoes, Lansingburgh, North Greenbush, and even a part of Schenectady. The district was, however, abolished in the spring of 1870.

Another serious threat to public order came in 1882 when Troy had two rival police forces. It began as a political squabble when the Democratic members of the Board of Police Commissioners walked out of the sessions and the Republican members appointed a new force. After a brief confrontation between the opposing two police forces, the courts provided a compromise.

Broad social changes had already begun before the Civil War as large numbers of Irish and Canadian immigrants moved into the Gateway area. These new arrivals, coming to work in the iron or cotton mills, had by the 1870s caused political life to change. While the French Canadians in Cohoes were accommodated by the old political order, the Irish in Troy gradually gained control over local political affairs. As they became more settled in Troy, the Irish demanded a greater role in politics. Hard work, commercial and professional success, and the emergence of a political machine using patronage and block voting aided the Irish of Troy to gain and hold power. The new majority used some established methods in dominating political life.

In 1871, Troy's first Irish mayor, Thomas B. Carroll, took office. Three years later, Edward Murphy, another Democrat and also Irish, began an eight-year tenure as

Edward Murphy, Jr. served as Troy's mayor from 1875 to 1882 and as U.S. senator from 1892 to 1899. From Landmarks of Rensselaer County, *by George B. Anderson, 1897*

Cornelius F. Burns was mayor of Troy for eight terms, from 1912 to 1920 and from 1928 to 1936. From Troy and Rensselaer County, New York, *by Rutherford Hayner, 1925*

mayor. From Troy, Murphy went on to become an important political force in state and national Democratic Party affairs. Murphy was followed in office by Edmund Fitzgerald, an independent Democrat who, while remaining loyal to the Democratic Party and his working class constituents, often sided with the city's business leaders.

By the 1880s, a sizable Irish professional and entrepreneurial class had emerged in Troy, and Mayor Fitzgerald depended heavily on its support. The mayor represented these interests as well. He recognized that good business and prosperity demanded social order and industrial harmony. The Democratic Party in Troy clearly was maturing.

During the middle decades of the nineteenth century changes in the political life of other Gateway district communities were occurring. West Troy, originally called Gibbonsville, had its own post office already in 1817. The

state legislature, acknowledging the growth of this community, incorporated it on April 23, 1823. And in 1836, further legislation incorporated "the village of West Troy," which was made up of Gibbonsville and Port Schuyler.

Green Island, earlier known as Tibbits Island, received its articles of incorporation on April 5, 1853, and a strong sense of community began to appear. By the end of the century (and continuing through today), Green Island's political development has been strongly influenced by the McNulty family. Jack McNulty, one of seven candidates for the position, was elected tax collector in 1890. After the First World War, he won election to the Board of Supervisors and he became chairman in 1923. A year later, Governor Alfred E. Smith appointed McNulty superintendent of buildings for the state, a position which gave him control over most of the state's construction proj-

City Hall in Cohoes was constructed in 1895. Photo by Robert Thayer

ects. McNulty held this position through the terms of three governors and thereby gained a powerful political base.

In Troy the Democratic Party remained strong until after 1918 when the machine started losing some of its power. The new strength of the Republican Party came from its reorganization introduced by Dean P. Taylor and a group of young reformers. While Republicans held the mayor's office from 1924 to 1928, the Democrats regained that office and controlled it for the next two decades. Af-

ter the November 1934 election victory, local Democrats were jubilant and the party chairman insisted that:

This indicates conclusively that the people of Renssalaer County have heartily endorsed the program of President Roosevelt and Governor Lehman and that they fully recognize the ability and character of the leadership of the Democratic organization in Renssalaer County, headed by Joseph Murphy.

After 1944, the Republicans again gained control of local government. Mayor Edward Fitzgerald, who held the post for six years, emerged as a powerful mayor, and prominent Trojans increasingly viewed the mayoralty form of government as outdated. They feared that the concentration of so much power in the hands of one leader was a source of potential abuse. In 1958, Congressman Dean Taylor stated that "Troy is reaching a dangerous degree of stagnation," and he led the drive for adoption of the city manager type of government.

A revised charter took effect on January 1, 1964, and Robert Stierer became Troy's first city manager. Over the next decade, four other city managers directed local affairs. Political battles with the city council became increasingly common and acrimonious. Some observers wondered how any governing was done.

Leaders in Troy recognized the need for an economic revival, and they set up the Troy Urban Renewal Agency in 1966. Funded by President Johnson's Great Society programs, this "first-of-its-kind revitalization project for the city's entire shopping district," as the *Times Record* described it, was launched with a fourteen-million-dollar grant. But as the economy slowed, the project stalled, and it was abandoned in the mid-1970s. Local builder Carl Grimm soon came forward and built a two-level mall in downtown Troy, thereby providing some economic relief.

Residents of Cohoes inaugurated far-reaching changes and reforms when in 1967, they voted the local political machine out of office. Civic pride blossomed and Cohoes was identified as an "All America City," and was selected as one of 150 municipalities to receive special funding under the federal government's highly competitive Model Cities Program.

In recent years, the communities of the Gateway district have witnessed a modest economic and political revival. After some hard times the residents are again showing their determination to work together for the benefit of the area, much as the first settlers had done long ago.

The Laureate Boat Club was located at the foot of Glen Avenue in Troy just above the present Federal Dam. This view was taken circa 1910. Courtesy, Gene Baxter

CHAPTER SEVEN

THE SOCIAL AND CULTURAL ENVIRONMENT

As a commercial center the Gateway area from its earliest days offered room and board to weary travelers. Near the ferry landing in Troy were Ashley's Tavern and Moulton's Coffee House. Troy's Washington Square was a central location for many long-lasting establishments. The Mansion House, which opened in 1822, operated until 1926 when it was replaced by the Hendrick Hudson Hotel. On the corner of River and First streets stood Platt Titus' Eagle Tavern, later replaced by the Troy Hotel. Next door, the site of the Cannon Building in the square earlier hosted a tavern built in 1806 known variously as the Bull's Head, the Indian Queen, and the Rensselaer House. The Eldorado Hotel, dating back to the late nineteenth century, once gave shelter to William McKinley, as well as John Philip Sousa's band and Victor Herbert's orchestra. Theatrical troupes playing at the old Griswold Theater and at Proctor's also sought respite there.

Lansingburgh had an early inn on what is now Second Avenue at 116th Street. It burned in 1834, and a new hotel rising from the ashes was named, quite appropriately, the Phoenix. It still stands as a sole survivor of the thirty-five inns that once dotted nineteenth-century Lansingburgh. Across the river in Waterford, at 87 Broad Street, was the City Hotel, also called the "Foxes," which dated from 1784.

Cohoes boasted a famous resort hotel, the Cataract House, built in 1860 on the bluff overlooking the falls. A broadside issued by manager William H. Glynn noted that "the scenery from the many windows in the large Billiard Room is surprisingly beautiful, and a spacious Ball Room for the accommodation of Sleighing Parties is attached to the house." Cohoes is also the home of the area's most famous restaurant, Smith's, currently owned by Eunice Antonucci, but earlier run by Michael T. Smith, chairman of the Democratic Party and host to Albany's political

Right: This was the Phoenix Hotel on Second Avenue (formerly State Street) in Lansingburgh as it looked circa 1880. Courtesy, Lansingburgh Historical Society

Below right: The bar room in the Eldorado Hotel on Fourth Street in Troy has been restored to its 1890s appearance. Photo by Robert Thayer

machine. Smith, an enormous man, was usually pictured wearing a stark white suit and ten-gallon hat surrounded by ward leaders of lesser physical stature dressed in darker, more somber tones. In addition, there was the Elliot Hotel, now the Park Hotel, in Green Island, which opened its doors more than a century ago. Innumerable small hotels also dotted Gibbonsville and, later, West Troy.

While inns, hotels, and restaurants eagerly welcomed travelers, a multiplicity of Gateway churches willingly accepted worshipers. If sheer numbers are any indicator, nineteenth-century religion flourished. By 1900 Troy alone had seventy-two churches, more than one for every 1,000 residents. The Protestant Dutch Reformed Church, whose members follow the teachings of John Calvin, was the first church in the area. One such congregation was organized in Lansingburgh as early as 1784. Its life span was short, however, due to the influx of many Presbyterians, another Calvinist-inspired tradition, from New England.

An old Dutch church was established in Waterford in 1799. Originally standing on the site of the Grand Union warehouses on the Mechanicville road into the village, it became the "Mother Church" of Waterford Protestantism. In 1838 a Dutch Reformed community was organized within the current limits of Cohoes. Earlier, local Dutch farmers worshiped at the Reformed Dutch Church of the Boght, formed in 1784. Dutch Reformed communities were begun in Watervliet in 1814, 1840, and 1844. In fact, Watervliet has the distinction of housing Christ Church—the only Reformed congregation still flourishing in the Gateway area.

The Scots/Northern Ireland Calvinist tradition of Presbyterianism made its regional debut in Troy when a congregation was organized in 1791. Initially meeting at Ashley's Tavern, its members quickly constructed their first church edifice. There, the minister, Reverend Jonas Coe, just as hastily stirred controversy by introducing into the church building a stove, carpeting, and soon thereafter, a bass viol and other musical instruments. These creature comforts were more than some Calvinist souls could bear. Presbyterian congregations prospered in many other Gateway cities as well, and, over the years, as many as fourteen such churches were established in Troy alone. Baptist congregations flourished as well, including a church founded in Troy in 1793, and others in Lansingburgh, Waterford, Watervliet, and Cohoes shortly there-

after.

The Methodist church was also active. Freeborn Garrettson, the great apostle of Methodism in the Hudson valley, visited Lansingburgh in 1788, while Thankful and Zadok King conducted Methodist prayer services in their home in Waterford. Circuit riders, the early Methodist traveling preachers, visited both Lansingburgh and Waterford in the late eighteenth century, and congregations were soon organized throughout the area.

Episcopal churches were also founded in the Gateway with the original parishes of St. Paul's and Trinity being established in Troy and Lansingburgh in 1804. A Quaker community was created in Troy as early as 1803, but began to decline after 1840.

Roman Catholicism grew rapidly in the Gateway as immigrants arrived first from Ireland and French Canada and later from southern and eastern Europe. The premier Catholic parish was St. Peter's in Troy, established in

The Mansion House was a landmark in Troy for over 100 years. This view shows the hotel and Washington Square in 1870. Courtesy, Rensselaer County Historical Society

Right: St. Bernard's Church, on Ontario Street in Cohoes, is shown here at the turn of the century. Completed in 1866 to serve the growing mill community, it still has the original stained glass windows donated by the iron works, cotton mills, woolen mills, and citizens of Cohoes. Courtesy, New York State Library

Facing page, left: The Reverend Henry Highland Garnet, pastor of the Liberty Street Presbyterian Church in Troy in the 1840s, became a national figure upon his delivery of a discourse against slavery at the House of Representatives in 1865. From A Memorial Discourse, *by H.H. Garnet, 1865*

Right: The Reverend Peter Havermans worked to establish numerous schools, orphanages, and hospitals in the Gateway area. From Landmarks of Rensselaer County, *by George B. Anderson, 1897*

1824. The potato famine in the late 1830s brought a great influx of Irish immigrants, spurring the creation of many additional parishes in other Gateway cities.

Lutherans were not organized in the Gateway until 1870 when Troy's Trinity Church was established. However, the Gilead Evangelical Lutheran Church of Center Brunswick, formed in 1742 by Germans from the Palatinate, served area Lutherans before that time.

Trojan Jews first organized a Reformed congregation, B'rith Sholom, in 1866. Its members built a temple four years later. Still in use, the structure is the oldest Reformed Jewish synagogue in New York State. The current Orthodox congregation, Beth Tephilah, is the result of the union of Beth Israel Bikor Sholom, which gathered before 1870; congregation Chai Adam, dating from 1890; Sharah Tephilah, organized in 1873 by Polish and Russian Jews; and Beth Jacob of Cohoes. It is located in Troy. The Conservative congregation Beth El is also headquartered in Troy.

The abundance of churches and synagogues in the Gateway was due primarily to an early lack of public transportation. Before the advent of street railways in the 1860s, the poorer classes were confined to an area which could easily be traversed on foot. Occasionally, doctrinal disputes, and more often ethnic and class distinctions, led to the formation of new congregations. In some instances, well-to-do worshipers erected memorials as monuments.

In an age of better transportation and declining religious affiliation, a multitude of small denominations, each supporting its own clergy and building, became harder to justify. Since World War II, then, the trend has been toward merger and, in some instances, closure of many congregations. However, the arrival of newer fundamentalist Christian bodies has been cause for the reuse of some old structures and the erection of many simpler religious buildings.

Another major influx of Eastern Europeans and Asians brought the orthodox Christian churches of Greece, Russia, and the Ukraine, as well as the early Christian Church of Armenia. If religion today is not the force that it was in the nineteenth-century Gateway, worship is certainly more diverse and varied.

During the nineteenth century the area witnessed the ministry of some towering religious figures. Nathan Beman, "haughty, cold, overbearing, and tyrannical," was the most controversial. Arriving from Georgia in 1822,

Beman became pastor of the First Presbyterian Church of Troy. Denouncing both liquor and slavery, which was still very much alive in the upper Hudson valley, he was usually embroiled in controversy with his congregation. Nevertheless, he served as pastor for some forty years.

Henry Highland Garnet was also a Presbyterian divine and a major black leader of national stature in America's emancipation movement. The grandson of a Mandiggo warrior chieftain and the son of slaves, he escaped with his family to Troy when his slaveowner died in 1824. He served as pastor of the black Liberty Street Presbyterian Church in Troy from 1840 to 1848, and then moved to New York City to become minister of the Shiloh Presbyterian Church. During his lifetime, Garnet became a distinguished writer, newspaper publisher, and preacher with enormous influence not only in Troy but throughout the country. "Let your motto be resistance" was his cry. In 1881 he became U.S. minister to Liberia and died there the following year.

Peter Havermans, a Dutch native of Flemish lineage, arrived in Troy in 1841 and subsequently served as pastor of St. Mary's Roman Catholic Church for more than fifty-two years. When he died in 1897 at age ninety-one, he was the oldest Catholic priest in America, having served in the priesthood for sixty-seven years. As part of his ministry, he helped to establish other Roman Catholic

churches in the area, as well as innumerable schools, orphanages, homes for the aged poor, and hospitals to serve the social needs of working-class Catholics. Havermans was ecumenical at a time when ecumenism was hardly the rule, and he was a prime mover in winning acceptance for Roman Catholics and their church in an alien environment.

Another towering nineteenth-century religious figure was John Ireland Tucker, first, and for fifty years, rector of Troy's Holy Cross Episcopal Church. Tucker's greatest fame resulted from his talents as a musician. In 1870 he completed the *Parish Hymnal*, and two years later, brought out the *Church Musical Hymnal*, which was said to have "raised the standard of psalmody from Atlantic to Pacific."

One twentieth-century religious figure, recently deceased, stands out above others. William M. Slavin was the first resident Catholic chaplain at Rensselaer Polytechnic Institute and later served as pastor of Our Lady of Victory Church in Troy. In the pre-World War II period, when America first broke out of its isolationist bonds, Slavin broadcast a nationally acclaimed Sunday radio program called "News of the Week from a Catholic Viewpoint." When he entered the U.S. Navy as a chaplain in 1943, a glowing editorial in the Troy newspaper acknowledged his contribution toward expanding and broadening Americans' view of the world. Active in a variety of community affairs, Slavin was instrumental in founding the Troy Human Rights Commission, for which Roy Wilkins, long the guiding spirit of the NAACP, bestowed on him honorary life membership. Undoubtedly his greatest contribution, however, was his ecumenical spirit.

In an age when government had not yet assumed responsibility for human services, churches filled the need. For example, during the past 150 years, four out of five orphanages established in the Gateway were church-related.

In the nineteenth century industrial accidents were not a rarity: when one working parent was killed or incapacitated, the surviving spouse assumed the responsibility of sole breadwinner. The children were often placed in institutional care. The earliest orphanage, the Troy Orphan Asylum, privately founded in 1833, still operates today in Wynantskill as Vanderheyden Hall. Four other orphanages were created by the Roman Catholic Church. Of these, however, only St. Colman's Home, located outside Watervliet in the town of Colonie, is still functioning.

Aged, sick, infirm, and destitute residents are still looked after by the Church Home of Troy, founded in 1854; the Little Sisters of the Poor (now moved to Latham); and the Presbyterian Home Associates of the City of Troy. The privately-endowed Deborah Powers Home for Old Ladies went out of existence a few years

ago. Much of the former work performed by these institutions has been taken over by county affiliates and private nursing homes. And for the active elderly, senior citizen centers abound.

Youngsters were once cared for by the Mount Magdalen School of Industry, the Reformatory of the Good Shepherd, and the Guardian Angels Home and Industrial School for young women. This institution survived under the latter title until the 1960s. Martha Memorial House, adjacent to St. Paul's Episcopal Church in Troy, was founded in 1881 to promote missionary work among working women. There also existed Seton House for Working Girls in Troy, as well as a Bethesda Home for homeless and friendless girls and women, which after several moves, survives today in Lansingburgh.

Perhaps no organizations epitomized the Gateway's spirit of social service better than the Mary Warren Free School of Troy and the Harmony Hill Union Sunday School of Cohoes. In 1839 Mary Warren initiated a charity day school for the daughters of the working class at St. Paul's Episcopal Church. As part of the music curriculum, the girls became members of the choir, a move which was apparently unacceptable to some parishioners. So Mary Warren founded the Church of the Holy Cross as "a house of prayer for all people, without money and without price." The Warren Free Institute of the City of Troy was incorporated in 1846 "for the instruction of in-

The Society of Friends meeting-house was located at the southwest corner of Fourth and State streets in Troy in the early nineteenth century. St. Anthony's Roman Catholic Church now occupies the site. Courtesy, Rensselaer County Historical Society

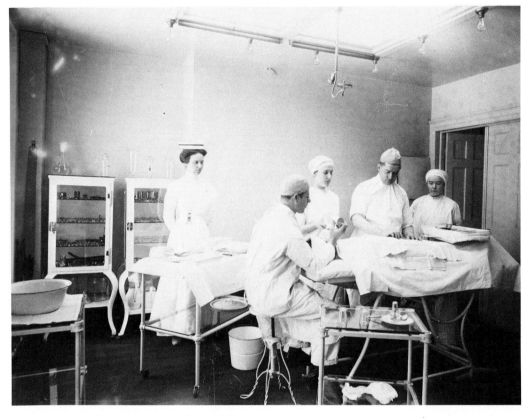

The operating room at Leonard Hospital in Lansingburgh is seen here at the turn of the century. Courtesy, Warren Broderick

digent female children" and a building adjacent to the church housed the school.

The Harmony Hill Union Sunday School was shorter lived but flourished under the aegis of David J. Johnston, whose family managed the Harmony Mills. Founded in the winter of 1853-54, the school maintained ties to the Baptist Church, but was nondenominational. It probably offered the bulk of formal education received by mill children. The number of pupils attending the school grew from eleven in 1854 to 1,124 in 1877. Supported by the mills, it offered "artistically" decorated rooms, pictures, maps, blackboards, an excellent organ, and a library of over 1,000 volumes. In December, yuletide festivities were held in Harmony Hall where the children unwrapped Christmas presents. A spring strawberry festival and a summer picnic were other annual highlights. However, by 1890 attendance was down to 540 students. One year after David J. Johnston died in 1894, the school closed its doors.

Hospitals also sprang up in the Gateway to serve the health needs of local residents. The oldest such institution, the Troy Hospital, was opened in 1850 by the Roman Catholic Church under the guidance of Father Peter Havermans. That building proved inadequate to meet the

needs of the community and the rapid medical and nursing advances made during the Civil War. A new structure on Eighth Street at the head of Grand Street was subsequently opened in 1871. In 1914 the hospital moved to its present location on Oakwood Avenue, and at midcentury was formally renamed St. Mary's Hospital.

An early hospital for the insane was the private venture of Benjamin Marshall, the entrepreneur known for developing the third and greatest water power system in the Poestenkill Gorge in Troy. The Marshall Infirmary and Rensselaer County Lunatic Asylum was built in 1850 on a bluff to the south of the gorge. One of the patients was Marshall's son, who suffered from severe emotional illness. Eventually, as New York State took over the care of the mentally ill, the number of patients declined. Marshall's sanitarium was razed about twenty years ago.

The Cohoes Hospital had its origins in 1891 when the city appointed a commission to purchase a suitable site. In the 1950s the hospital board purchased twenty-three acres on Columbia Street and after two major fund drives opened the modern Cohoes Hospital in 1960.

Lansingburgh's hospital owed its existence to the beneficence of Dr. Frederick B. Leonard who left his home to be used as a hospital. New wings were added in 1926 and

1933, and in 1972 a completely new 159-bed facility was
opened. It is the only hospital-based, certified Home
Health Care Agency in Rensselaer County.

The largest hospital in the Gateway area, offering 300
beds, is the Samaritan Hospital of Troy. It is equipped
with a medical office building, a mental health division,
and a detoxification unit. The Eddy Geriatric Center, associated with the hospital, is presently constructing nearby apartments with "assistive living services" to provide
maximum independence for the elderly.

The Howard and Bush Foundation, serving the needs
of residents in the Hartford, Connecticut and Troy areas,
has contributed funding to numerous hospitals and all
forms of social and community services. In fact, there are
monuments to the extraordinary generosity of Edith
Mason Howard and her niece, Julia Howard Bush, in al-

most every community service institution in the area.

The Gateway has long provided a wide variety of social
and service clubs for its residents. In 1900 the Troy
Chamber of Commerce developed out of a group calling
itself the Commercial Travelers' Association. The chamber
initiated a Troy Week some eight years later. Former Trojan sons and daughters returned home to a seven-day
celebration of Troy's industrial and business greatness.
Chamber members have enjoyed a long tradition of active
involvement in community affairs. In 1924, for example,
after determining that there were fifty-two private, non-
church-related welfare organizations in Troy, the members
helped to form a Community Social Welfare Chest which
developed into today's Mohawk-Hudson Area United
Way. In more recent years, the Chamber enlarged its
scope to encompass most of the Gateway.

Area women have long been meeting to pursue personal, social, and political concerns. The Women's Improvement Society of Troy, which first met in 1906, later became the Women's Civic League. Members sought basic reforms which are now taken for granted, such as food inspection, health regulations, and garbage disposal. The Troy Women's Club, founded in 1920, has had as many as 500 members and continues to attract a significant number of women, and the Junior League actively satisfies its community service goals.

Service clubs such as Rotary, Kiwanis, and Lions draw area business people together in a combined spirit of camaraderie and humanitarianism. And fraternal organizations, especially the Masons, have flourished in almost all Gateway communities from their earliest days. Apollo Lodge No. 49 first met in Troy's Moulton's Coffee House in 1796, and Troy Masonry still boasts three lodges and eight coordinate bodies housed in the former Robison Mansion on Brunswick Road. Odd Fellows have had lodges in Troy, Watervliet, Green Island, and Cohoes, and the Elks boast very active chapters in Troy and Watervliet. The Knights of Columbus have councils in all Gateway communities. At various times, the Order of Druids, Knights of Pythias, Maccabees, Red Men, Owls, Moose, Knights of Malta, and Royal Arcanum have also attracted followings in the region.

Ethnic organizations have also thrived in the Gateway. Danes were once served by a Danish brotherhood in Lansingburgh. Germania Hall continues to flourish in the same section of the city of Troy. Clubs for Poles and Ukranians have found homes in Troy, and Ukranian-American Citizens Clubs, in both Watervliet and Cohoes. A Federation of Armenians Picnic Grounds once flourished in North Greenbush, while French Canadian interests are still very much alive in Cohoes. Church-sponsored activities continue to meet the needs of other ethnic groups like the Greeks. Troy has a community center for Italians housed in an old mansion on Washington Park. Green Island has a modern, circular center for its Italian Fraternal Society. Irish residents in Troy and Watervliet enjoy very active chapters of the Ancient Order of Hibernians. And each year on the feast of St. Patrick, the Friendly Sons of St. Patrick, a society which welcomes persons of all ethnic origins, holds a gala black tie dinner.

Troy's black residents have played a significant role in that city's history. In the 1840s regional, state, and national meetings of blacks working toward abolition were

Sojourner Truth attended an abolitionist meeting in Troy in the 1840s. Courtesy, National Portrait Gallery, Smithsonian Institution, Washington, D.C.

held in Troy. The last of these sessions was attended by Frederick Douglass, Harriet Tubman, and Sojourner Truth. The NAACP has long been active in Troy as well.

Troy was also an important station for runaway slaves on the Underground Railway to Canada. While Harriet Tubman was visiting the city in 1860, an escaped slave, Charles Nalle, was arrested on a warrant from Virginia. As he was being taken away, an angry crowd gathered and someone raised a cry. Nalle escaped during the ensuing melee. Later Uri Gilbert, Nalle's employer, raised $650 from the Trojan community to purchase Nalle's freedom. This is not to say that blacks have always been treated well in Troy. During the nineteenth century black residents were forced to attend separate and less-than-equal schools, confined to work in lower-paying positions,

"Uncle Sam," by sculptor George Kratina, stands at the entrance to Riverfront Park in Troy. Photo by Robert Chase

and denied participation in the industrialization process. Because their freedoom was seen as a threat to immigrant job security, blacks were also harassed by white workers during the Civil War. Between 1829 and 1856 the names of black families were italicized in city directories. After World War II the Gateway's black population increased substantially as many black southerners migrated north from South Carolina to Troy.

The arts have always enjoyed a receptive atmosphere in the Gateway. During the nineteenth century the region was the home of several significant painters and a host of lesser artists. One outstanding painter was Abel Buell Moore, who arrived in Troy in 1823 to paint portraits, an important art form in the era before photography. Moore soon became the portraitist for many of Troy's wealthiest citizens. William Richardson Tyler came to Troy in 1841 to work as a railroad car muralist for the highly respected firm of Eaton and Gilbert. He later opened his own studio and painted landscapes and seascapes after the manner of the Hudson River School.

Like Tyler, Green Island's David Cunningham Lithgow started out as a muralist for the Gilbert car works, but later opened his own studio in Albany. He became a familiar figure on Gateway streets, fashionably dressed in an elegant outfit that was accented by a black derby and pince-nez glasses.

The area's music lovers have enjoyed a justifiable pride in the Troy Music Hall. One of America's acoustically greatest musical spaces, it opened on April 19, 1875, with a concert by American composer Edward A. MacDowell. Great performers including such notables as Ignace Paderewski and Sergei Rachmaninoff have given concerts there, as have the world's greatest symphony orchestras.

One of the area's most famous and longest-lived musical organizations was Dorings Band founded as the Troy Band in 1846. During the Civil War most of its members joined the Union forces to entertain the soldiers of the 2nd Regiment, and some years later, in 1898, the performers again enlisted to play for the troops in the Spanish-American War. The band subsequently served on the Mexican border in 1916 and again in World War I. The musicians, led for nearly eighty-five years by Charles Doring and then by his son, George, have recently faded from the local scene. However, Robert Weiss of Lansingburgh, the band's last leader, still retains the music and the uniforms. If called upon, he could still reunite a group of musicians under the old name.

In the realm of literature the Benet siblings, William Rose, Stephen Vincent, and Laura, as well as Herman Melville, placed the Gateway on the literary map. The Benets' father served as commandant of the Watervliet Arsenal between 1919 and 1921. His talented offspring wrote fiction, poetry, and criticism. Herman Melville resided in Lansingburgh during nine of the most eventful years of his early manhood. In fact, his first published piece of fiction, "Fragments from a Writing Desk," appeared in the *Democratic Press and Lansingburgh Advertiser* on May 4,

This is the interior of Rand's Opera House at Third and Congress streets in Troy as it appeared after remodeling in 1872. The hall seated 1,450 people. Courtesy, Rensselaer County Historical Society

1837. His ties to Lansingburgh ended, however, with his 1847 marriage to Boston-born Elizabeth Shaw.

Vaudeville flourished in the Gateway from the 1890s to the 1930s. Cohoes, in fact, was the hometown of that era's greatest star, Eva Tanguay. Eva came from a poor French Canadian family that had taken up residence in Cobble Alley. She was short and plump with an engaging personality, but a most unexceptional singing voice. To make up for this deficiency, she appeared as an outrageously

dressed, tousle-haired, bleached blonde, warbling her favorite tune, "I Don't Care." In her heyday in 1918 she was paid up to $3,000 a week, an enormous sum for that time.

Theater was very much a part of Troy's entertainment scene. The first performance of "Uncle Tom's Cabin" took place in Peale's Troy Museum, and the city also boasted such great palaces as Rand's, Shea's, Griswold's, and the Troy Opera House. Legendary vaudevillians such as Lillian Russell, Eddie Cantor, and Al Jolson brought live diversion to the common Trojan, bequeathing one of vaudeville's greatest gifts.

The Cohoes Music Hall carried on into the early years of the twentieth century, hosting celebrities like Buffalo Bill Cody, John Philip Sousa, Sarah Bernhardt, and Harry Houdini. After changing hands several times, the building was perfectly restored with the help of federal, state, and local aid. It reopened in 1975, headlining the same play it

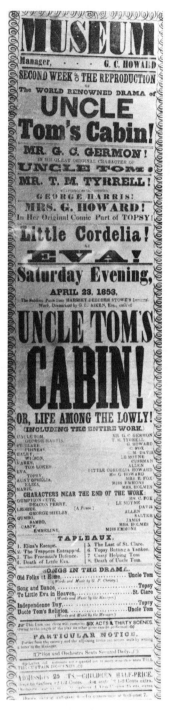

Above: This broadside advertised an 1853 performance of "Uncle Tom's Cabin" which had its debut in Troy the year before. Courtesy, New York State Library

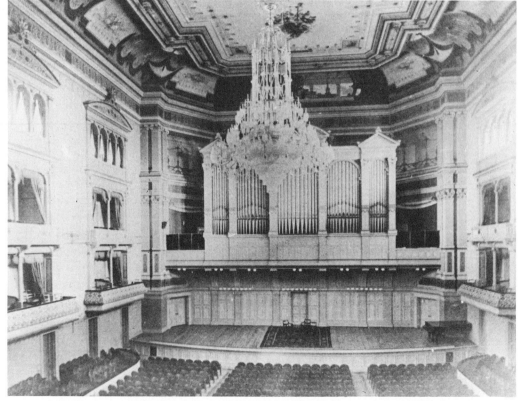

had featured nearly 100 years earlier, "London Assurance."

Sports have formed a lively part of the Gateway's recreational activities. The area produced three world heavyweight boxing champions: John Morrissey, Paddy Ryan, and John Carroll Heenan. John Morrissey of Troy was by far the most colorful. During his lifetime, he was a bartender, saloon-brothel bouncer, riverboat deckhand, gang leader, ward heeler, Tammany leader and opponent, bigtime gambler, an owner of the Saratoga Race Track, friend of the socially and financially elite, state senator, and congressman. He was also heavyweight champion of the world. One story particularly illustrates his fiery temperament. To celebrate his success, Morrissey decided to build himself a splendid mansion in his hometown. However, Troy's business and financial elite successfully stymied his plans by blocking the purchase of the property, so Morrissey built a soap factory downwind from the city's residential district. Daily, the fumes of the industrial process wafted slowly over the elegant homes of Troy's leading citizens. The resulting stench was Morrissey's revenge.

In 1866 a newly-organized baseball team, the Haymakers of Lansingburgh, played the Mutuals of New York on the home green. They defeated the visitors by a lopsided score reported to be 150 to 32. Five years later the Haymakers came in third in the first season of professional baseball organized under the National Association, which was succeeded by the National League. In 1882 six of the players, including Buck Ewing, one of early baseball's greatest catchers, went to New York City to form the nucleus of the New York Giants. It was John J. Evers, however, who became the area's greatest contribution to professional baseball. Traded to the Chicago Nationals in 1902, Johnny Evers was touted for his deft fielding, mighty batting, and brilliant mastery of the "inside play." In 1914 he joined the Boston Braves as a member of the "miracle team" which won both the National League championship and the World Series.

Facing page, top right: The Lansingburgh Historical Society, at First Avenue and 114th Street, occupies what was once the residence of Herman Melville. Frances D. Broderick painted this watercolor. From the artist's collection

Bottom: This is a view of the Troy Music Hall in the Troy Savings Bank building circa 1890. From Troy Illustrated, *1891*

Journalism formed another dynamic part of the Gateway's tradition. The early municipalities published a multiplicity of newspapers. In Waterford, for example, during a century and a quarter, some ten newspapers were produced. However, these early publications were not particularly *news* papers. The front sheet was usually consumed by short advertisements, while the inner sheets contained acts of Congress, a little federal news, essays, and lugubrious obituaries written in verse. The articles focusing on local personages would most certainly be considered libelous today. Local news coverage did improve as the nineteenth century progressed but Gateway publications had more than their share of lengthy, often pointless, editorials.

Watervliet had the *West Advocate* from 1834 to 1865. The *Watervliet Journal,* founded in 1860, subsequently changed its name to the *Watervliet Journal and Democrat.* Cohoes' earliest paper, the *Cohoes Advertiser,* was created in 1847, soon becoming the *Journal* and the *Cataract.*

The number and variety of general and special interest papers published in the Gateway since 1787 is testimony to the fact that national magazines, radio, and television have only recently arrived on the scene as mass communication vehicles. One local paper of particular interest was the *Northern Budget,* founded in Lansingburgh in 1797. Colonel Charles L. MacArthur joined another great Troy newspaperman, John M. Francis, to purchase the *Budget* in 1867, transforming it into one of the foremost Sunday journals in New York State. The paper continued to be published by MacArthur's heirs until 1917, when it was finally sold out of the family.

John M. Francis, Colonel MacArthur's partner in the 1847 purchase of the *Budget,* was only twenty-two years old at the time. He left the *Budget* in 1849, and two years later established the *Troy Daily Times* which, under his management, soon grew to be one of the most powerful newspapers in the state.

One other Trojan newspaperman stands out in the history of Gateway journalism. Dwight Marvin, a lawyer, became editor of the *Troy Morning Record and the Evening Record* in 1915. He remained in that post for forty-three years until his retirement in 1958. His career was a distinguished one. His excellence and influence as a journalist were recognized not only in Troy, but throughout the state and the nation at large. During his editorship, the *Record* merged with the *Troy Daily Times* to form the *Troy Times Record,* creating the sole daily newspaper remaining in the Gateway area today.

This Pawling Avenue villa featured a wrap-around porch, a picket fence, and a landscaped yard. The house still stands but is devoid of some of its whimsical decoration. Courtesy, Carl S. Erickson

CHAPTER EIGHT

THE ARCHITECTURAL ENVIRONMENT

Buildings define and distinguish each of the communities of the Hudson-Mohawk Gateway and daily provide tangible evidence of their history. These buildings and the streetscapes they form testify not only to the skills of architects and contractors but also to the aesthetic standards and civic-mindedness of their clients. While much has been lost to fire, neglect, or deliberate demolition, each Gateway community retains scores of notable structures, and Troy boasts some of the finest architecture to be found in any small city in America.

The earliest remaining buildings reflect the Dutch settlement of the Hudson Valley. The Van Schaick House, situated on Van Schaick Island, is believed to have been built about 1735. Its Dutch origins are evident in the gambrel roof (a distinctive form with a broad, steep lower slope topped with a narrower, flatter upper slope), sturdy walls of local brick, chimneys inside each end wall, and a central doorway. Just across the Hudson in Lansingburgh, the dwelling at 580 First Avenue (c. 1770) has an additional half-story tucked beneath a gambrel roof, which is supported by walls laid up in English bond—alternating rows of stretchers (the broad sides of the brick) and headers (the narrow ends). Two blocks south, the two-story house at 524 First Avenue, built a few years later, is significantly larger in size as well as scale.

These two Lansingburgh houses stand near the western boundary of the town plan laid out by 1771 at the direction of trader Abraham Jacob Lansing. Delineating the area between the river and what is now 111th and 114th streets and Seventh Avenue, the plan had as its centerpiece a rectangular village green "reserved to Public use" and framed by a grid of streets and alleys which formed building lots measuring 120 feet by 50 feet. The Lansingburgh plan is a notable example of pre-Revolutionary town planning in upstate New York, and the green is still a public space.

The close of the Revolution brought waves of immigrants from New England who settled in Lansingburgh

The Hart-Cluett mansion, at 59 Second Street in Troy, was built in 1827 by William Howard of New York City as a wedding gift for Richard P. and Betsey Hart. Courtesy, Rensselaer County Historical Society

and the newer villages of Troy and Waterford. Dwellings of this period are typically two-stories with window trim nearly flush with exterior walls and hipped or gabled roofs. Smaller houses of this era have a stair hall along one end wall, while larger houses have a center hall plan. Important survivors are the substantial four-square, brick Janes House at the foot of 116th Street and the block of row houses at 612-616 Third Avenue, whose doorways are framed by brick archways. The Lansingburgh Academy (1820), whose function is signaled primarily by an eight-sided, louvred lantern rising from a truncated tower, is only slightly larger in scale than its residential counterparts. Two handsome brick houses attest to Waterford's contemporaneous growth—the Nathaniel Doe House at 60 Third Street and the Isaac Eddy House at 37 Middle Street. Both have elegantly detailed doorways and brick walls laid up in Flemish bond, where headers and stretch-

ers alternate in every course.

In 1793 Troy became the seat of Rensselaer County, demonstrating its increasing vigor and predominance over Lansingburgh. Two remarkable residences were harbingers of Troy's economic growth, as well. The Vail House (1818) at the corner of First and Congress streets has a Flemish bond facade enriched with carved stone trim and iron grilles; the interior has a spectacular, circular three-story stairway and finely detailed wooden trim with decorative painting dating from 1875. The Hart-Cluett Mansion at 59 Second Street is architecturally an equal of prominent houses in New York City. Completed in 1827, it has a white marble facade, elaborate wrought- and cast-iron railings, plaster cornices with egg and dart moldings, and a cantilevered stairway.

Captivated by accounts of the Greek war for independence, Americans during the 1830s looked to antiquity for its building forms and details and adapted them into a truly American architectural style: the Greek Revival. Fortuitously, this fervor for the Greek Revival coincided with a period of economic growth in the Gateway region and resulted in the construction of outstanding examples of high style and vernacular Greek Revival buildings for civic, commercial, religious, industrial, and domestic purposes. Three building forms predominated. The fully developed temple front has a gable and freestanding columns boldly facing the street; examples include houses at 713 and 819 Third Avenue in Lansingburgh, the First Baptist Church in Troy, and the White Homestead in Waterford. In other buildings the portico was compressed to form subtly projecting pilasters and pediments, as in the Atheneum in Troy and the United Methodist Church of Lansingburgh. Brick residences with simple, broad cornices and recessed entrances with fluted columns or pilasters are a third form; remaining examples include 554 First Avenue in Lansingburgh, 110 Third Street

Above: This was the front parlor of the Hart home in the 1880s. The classical details of the woodwork are from the original construction although the Victorian furnishings reflect the family's desire to keep up with changing styles. Courtesy, Rensselaer County Historical Society

Left: The Van Schaick house in Cohoes is one of the few remaining buildings representing the Dutch settlement of the Gateway region in the seventeenth and eighteenth centuries. Courtesy, Rensselaer County Historical Society

Above: This is the First Presbyterian Church on Seminary Park in Troy as it appeared in the late nineteenth century. Courtesy, Rensselaer County Historical Society

Left: The White Homestead, a Greek Revival house with a temple front, is now the Waterford Historical Museum. Photo by Robert Chase

Right: This is Quarters One at the Watervliet Arsenal as it appeared in the 1870s. Courtesy, Watervliet Arsenal Museum, U.S. Army photograph

in Troy, and the Commandant's House at the Watervliet Arsenal.

These buildings incorporate generous quantities of Greek Revival motifs—Doric, Ionic, and Corinthian columns or pilasters, anthemions, dentil moldings, and cabriole brackets, but even in industrial and commercial buildings where detailing is minimal, the studied proportions and simplicity that characterize the Greek Revival are apparent. Examples include the River Street warehouses north of Congress Street and the Cannon Building (1835) designed by Alexander Jackson Davis in Troy

and the Benet Laboratories at the Watervliet Arsenal.

In Troy the wide appeal and versatility of the Greek Revival is well-illustrated by three outstanding structures. Designed in 1834 by architect James H. Dakin, the former First Presbyterian Church, now the Julia Howard Bush Memorial Center, ranks nationally as one of the earliest and most accurate examples of a hexastyle, or six-columned, Doric temple. Its unobstructed auditorium retains the original shallow, coffered dome. To the south Washington Park was laid out in 1840 in the manner of London's private residential squares; the ten rowhouses along

encrusted with crockets, and rib vaults were common features. Consecrated in 1828, Saint Paul's Episcopal Church in Troy recalls the boxy form of a New England meetinghouse, but the lancet windows, tracery, and pinnacles of the tower signaled a rising interest in Gothic forms. Smaller Episcopal congregations embraced Gothic forms reminiscent of rural English parish churches; their buildings typically had stone walls braced with buttresses, steeply pitched roofs, and a corner tower. Notable examples include Saint John's in Troy and Saint Mark's in Green Island.

The Warren family of Troy, prosperous from their businesses and rich in intellectual curiosity, traveled to England where they studied church architecture and choral services. The Warrens brought to Troy three prominent architects from New York—Alexander Jackson Davis, Richard Upjohn, and Henry Dudley—and became important architectural patrons, commissioning the Church of the Holy Cross, its parsonage, the Mary Warren Free Institute, a crenellated villa on Mount Ida (whose steep-roofed, picturesque Gothic gatehouse survives at 95 Cottage Avenue), and a private family chapel atop a knoll in Oakwood Cemetery. The Warrens also supported Saint Paul's, which is embellished with plaques in their memory.

Many other congregations also built with the finest materials and craftsmanship. The Jermain Memorial Church (1874) in Watervliet remains resplendently intact with a wood-paneled sanctuary, limestone and sandstone facades, a Victorian Gothic fence, and a pinnacle encircled with an iron railing. Equally distinctive in the skyline is Christ Church United Methodist in Troy, whose soaring limestone spire recalls the steeples of English towns. Many other mid-nineteenth century churches have facades of red brick with corbelled cornices, round-headed windows, and brownstone trim. Remaining examples include the First United Presbyterian Church and Saint John's Lutheran Church in Troy, Saint Agnes Church in Cohoes, and Saint Patrick's Church in Watervliet. Saint Joseph's Catholic Church in South Troy is remarkable for its massive tower and stained glass windows by the studio of Louis Comfort Tiffany.

Mid-nineteenth century American landscapes were influenced by an interest in the picturesque—seemingly casual but carefully arranged grounds dotted with fanciful structures connected by undulating paths. Consecrated in 1850, Oakwood Cemetery in Troy grew from this tradition. Troy industrialists and merchants erected extraordi-

the south side, called Washington Place, have a common pediment, massive brownstone stoops, and elaborate ironwork with female figures and miniature columns. On Second Street, midway between these two monumental structures, are three wooden temples, originally known as Cottage Row, which though more modest in scale, received national recognition in 1843.

For religious buildings, congregations and their architects often looked to a different past for inspiration and created from medieval forms new buildings in a style known as the Gothic Revival. Pointed arches, pinnacles

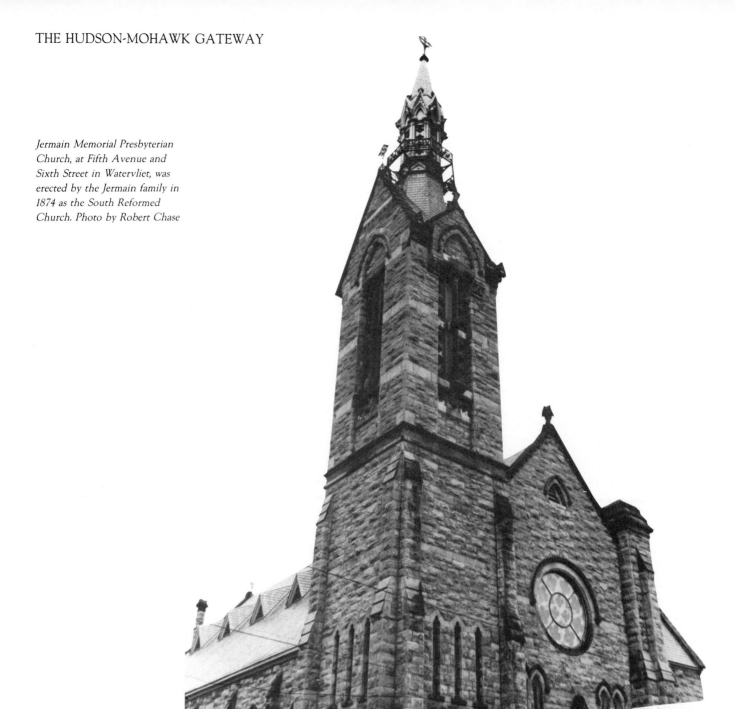

Jermain Memorial Presbyterian Church, at Fifth Avenue and Sixth Street in Watervliet, was erected by the Jermain family in 1874 as the South Reformed Church. Photo by Robert Chase

nary monuments and mausoleums with Greek, Gothic, and even Egyptian motifs amid "its shady dells and breezy heights, its crystal water and noble shade trees."

By mid-century, the Gateway's industrial products—bells, stoves, valves, cotton cloth, and shirts and collars—had won international acclaim. Blocks of modest, flat-roofed brick row houses and detached frame dwellings were erected to meet new demands for workers' housing. Their two-story facades were typically ornamented with bracketed cornices, flat-arched windows, and slightly recessed, paneled doorways. Hundreds of examples remain in South Troy and on Cataract Street and Harmony Hill in Cohoes.

A fire that swept through central Troy in 1862 enabled

the newly prosperous industrial and merchant class to build imposing residences of brick and brownstone, rivaling those found in New York and Brooklyn. Still standing along Fifth Avenue and on First, Second, and Grand streets, their three-story facades have high brownstone stoops, elaborately bracketed cornices, and bay windows, a hallmark of the Troy row house. Only twenty to twenty-eight feet in width, these dwellings were spatially efficient and often lavish; interiors feature deep plaster moldings, marble mantels, paneled woodwork painted in imitation of exotic hardwoods, and parlors of impressive proportions.

Illumination was provided by the Troy Gas Light Company, which constructed a circular, brick gasholder house

*Above: The Vail family mauso-
leum in Oakwood Cemetery is a
Gothic masterpiece constructed in
sandstone. Photo by Robert Chase*

*Left: Washington Place in Troy is
shown here in the late nineteenth
century. The common pediment
was still intact although the central cupola had been removed and
Victorian bay windows had been
added to the second floors. Courtesy, Rensselaer County Historical
Society*

Right: This is an early view of the Hall Building (now Rice Building) at River and First streets in Troy. Courtesy, Rensselaer County Historical Society

Facing page, top: Mid-nineteenth-century housing for the Harmony Mill complex is still standing on North Mohawk Street in Cohoes. Photo by Robert Chase

Bottom: This is the architectural rendering of the building designed by M.F. Cummings & Son for the George P. Ide & Co. in 1907. It was one of the many steel-framed, "fire-proof" collar factories built along River Street in Troy in the early twentieth century. Courtesy, Rensselaer County Historical Society

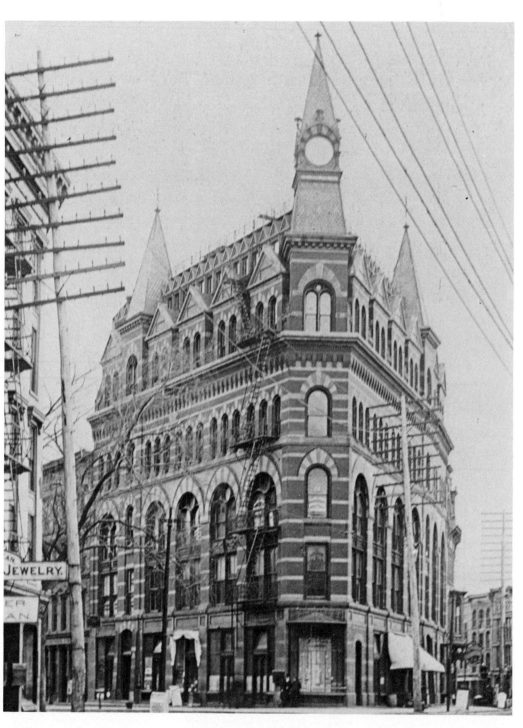

(1873) embellished with corbels and piers and pierced with slender windows—a commodious structure appropriately scaled to its neighborhood. The four-story W. & L.E. Gurley Company Building, which sits comfortably beside narrow, three-story row houses, is another example of architectural good manners.

The ornamentation for these new structures was seldom made by hand by skilled carvers of stone or wood; usually it was produced by machine for sale at prices the burgeoning middle class could afford. Brackets, doors, windows, balusters, shutters, marbelized slate mantels, and cast-iron window trim could be ordered ready-made from catalogs or purchased from manufacturers in Troy or Cohoes. Other prefabricated building components, such

as cast-iron storefronts and sheet metal cornices, can be found on mid-century commercial structures along Remsen Street in Cohoes, 19th Street in Watervliet, Broad Street in Waterford, George Street in Green Island, and throughout Troy. A prefabricated cast-iron storehouse at the Watervliet Arsenal was supplied ready to assemble by the Architectural Iron Works in New York. The practice of standardized building assumed another form under Troy architect Marcus F. Cummings, who wrote three architectural pattern books between 1865 and 1873 which spread deliberately replicable forms nationwide.

Beginning in the eighteenth century, buildings of the Gateway area were usually built upon the alluvial planes along the rivers, but the close of the Civil War brought suburbanization. Along the thoroughfares ascending the hills—Pawling and Pinewood avenues in Troy and Saratoga Avenue in Waterford—architects and builders took advantage of this spaciousness by building asymmetrical villas, decorated with projecting towers and porches that created fanciful silhouettes against sky and foliage. Later in the century, their verticality and planar boldness gave way to the more horizontal emphasis of Queen Anne houses, which had decorative wooden siding and shingles, capacious porches, and round towers with conical roofs.

Examples stand in Lansingburgh at 842 Second Avenue and in Troy at 162 Pawling Avenue and 7 Collins Avenue.

Another distinctive profile is created by the enormous, curvilinear red slate roof and monitor of the Troy Music Hall, designed by New York architect George B. Post and built in 1871-75. Sheltered within is one of America's most acoustically perfect auditoriums; on the first floor is the banking room of the proprietors, the Troy Savings Bank. The more modest Cohoes Music Hall (1874) is notable for the painted interior.

Industrial growth demanded expanded factories. Between 1857 and 1872 the Harmony Company erected three spectacular mills along North Mohawk Street in Cohoes, including Mill No. 3, an expanse of red brick 1,100 feet long with four tiers of large windows topped by a Mansard roof lighted by tall dormer windows. In Troy and Lansingburgh the demand for collars and cuffs created a new scale of brick construction. The block-long Lion Factory at 120th Street followed a traditional building form, but the steel-framed factories at 547, 599, and 621 River Street have grouped windows that admit large amounts of daylight.

Community growth and civic pride spurred the con-

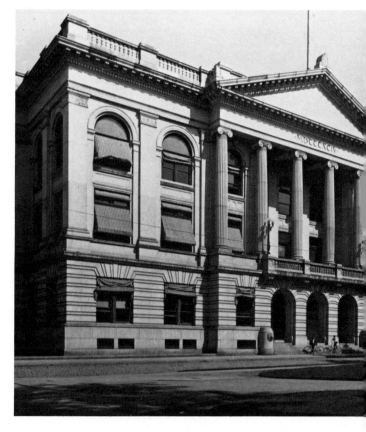

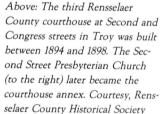

Above: The third Rensselaer County courthouse at Second and Congress streets in Troy was built between 1894 and 1898. The Second Street Presbyterian Church (to the right) later became the courthouse annex. Courtesy, Rensselaer County Historical Society

Left: Built as the Manufacturers National Bank in 1922, this building became a branch office of Marine Midland Bank in 1965. It stands at the corner of Fourth and Grand streets in Troy. Courtesy, Rensselaer County Historical Society

Right: The interior of Frear's "Troy Cash Bazaar" was as elaborate as its exterior. Here the employees pose on the main staircase in 1908. Although the first floor of the staircase is now gone, the upper part remains and may eventually be incorporated into the Uncle Sam Atrium. Courtesy, Rensselaer County Historical Society

struction of public buildings. By 1884 Troy boasted fourteen brick schoolhouses and firehouses. Similar civic needs and architectural values prompted construction of the Whipple, Powers, and Haskell schools in Lansingburgh, the city hall in Cohoes, and Corporation Hall in Green Island.

As the turn of the century approached, an interest in polychromy—the use of contrasting masonry—overtook the earlier combinations of brick and brownstone. An early example is the Rice Building (1871) at the junction of River and First streets in Troy; its red brick walls are

only a backdrop for the brown and tan voussoirs above the windows. Twenty years later, Marcus Cummings experimented with rusticated light and dark masonry in the Gurley and Plum buildings on what is now the Russell Sage campus and the Young Women's Association at 33 Second Street.

This delight with building materials was carried over to interiors, notably at Saint Paul's Episcopal Church, where the studio of Louis Comfort Tiffany was commissioned to design splendid chandeliers and pews, and J.A. Holzer created stained glass windows and a baptistry. At Oakwood

Cemetery the parents of Gardner Earl constructed a memorial chapel and crematorium embellished with quartered oak, exotic marbles, and mosaics. The extravagant Paine House (1894) at 49 Second Street, designed by Washington architect P.F. Schneider, has a richly carved limestone facade and tower. The Troy Public Library (1897) was constructed of elegantly tooled white marble and recalls the Boston Public Library at a smaller scale; the collection is stored in steel-framed stacks divided by floors of translucent glass.

As the twentieth century opened, a progressive spirit prevailed, bringing considerable new construction, especially in Troy. The growing influence of classicism is apparent in the Ionic portico of the Rensselaer County Courthouse (1894-98). A later, elegant example of the use of classical forms is the limestone Marine Midland Bank Building (1922-23) at Fourth and Grand streets.

Blocks of small domestic buildings were replaced by six- or seven-story commercial buildings. Two notable examples are the Ilium Building and the National State Bank Building, both built in 1904. Located just two blocks apart, they echo each other's configuration—rusticated ground floors surmounted by clustered windows and an arcade of smaller openings. Located midway between them is the monumental Frear Building (1897), with Corinthian capitals and richly carved spandrels.

Lighter facades and fanciful ornament were considered tasteful at the turn of the century. In Troy white terra cotta was used at Proctor's Theatre and in the McCarthy Building with its remarkably expansive showcase window.

The Caldwell apartment building (1907) was constructed of buff brick and gray litholite, an artificial stone, and had a dining room for tenants; at the opening it was heralded for its "metropolitan-like touch" that marked "another step toward a greater and better Troy." The Arts and Crafts movement is suggested by the facade of the YMCA on Second Street, which has copper roofs that project over broad windows. Emma Willard School boasts a fine campus with Collegiate Gothic elements, the work of Troy architect Frederick M. Cummings.

At the same time many area structures continued to be built of red brick, oftentimes in buildings that recall varied antecedents. The First Presbyterian Church in Waterford, for instance, is reminiscent of New England meetinghouses. The Troy Record newspaper plant (1908-09) operates behind a facade laid up in Flemish bond and surmounted by a Dutch bell gable. The entrance to the Union National Bank (1936) recalls a Roman basilica. Meanwhile, the popularity of the automobile spawned new neighborhoods that spread further up over the hills;

new houses often had traditional center hall plans but the exteriors showed a richness of historical and aesthetic influences. A notable example of a planned "residential park" is Whitman Court in Troy, where architect Frederick Cummings designed comfortable dwellings for himself and others in "modified English, cottage, mission, and colonial forms."

Significant mid-twentieth century architecture has been commissioned by Troy's educational institutions. Among the best examples are the Chapel and Cultural Center (1967-68) on Burdett Avenue, designed by Levatich and Miller of Ithaca, and, at the Emma Willard School, the library and music building (1966-67) by Edward Larrabee Barnes, and the gymnasium (1976-77) by Bohlin and Powell. Other recent building activities have included the adaptive use of significant historic buildings, such as the Julia Howard Bush Memorial Center at Russell Sage, the commercial facade programs in Troy, Lansingburgh, and Cohoes, and the rehabilitation of dwellings by individual owners.

This was graduation day at the Lansingburgh Academy in the late nineteenth century. In 1900 the private school was discontinued and it became part of the public school system. Courtesy, Lansingburgh Historical Society

CHAPTER NINE

A MAJOR EDUCATIONAL CENTER

From its earliest days, the Hudson-Mohawk area has been home to outstanding educators and outstanding educational institutions. Lansingburgh Academy, Emma Willard School and Rensselaer Polytechnic Institute, especially, have each played important roles in the history of American learning. Innovative educators, like Emma Willard, Amos Eaton, Benjamin Franklin Greene, the Kevenys of Cohoes, Palmer C. Ricketts, Lewis A. Froman, and George M. Low were attracted to the Gateway and did their influential work in the area. Harry Pratt Judson, who was teacher and later principal of Troy High School between 1870 and 1885, went on to become President of the University of Chicago in 1907. Educational efforts at all levels were encouraged by the nineteenth century merchants and industrial elites. The twentieth century has witnessed a continuation of this tradition.

Emma Willard was one of the two most innovative educators to settle in the Hudson-Mohawk area. She insisted that young women be schooled in the same disciplines as young men. While living in Middlebury, Vermont, she first learned these subjects from her husband's nephew, a student at what is now Middlebury College. Contact with Amos Eaton, when she moved to Troy in 1821, further broadened her education.

During her residence in Middlebury, Willard authored a "Plan For Improving Female Education" which so inspired Governor DeWitt Clinton of New York, that he invited her to the state. She opened her school in Waterford in 1819, but when financial backing was not forthcoming from that community or the state, the educational pioneer was given a great deal of support by Trojans and moved to their city. The town's Common Council raised $4,000 and initiated "another fund." Moulton's Coffee House, set back from the southwest corner of Congress and Second streets, was subsequently purchased, renovated, and retrofitted. The Troy Female Seminary, with Emma Willard as principal, opened in 1821 with ninety

pupils from as far away as Georgia and South Carolina. Its student body doubled the following year.

Emma Willard was a "pioneer in securing advanced education for women." She instructed her own teachers and wrote textbooks where none existed. Proceeds from these publishing efforts allowed worthy students to enroll in her school, receiving an education which otherwise would have been unaffordable for them. But Emma Willard's interests were hardly parochial; after a trip to Europe in the 1830s, she compiled her *Journal and Letters from France and Great Britain,* using the earnings to found a girls' school in Greece. She also encouraged her teachers to broaden their perspectives through travel.

Following several expansions, in 1837 the school began receiving monies from the state "Literature Fund," which had up to that time supported boys' schools exclusively. The educational innovator retired from the principalship in 1838. She was succeeded by her son, John, as business director, and his wife, Sarah, as principal. When the lease on the buildings ran out in 1872, the trustees raised $50,000 to purchase them from the city. In that same year, John and Sarah Willard retired and Emily Treat Wilcox, a grandniece of the founder, was chosen principal. She discontinued the boarding division and conducted the school as a day school exclusively. During the 1890s, the gift of donors brought new facilities: Gurley Memorial Hall, the Anna M. Plum Memorial (a music and arts building), and a residence hall awarded by Mrs. Russell Sage. As a result of this latter gift, the school reopened its boarding division.

During the principalship of Anna M. Leach, Russell Sage's widow, Margaret Olivia Slocum Sage, contributed one million dollars for the construction of a new campus on Pawling Avenue. The generous benefactor took a personal interest in this project, helping to select an architect and oversee the design. Its beautiful collegiate Gothic

Left: This was the Troy Female Seminary as seen from Second Street in 1822. Moulton's Coffee House was purchased by the city in 1821 and remodeled for use as the school. The upper floors contained lodging and study rooms for boarding students. From Emma Willard and Her Pupils, *by Mrs. Russell Sage, 1898*

Right: Emma Willard was a pioneer in securing advanced education for women by insisting that they be schooled in the same disciplines as men. In addition to opening the Troy Female Seminary (Emma Willard School), she instructed teachers, wrote textbooks, and founded a girls school in Greece. From Emma Willard and Her Pupils, *by Mrs. Russell Sage, 1898*

Following page: The Emma Willard School campus on Second Street in Troy is seen here at the turn of the century. From the left are Plum Hall, Gurley Hall, and Russell Sage Hall. These buildings were the nucleus of Russell Sage College upon its founding in 1916. Courtesy, Rensselaer County Historical Society

campus remains in use to the present day. Renamed for its foundress in 1895, the school has experienced a continuing prosperity. William M. Deitel, the first male to head the all-girl school, updated both campus and curriculum in the 1960s, making Emma Willard School one of America's first-ranking schools for young women. Faculty housing, an art and music building, and a library were built during Deitel's principalship. Dennis Arthur Collins succeeded as principal in 1970. A children's division, then begun as a nursery school, now extends up to the third grade. Frances Roland O'Connor was appointed principal in 1974 and the new gymnasium was completed three years later. The school continues to flourish under the principalship of Robert Curtis Parker.

The Emma Willard School has graduated many notables from Elizabeth Cady Stanton in the nineteenth century to today's activist-film star Jane Fonda. Mary Lyons, the foundress of Mount Holyoke College, was an early alumna. Both the nineteenth and twentieth century women's movements have been well-served by a school founded on the premise that young women should have educational opportunities comparable to those offered young men.

In the meantime, quality academic training for boys was offered by the Lansingburgh Academy. Chester A. Arthur, twenty-first President of the United States, and Herman Melville, author of *Moby Dick,* were sometime students there, and its most distinguished principal, the Reverend Dr. Samuel Blatchford, became the first president of what was to become the Rensselaer Polytechnic Institute. One of only thirteen academies (the basic equivalent of our high schools), founded in New York State before 1800, the Lansingburgh Academy was also the last survivor of this tradition. It had been chartered by the New York Board of Regents in 1796, and was dissolved by the same body in 1911, after having been absorbed into the public school system at the turn of the century. The academy originally occupied a building on the west side of the village green until 1820, when it moved to a new two-story brick structure on the corner of 114th Street and Fourth Avenue.

While the Lansingburgh Academy and Troy Female Academy were precursors to the college preparatory movement, public education also took an early lead in

the Gateway area. In the seventeenth and eighteenth centuries, the Dutch prized both religion and academic training, so it is not surprising that the Lansingburgh community sponsored a tuition-free school, open to boys and girls, as early as 1774. By 1830 William Powers introduced the Lancasterian method which relied on older students to teach younger ones. This method was inexpensive and, therefore, was used in the education of the poor. In 1847 Lansingburgh School District No. 1 was permitted to tax and operate what is reputed to be the oldest free school in the state. The jurisdiction had no high school until 1899, however, and sent its secondary students to the Lansingburgh Academy or to Troy High. On January 1, 1901, the village of Lansingburgh was consolidated into the City of Troy, with the stipulation that the school systems remain separate. For a city of its size, Troy is rather unique in its possession of two school districts.

What is perhaps most unique about Lansingburgh is that the old Lansingburgh Academy building, a relic of the past constructed in 1820, has been completely renovated with community development funds. It now houses the Lansingburgh Arts Center, a branch of the Troy Public Library, and the offices of Camp Fire, Inc.

Troy's first school had been established in 1791 on the site of the Rensselaer County Courthouse. Two years after its founding, the school moved to the new government building, occupying a single room. In 1796 a brick English grammar school was constructed on First Street north of Ferry, only a block west of the site of the earliest school. The village was divided into four districts in the first sixteen years of the nineteenth century. A Lancasterian school was built on State Street at Seventh Avenue, and, although the original building was soon destroyed by fire, it was rebuilt in 1819 and eventually became the home of

Troy Academy. Troy Academy evolved into a private preparatory school for Rensselaer Polytechnic Institute, with which it shared teachers. The second school building was razed in the great fire of 1862, but replaced with yet a third structure which served until 1917 when the academy closed its doors. Troy had separate schools for blacks (1821 and 1829) and this minority group was not integrated into the school system until 1873. During the first half of the nineteenth century, the schools were maintained by payment of tuition as follows:

$2.00 per quarter in the upper departments. (above seven yrs of age).
.75 per quarter in the infant schools (4-7 yrs of age)
.0625 per quarter in "African" schools.

Teachers received ten percent of what they collected; books and supplies were furnished.

An early form of high school was established in the top floor of the Lancasterian school in 1828. It employed the same system as its downstairs neighbor: the more advanced instructed the less advanced. There were two grades, junior and senior, and separate classrooms were provided for boys and girls. Troy High School was opened in 1854 and continues to offer secondary education to this day. With the establishment of public schools in 1849, each of Troy's twelve wards developed separate districts and their own schools. Education became free for children five through sixteen years of age, and teachers' salaries at this time were $275 a year. A Board of Commissioners and clerk were authorized in the legislation establishing the free schools. School opened with a rhythmic rendition of the Lord's Prayer and closed with the recitation of the Ten Commandments. Writing and arithmetic were taught in the morning; spelling, reading, and geography filled the afternoon schedule.

The primary and secondary educational systems of Troy have evolved from these early beginnings. In recent years, the number of public schools has been reduced from fifteen to nine. However, in the 1970s, Brunswick School Districts 10 and 11 joined with the Troy School District to form the Enlarged City School District of Troy. Today's Troy High School building opened its doors over three decades ago, offering opportunities for vocational training, as well as traditional academic education.

Waterford's record of education dates back to 1788, when one James Dugan taught there. We also know of the appointment of the Waterford-Halfmoon School Commission roughly eight years later. A district school located in the Waterford-Halfmoon area is first mentioned in 1812. Within a quarter of a century, this institution

Right: The marble plaque of Classic Hall pays tribute to this early private school on First Street in Waterford. Photo by Robert Thayer

Previous page: This was the Troy Female Seminary in the 1880s, looking southwest from Congress and Second streets. The main building was replaced in the 1890s by those currently used by Russell Sage College. To the right is the First Presbyterian Church, also now part of the college campus. Courtesy, Rensselaer County Historical Society

boasted 232 pupils, but only two instructors. What came to be known as the public schools, and in their early days the "free schools," came into existence with the legislation passed by New York State in 1849. In Waterford a new, three-story structure was erected to accommodate three teachers per floor. Students were not graded at first, and graduating classes were rare, since many children left for private schools. As the century progressed, three schools enlarged the system and its name changed to Union Free School District No. 1. Finally, in 1959 Waterford's District No. 1 and District No. 2, encompassing all of Halfmoon and part of Waterford, were merged. Three years later the new system opened a school which serves kindergarten through senior high. The Waterford-Halfmoon District celebrated its 100th graduating class in 1984.

Aside from its public schools, early Waterford enjoyed considerable private education. The Waterford Classical Institution, housed in the "Classic Hall," was a young men's school with a tuition of three dollars per term for reading, writing, and arithmetic; and an additional four dollars per term for English, grammar, and geography. What was called "higher education," something like secondary education, cost five dollars per term. At the Waterford Ladies' School (1822) a Miss Haight charged her pupils twenty dollars a year for instruction in eight sub-

jects. An additional ten subjects, including chemistry, astronomy, and philosophy cost twenty-four dollars per year, while drawing and painting on velvet hiked tuition by thirty-two dollars. French and music were taught when enough pupils were interested.

Up to approximately 1813, the only school in the Cohoes vicinity was located at the Boght. About this time, however, two institutions opened their doors: the first, "in a building on the main road," and the second, "a short distance above the Heamstreet farmhouse." The latter was apparently the "Red School House." A second school district was formed in 1828. Located near the site of the old freight house of the Rensselaer and Saratoga Railroad's freight station on Oneida Street, its offices were formerly boarding house lodgings. School trustees, chosen in 1850, soon identified a need for more classroom space. The basement of the Reformed Church was rented while the Messrs Fuller built the two-story schoolhouse on Remsen Street, which was subsequently leased by the trustees. Just five years later, in 1855, the *Albany Knickerbocker* noted that:

The advantage of having new public schools entirely free is shown by the experience of Cohoes. Under the past pay system, the number of pupils who attended was less than four hundred. At present, it is over eight hundred.

There were seven schools in Cohoes at the time. By 1876 the Board of Education operated 25 primary, four intermediate, one grammar, and one high school in eight buildings, seven of which belonged to the city. Thirty-eight teachers served the needs of approximately two thousand students. Today's school district is directed by a five-member Board of Education which oversees three elementary schools, one middle school, and one high school. One hundred and fifty-three teachers are charged with the instruction of approximately 3,200 pupils. The only documented private school in Cohoes was opened in the mid-nineteenth century under the direction of Rev. Stephen Bush.

Green Island had two schools prior to the passing of the Union Free School Law of the State. A Mr. Doolittle taught in one schoolhouse, while Mrs. Dodge, "a very refined and well-educated woman" who was "held in the greatest respect," headed the other. This sophisticated educator inspired a love of learning in nineteenth-century Green Island residents. On November 17, 1854, Green Island voted for a reorganization of the town district and compliance with the state's public school mandate. Two schools were subsequently built, in 1865 and 1879. James Heatly served as superintendent of schools from 1880 through 1924. Heatly School, built in 1930, commemorates his long service to the education of citizens of the village. Green Island's two earlier schools, in the meantime, were merged and a ninth grade was added, inaugurating a junior high. When a 1934 decision urged further education, the ninth grade expanded into a four-year secondary school program. Completely renovated in 1956, the Heatly School, housing all primary and secondary grades, continues to serve the educational needs of Green Island.

Called "West Troy" until 1897, the city of Watervliet included what had earlier been Gibbonsville, Washington, and Port Schuyler. An infant school existed there in 1818, and schoolhouses are mentioned in 1828, 1832, and 1833. The West Troy Female Seminary, with S. Harris and Elizabeth O. Stowe as teachers, was founded at this time; according to Watervliet's historian it just "bloomed and faded away." Other records describe first and fourth ward "select schools" in the late 1830s. A high school is mentioned in 1881, though it can be assumed that sometime after the mid-nineteenth century when public education came into existence, a whole system of primary and secondary programs was established.

Watervliet's next benchmark in the field of education came much later, in 1952. City schools then became independent of the government. As the sixties drew to a close, an Enlarged City School District commenced operation, starting out with five elementary school buildings. These buildings were eventually closed, and a Norton Company building was converted to a single primary school, serving the entire district. Along with the Watervliet Junior-Senior High School, this institution meets the educational needs of the jurisdiction.

Parochial and other church-related schools, too, have played an enormous role in educating Gateway youth. In fact, at times these schools have enrolled as many pupils as the public schools. As early as 1825, the Quakers built a schoolhouse adjacent to their meeting house on the corner of Fourth and State streets in Troy. This institution served Trojan children for forty-three years. And in Cohoes, St. John's Episcopal Church was operating a parochial school in the mid-nineteenth century. Nevertheless, the Roman Catholic Church, religious beacon for the immigrant masses, has been responsible for most of the Gateway's parochial and church-related academies.

The first parochial elementary school was connected with St. Mary's Church in Troy. The Sisters of Charity began to educate girls in 1847 and the Christian Brothers took boys under their tutelage three years later. St. Peter's, also of Troy, initially employed lay teachers in its school (1854) but the Sisters of St. Joseph took over within a decade. Boasting an enrollment of 500 elementary students from its start in 1861, St. Bernard's of Cohoes operated an evening program for children who worked in the mills. The school became coeducational thirty-one years later. With the devotion of several religious teaching orders, the Gateway area counted roughly twelve other primary schools. These nineteenth-century institutions had opened with lay faculty, but soon turned to teaching sisters.

The twentieth century has witnessed the continuation of this trend toward parochial education. Some of the schools opened in this century are the strongest primary parochial schools still open today. They include: St. Joseph's, Green Island (1922); Sacred Heart, Troy (1927); St. Michael's Ukranian, Watervliet (1940); Our Lady of Victory, Troy (1952); and St. Mary's, Waterford (1953). In fact twelve Roman Catholic elementary schools continue to operate in the Gateway area.

In addition no less than thirteen of the Roman Catholic elementary schools had high schools attached to them at one time. By 1923 the five remaining Troy and Watervliet academies were phased out in favor of Catholic

The first home of Rensselaer Polytechnic Institute, the former Farmer's Bank was at the corner of River and Middleburgh streets in Troy. Courtesy, Rensselaer County Historical Society

Central High School, which was to serve a much larger part of the Gateway. The former Troy Hospital building on Eighth Street in Troy was renovated to house a secondary program, with Rev. Edward J. Burns as its founding principal. He left his stamp of quality education on the school. In 1952 the school purchased the Cluett Peabody Research Laboratory at 116th Street between Sixth and Seventh avenues. Moving there, it annexed the old Country Day School property which had more recently been owned by LaSalle Institute. A gymnasium was erected and, later, a wing was added to the original structure. The school topped off at approximately 1,500 students, and has been taught over the years by Sisters of

Mercy, Sisters of St. Joseph, priests of the Diocese of Albany, Augustinian Fathers, and lay teachers.

The old St. Bernard's Academy, founded in 1878, entered its new building in 1930. To honor three priests, all related, who had been prominent in parish education, the school's name was changed to Keveny Memorial Academy. At last count it had more than 200 students. St. Joseph's Academy of Troy (1851) later became La Salle Institute in commemoration of the Christian Brothers' contribution to the learning arts. The school moved from South Troy to a new campus adjacent to Hudson Valley Community College in 1966. A middle school was opened within five years. Today, La Salle is a private middle and secondary school with a Junior Reserve Officers Training program. It presently enrolls over 500 students.

If the Hudson-Mohawk area has done an excellent job of teaching its children and youth, it has also offered outstanding opportunities for advanced education. Earliest and most famous among its institutions of higher learning is Rensselaer Polytechnic Institute, originally the Rensselaer School, founded in 1824. It was named for its founder and patron, Stephen Van Rensselaer, eighth patron of the Upper Hudson who, in a letter addressed to the school's first president, the Rev. Samuel Blatchford, stated:

I have established a school at the north end of Troy ... for the purpose of instructing persons who may choose to apply themselves, in the application of science to the common purposes of life.

Van Rensselaer went on to say:

My principal object is, to qualify teachers for instructing the sons and daughters of farmers and merchants ... I am inclined to believe that competent instructors may be produced ... who will be highly useful to the community in the diffusion of a very useful kind of knowledge, with its application to the business of living. ...

Insofar as this primary document was concerned, the Rensselaer School sought to train teachers of applied science for service in New York schools; it was an innovative educational venture. The patroon may have also had a personal objective in mind, namely, the development of his estate's roughly 900 farms and other holdings which were spread over a three-county area. In the same letter to President Blatchford, Van Rensselaer named as senior professor, or head of the faculty, Amos Eaton, who was to carry the title "Professor of Chemistry and Experimental Philosophy, and Lecturer on Geology, Land Surveying and laws regulating town officers and jurors." Lewis C. Beck, "Professor of Mineralogy, Botany and Zoology, and lecturer on the social duties peculiar to farmers and mechanics," was chosen junior professor.

From its inception the Rensselaer School came under the dominating influence of Amos Eaton. Courses and professorships in science already existed in America's colleges, some dating back to the preceding century, but these were academic in character. Quite apart from the classical tradition, Eaton was interested in popular and practical technical education. His intent was by no means unique, but his methods certainly were. He threw his imaginative and innovative mind into the development of what we now know as the oldest technological university in continuous existence in the English-speaking world. Interestingly, the Rensselaer School from the beginning aspired to grant women an opportunity to prepare them-

Stephen Van Rensselaer III, founder and benefactor of RPI, was the eighth patroon of the Manor of Rensselaerwyck, a vast semi-feudal estate including most of Albany and Rensselaer counties and part of Columbia County. Farmers were bound to him by a leasehold system in which they paid annual rent for the use of his land. Courtesy, Rensselaer Polytechnic Institute Archives

selves for teaching careers. In 1828 Eaton even proposed a "Ladies Department." Finally, a class of eight women was actually presented for public examination seven years later. But the experimental method, involving the student in lecture and demonstrations, was Eaton's most original and significant contribution. Perhaps he was applying Lancasterian techniques to higher education. Whatever the case, in 1826, this noteworthy educator established a "Preparation Branch," intended for students thirteen years of age

111

*Amos Eaton, the progressive
senior professor at the Rensselaer
School, instituted the experimental method of instruction which
involved students in lectures and
demonstrations. Courtesy, Rensselaer Polytechnic Institute
Archives*

and upward who had already completed basic schooling.
Within a decade the state legislature enacted a bill author-
izing the Rensselaer Institute, as it then became known, to
develop a department of mathematical arts for instruction
in "Engineering and Technology." The trustees, acting on
this mandate, established two branches with correspond-
ing degrees, both new to American education. One was
the degree of Bachelor of Natural Science for the course
already in existence, and the other, the degree of Civil
Engineer, accommodated new technical programs. This
second branch and credential were to set the course for
the future development of the Rensselaer Institute. By the
time Eaton died in 1842, it had awarded ninety-seven degrees in Civil Engineering and forty-two in Natural Science.

Eaton had always had to struggle mightily to keep his
fledgling institution fiscally solvent. He turned regularly
to his benefactor, the patroon, for approximately $3,000

per year. But Van Rensselaer died in 1839, and Eaton
spent his last years struggling to keep the Institute open.
He made a claim for $10,000 on Stephen Van Rensselaer's
estate, expecting a similar sum to be raised among the
Trojans. However, Stephen's son, Alexander, a graduate of
the school, replied, "My father no doubt felt vexed to
think that they (the Trojans) so little appreciated the vast
sum of money he had expended in founding a school in
their very midst." Rensselaer's scion therefore declined
Eaton's request, calling it "absurd." On his death, Eaton's
property and that of the Rensselaer Institute were sold for
$382.26 to Dr. Thomas Brinsmade. Brinsmade then con-
signed all of the holdings to George B. Cook, Eaton's suc-
cessor as senior professor. Finally, in 1844, Troy turned
over the Infant School, appraised at $6,500, to the Insti-
tute. William Paterson Van Rensselaer, one of Stephen's
sons, matched this with $6,500 to create an endowment
which provided an annual income of $455.

Another one of the Institute's exceptional senior pro-
fessors was Benjamin Franklin Greene. Only twenty-nine
years old when he was named senior professor, Greene,
like Eaton, his teacher, possessed a brilliant and creative
mind. The young educator called Rensselaer "a Polytechnic" and wrote the "True Idea of a Polytechnic." He per-
sisted and after resigning from his post in 1859, this name
was legalized by an act of the legislature in 1861. Greene
called himself "Director and Professor" and established
three departments. The one-year curriculum was extended
to three years. He elevated the new Rensselaer Polytechnic
Institute to collegiate rank, suggesting a breadth of education which was realized only a full century later. Greene
also made Rensselaer a national and even international institution. As early as 1850, for example, a Brazilian student
was graduated. The director, too, introduced courses in
German, French, and English. Like Eaton, Greene had
grand visions and was constrained by limited means,
though he did convince the state legislature to appropriate $3,000 for the Rensselaer Institute in 1851. Added
funds allowed him to accomplish some of his goals.

Nevertheless, Greene's "True Idea of a Polytechnic" was
premature. The board of trustees—which included Greene
after 1855—consisted of local persons. State government,
in spite of some funding in 1851, was not ready to get involved in private educational enterprises, even the most
imaginative of sorts. Local support, too, was not adequate.
Finally, in 1859, in a crisis of personality and business behavior with the board of trustees, Greene's directorship
and professorship ended in resignation. Rensselaer's most

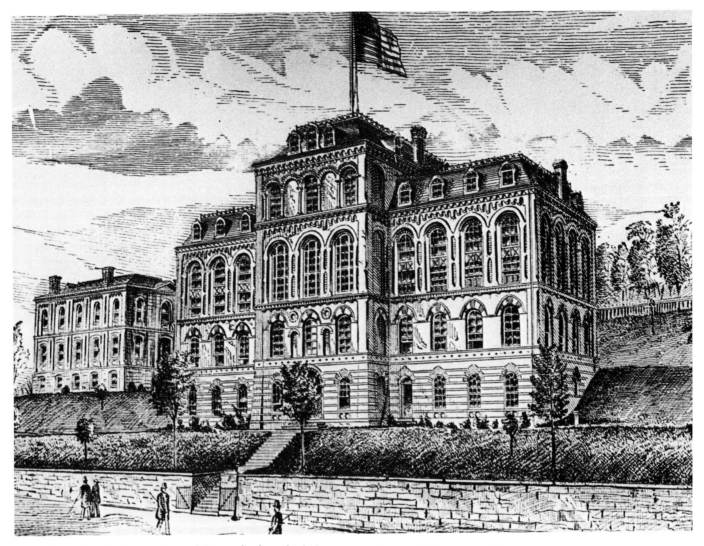

recent historian, Professor Samuel Rezneck, described the post-Greene period as one in which the school "contracted into just another technological institution, claiming age and antiquity rather than novelty of origin and purpose." Nevertheless, after the great fire of 1862 destroyed the Infant School Building near the railroad station which RPI had occupied since 1844, RPI moved into "Old Main," newly built on the site of the currently dilapidated "approach." A chemistry laboratory (1866) and the Proudfit Observatory (1878) enhanced the campus, and a creditable celebration marked the school's fiftieth anniversary in 1874. Famous graduates of the period included Henry A. Rowland, first professor of physics at Johns Hopkins; George Washington Ferris, inventor of the Ferris wheel; and Mordecai T. Endicott, founder of the Navy's Civil Engineering Corps.

An era of relative inactivity ended with the accession

The main building and smaller chemical laboratory of the Rensselaer Polytechnic Institute were constructed on Eighth Street at the head of Broadway after the fire of 1862. After the main building burned in 1904, the campus moved to its present location. From History of the City of Troy, *by A.J. Weise, 1876*

Several students from RPI's class of 1888 use the nearby Poestenkill Gorge as a classroom for surveying studies. Courtesy, Rensselaer Polytechnic Institute Archives

of Palmer Chamberlaine Ricketts to the directorship in 1892, and subsequently, to the presidency. Ricketts had come to RPI as a freshman in 1871 and remained at the school until his death sixty-three years later. He was a builder. The Carnegie Building was opened in 1904, and the following two years saw the ground-breaking of the Walker and Sage Laboratories, the latter named for former trustee Russell Sage, whose widow had given a handsome sum of one million dollars for the facility's construction. The host of successful Western Pennsylvania alumni made their contribution in the Pittsburgh Building (1907). Five years later the classes of 1886 and 1887 presented the school with an athletic field and gym, named for their respective years. A clubhouse was opened in 1914, as were the quadrangle dormitories. Between 1920-

24, the Troy Building was built, while 1928 saw the completion of Amos Eaton and the former Rensselaer Union, now the Lally Management Building. Greene and Ricketts began their service to the RPI community in the following year.

President Ricketts also fulfilled most of B.F. Greene's vision of the "True Polytechnic." Speaking to the first meeting of the American Society for the Promotion of Engineering Education, he said, "In general the engineer is not liberally educated. Beyond his profession his knowledge is not great. This is a mistake. . . ." Ricketts used some of the first Sage gift to initiate electrical and mechanical engineering and housed them in the Russell Sage Laboratory. Chemical engineering and graduate study in engineering were both introduced in 1913, as Mrs. Sage

Ricketts' first move to broaden the curriculum came in 1915 with the hiring of a young, Harvard-trained, English Ph.D., Ray Palmer Baker. Baker soon headed a Department of Arts, Science, and Business Administration, offering degrees in chemistry, physics, biology, and business administration. History, political science, economics, sociology, psychology, foreign languages, and English were introduced or strengthened, and architecture found its way into the course list as the 1920s drew to a close. Already seventy-seven years of age, Ricketts added three new curricula: metallurgical, aeronautical, and industrial engineering in 1933. When he died one year later, the faculty boasted 145 members. RPI's student body numbered approximately 1,350.

After a short *interregnum,* William Otis Hotchkiss moved from the Houghton School of Mines in Michigan to become Rensselaer's president, the first non-alumnus to head the Institute. His principal contributions were in the area of curriculum development. He also strived for improved faculty salaries, manageable teaching loads, more modern equipment, increased research activity, and better student-faculty relations. As the United States entered World War II, the president had the unenviable job of scaling back most normal activities and gearing up to wartime needs. Undergraduate enrollment slid to a low of 932 in 1945, two-thirds of which were Navy ROTC and V-12 students. The faculty, 160 strong in pre-war years, diminished to less than a hundred.

Taking over the reins from Hotchkiss in 1945, Livingston Waddell Houston, local industrialist and longtime RPI officer, reorganized the administration. He named Dr. Matthew A. Hunter dean of faculty and Dr. Ray Palmer Baker dean of students. An excellent manager, Houston prepared for the post-war boom, utilizing the Committee on Post-War Planning originally established by his predecessor. But no one could have predicted the number of students who descended on universities following the war. They were older, married, very career-oriented—and in a great hurry to get started. Curricular reforms, other than the introduction of an eight-course core of humanities and social sciences, had to be postponed. But an evening school, refresher courses, cooperative education, and ROTC programs by all three major services were introduced. New housing and classrooms came into being. Rensselaerwyck for married students and a large field house were built out of wartime surplus materials; an abandoned orphanage provided lodgings for new faculty. Classrooms and offices were added later. West

provided funds for the establishment of two masters-level fellowships. The publication of a Rensselaer Science and Engineering course also furthered research, but Ricketts was cautious. Restating his primary interest in undergraduate education in 1933, he wrote:

It is believed that teachers should do outside work in the line of their profession, in order that they may be better fitted to teach, but it must be explicitly understood that such work is wholly secondary to their duties as teachers. It's not intended to provide any teacher with a place from which he may pursue professional outside work of any character while neglecting his duty as a teacher. Abuse of this nature has caused endless trouble in another well-known school, and it cannot be permitted to arise here.

The Rensselaer Newman
Foundation's Chapel and Cultural
Center is on Burdett Avenue in
Troy. Photo by Jim Shaughnessy.
Courtesy, Rensselaer Polytechnic
Institute

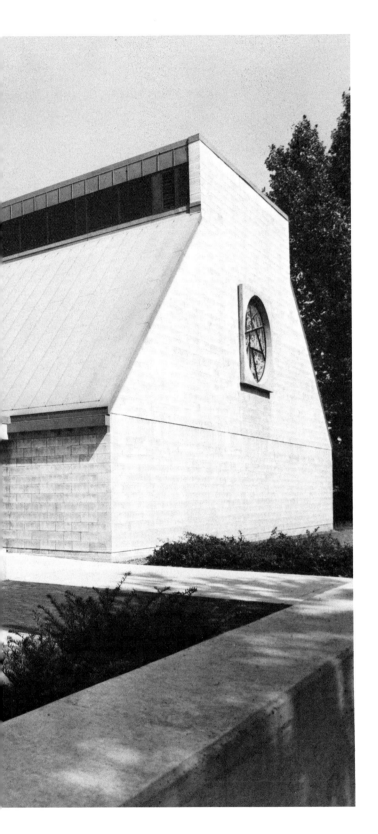

Hall, with all its teaching facilities sprung from the former Catholic Central High; freshman dormitories also arose. Enrollment reached 4,000 while assets climbed to fifty-one million dollars.

After the post-war boom, long-range goals were pursued and planning for their achievement followed. Houston raised $27,750,000 before his retirement in 1958. With it, he enlarged the RPI campus, increased student activities, and expanded the endowment. At about the same time, Houston divided the departments into schools, each headed by an academic dean. The School of Management came along a few years later. Dr. Paul Hemke, dean of faculty since 1949, was named vice president and provost. The graduate division was also made a school. On top of these developments, RPI established the Hartford Graduate Center in Connecticut. Houston, in fact, had been so successful as administrator and fundraiser that upon his retirement, he was named chairman of the board.

Richard Gilmore Folsom, director of the University of Michigan's Engineering Research Institute, replaced this managerial expert. Changing times demanded that an essentially undergraduate institution take advantage of growing graduate education and research opportunities. A numerically and qualitatively expanding staff formed a Faculty Council. And, under the new president, development took the form of a Science Center, the Materials Research Center, a Communications Center, the Rensselaer Union, and a new library, named, after his retirement, for Folsom. A linear accelerator was built as were many dormitories, and the old Troy Armory was converted into RPI's Alumni Sports and Recreation Center.

The former dean of engineering at Purdue University, Richard J. Grosh, succeeded Folsom in 1971. His tenure and a bold move towards top quality education, Engineering Initiatives, propelled the construction of the Jonsson Engineering Center. Presiding over RPI in 1976, George M. Low had directed the Apollo space program and served as deputy administrator of the National Aeronautics and Space Administration. Low's leadership brought Engineering Initiatives to a more than successful conclusion. His blueprint for the future, "Rensselaer 2000," states that by the end of the present century, "RPI will be one of a small number of first-rank, internationally renowned technological universities." Low, who died in 1984, spent his eight years at Rensselaer working towards the realization of this overarching goal.

The former chapel of St. Joseph's Seminary, now part of RPI, was converted into a computer center, an effective adaptation which nevertheless allows the previous use to remain obvious. Thelma and Kenneth Lally's name was placed on the management building, reincarnated from the Rensselaer Union Clubhouse, and Sage Laboratory was completely renovated as the home for the School of Humanities and Social Sciences as was the Playhouse. A former Norton Abrasives research laboratory in Watervliet became the Center for Integrated Electronics. Low also convinced the state to join RPI in the building and equipping of a Center for Industrial Innovation—a bold move which, along with the school's Incubator (industrial development) program and Technology Park, forms the basis for a "Second Industrial Revolution" in the Capital District of New York State. Even more importantly, the quality of the faculty and the quantity of research grew greatly during Low's presidency, bringing new national recognition to both the country's oldest engineering school and the Gateway area. At this writing, Dr. Daniel Berg, formerly Provost and Chief Academic Officer, has been named 15th President of RPI to succeed Low.

Although RPI's accomplishments could fill their own book, these educational ventures hardly exhaust the higher education offered in the Hudson-Mohawk Gateway. A mid-nineteenth century advertisement in the *Troy Whig* announced that if the local people could raise $100,000, the Methodist College at Charlottesville (Schoharie County) would move its campus to Troy. Given the city's heady atmosphere at that time, the proposition presented no great problems and the money was quickly subscribed. Jacob D. Vanderheyden's property, some thirty-six acres on the brow of the hill overlooking central Troy, was purchased. Surmounted by four tall spires, the cornerstone for a great neo-Romanesque structure was subsequently laid. Troy University opened in 1858, offering four-year B.S. and B.A. degrees, a three-year program in agriculture or civil engineering, and a bachelor of divinity degree in two years. However, the college's president never left New York City. Perhaps as a result, only four professors and fifty-five students appeared and Troy University soon closed down. The Provincial Theological Seminary of the Roman Catholic Archdiocese of New York came to occupy the site in 1864, but moved to Yonkers twenty-eight years later. After serving as a refuge for victims of disaster, the building eventually was purchased by the Sisters of St. Joseph of Corondolet. When they moved to new and larger quarters in Latham, the property and building were purchased by RPI.

After the Emma Willard School moved to its new cam-

George M. Low was president of Rensselaer Polytechnic Institute from 1976 to 1984. Courtesy, Rensselaer Polytechnic Institute

pus, Russell Sage College—housed on the old campus of the school—was created to provide young women with a practical, as well as a more classical education. Opening with 117 students, it blended secretarial, home economics, and nursing courses with the traditional liberal arts. By 1923 a full-fledged school of nursing developed, and one year later the college boasted a 310-member student body. It shared the Emma Willard School principal as its president, but by 1927, it became obvious that such a successful endeavor required its own full-time administrative head. James Laurence Meader, who greatly strengthened the liberal arts program, became its second president. Within three years, the Central School of Hygiene and Physical Education moved from New York City and joined Russell Sage College.

After Meader resigned to enter the military service, several short-term presidents assumed the leadership role. But Lewis A. Froman's twenty-one-year tenure, from 1948 to 1969, saw truly massive development of the school's facilities, constituent components, and curriculum. Enrollments grew to 1,250. A fine arts center, auditorium, and Ackerson Hall were constructed, and the James Wheelock Clark Library opened in 1955, to be expanded in 1966. Vail House, the federal period seat of a Poestenkill Gorge industrialist, became the president's residence. In addition, Russell Sage College added new campuses and broadened its schedule to include evening classes for both men and women (1941), an Albany division (1949), and the coed Junior College of Albany (1957). Froman then saw the need to unify the growing home campus and built a tunnel to carry traffic beneath Ferry Street.

In 1970 Charles U. Walker became president of Russell Sage and remained in that post for five years. During that period, the Greek temple-like First Presbyterian Church in the midst of the campus was given to the college as the Julia Howard Bush Center. The school's current president, William F. Kahl, arrived at Sage in 1976. His term has brought about the building of the Ellis and Doris Robison Athletic and Recreation Center. Enrollments at the three constituent elements of the college are approximately: 1,400 at Russell Sage, 1,000 at the Junior College of Albany, and 2,500 at the evening divisions in Troy and Albany. Master's degrees are offered in business administration, elementary education, reading, special education, health education, nursing, public service administration, health services administration, and community psychology. The Junior College also offers course work at three New York State correctional institutions and the Job Corps Center in Glenmont.

Yet another Gateway area institution of higher education appeared at mid-century and has grown by leaps and bounds over the past thirty years. Hudson Valley Community College, located in Troy and sponsored by Rensselaer County, had its origins in the Veteran's Vocational School (1946). The two-year program was initially housed in the vacant Earl and Wilson Shirt Company building on Seventh Avenue, a structure earlier occupied by an Army Signal Corps School. At first the school helped returning World War II veterans acquire the technical training necessary for the new industrial era. Having taken care of returning G.I.'s by the early 1950s, many people assumed that this technical institute would close its doors. However, Dwight Marvin, editor of the *Troy Record* newspapers, believed it to be the potential nucleus for a community college. Other new two-year schools were just beginning to gain recognition in New York State, so the Hudson Valley Technical Institute was opened in 1953, with Otto V. Guenther as its first president. Guenther had been chair of the Mechanical Technology Department at Buffalo's Erie County Technical Institute. He also had been recommended by the New York State Department of Education. There was little money during these early days, and instructors did the maintenance and routine construction work in the building.

Guenther's assiduous efforts and those of the first facul-

ty members paid off, however. The name of the institution was changed to Hudson Valley Community College in 1959, reflecting a broader mission. Plans for a new campus were announced as well. Taxpayers then challenged the county's right to assess its citizens for the support of a college, but the New York State Court of Appeals handed down a decision in favor of the taxing. The newly-named Hudson Valley Community College surged ahead. The former Williams farm on the southern border of the city and northern border of North Greenbush was purchased, and five structures costing five million dollars were built by the time of the move. The student body had grown from eighty-eight to 1,200 in just six years. Technical courses were still the bread and butter items of the curriculum, but banking, insurance, and real estate, as well as dental hygiene, were added in 1960. The first two years of the liberal arts program first appeared in 1961. Curricular expansion continued as the post-war baby boomers reached college age. In 1965 Guenther announced his retirement. He inspired a pioneer faculty and staff to create a new higher educational institution in the traditional northeast.

James J. Fitzgibbons, who had moved from department chair to dean at HVCC and later joined the state's education department, returned as second president. The latter half of the 1960s saw enrollment swell to 4,000 students. HVCC subsequently became administrator of new urban centers for the economically disadvantaged which sprang up in the inner cities of the Capital District. Educational offerings extended to some forty curricula. The Middle States Association granted these programs full accreditation in 1968, and a student union and library graced the campus within six years. By this time the HVCC student body had grown to 6,240. Fitzgibbons retired in 1979, to be succeeded by Joseph J. Bulmer, formerly of the General Electric Knolls Atomic Power Laboratory. The college's rapid development has continued apace under Bulmer's leadership. A health technologies building named for Fitzgibbons opened in 1982, and the college acquired the old Henry Burden property, later a Franciscan Seminary complex, two years later. Nearly 300 full- and part-time faculty now teach some 7,500 students at one of the largest community colleges in upstate New York.

Troy also claimed a small business college, founded in the early 1860s, which ultimately merged with the Albany Business College in the middle of the twentieth century. And, as might be expected, Samaritan Hospital still continues to sponsor a nursing school.

The Ford Motor Company plant
on Green Island continues to be
an important business in the area.
This was the dedication ceremony
for the manufacturing plant in
1923. Courtesy, Rensselaer County
Historical Society

CHAPTER TEN

DECLINE AND REVIVAL IN THE TWENTIETH CENTURY

The northeast's "gritty cities," areas that were industrialized earliest in this country, have generally experienced special adjustment problems in the twentieth century. Water was a key to the settlement of these early industrialized areas—falling water for power and waterways for transportation. Steam engines, and later electricity, made industries more independent of water, though water continues to be important for many industrial processes. The freedom provided by steam and electricity allowed industries like textiles to move closer to the center of raw materials. Labor unionization and labor-management conflicts forced industries towards cheaper and more pliable labor markets. There was also the matter of scale: early industry built on such a small scale that the visible remains are barely noticeable in our old cities. As the size of the industrial process and their buildings increased, the larger, open spaces much more easily found in the relatively flat midwest were in increased demand. In addition, there was the inexorable movement west in the second half of the nineteenth century. Those industries which stayed behind tended to become obsolete; this was evidenced in their unwillingness to pursue the research and development that would keep the companies up-to-date with the latest technological advances.

The Gateway area was a victim of all of these forces. By the late nineteenth century, creeping industrial decline was visible to the perceptive, and in the first half of the twentieth century, that decline was obvious and visible to all. Fortunately, however, there were other institutions still in their growth stages that gave the area its needed base for continued existence, and, in fact, relative prosperity even in difficult times like the great Depression. At the same time, Gateway communities in the late twentieth century have been undergoing extensive renewal programs.

Troy's business district was most affected by the ill-fated

Full Enameled Gas Range

| 16-4 | | GRAY FRONT | 16-5 | | WHITE FRONT |
| 14-4 | | | 14-5 | | |

The range illustrated is No. 16-4 in full enamel, castings gray and sheet metal white. May be had with white enameled castings in No. 16-5. The same selections of colors are supplied with the Nos. 14-4 and 14-5, these numbers signifying 14-inch instead of 16-inch ovens.

DIMENSIONS

	No. 16-4 or 16-5	No. 14-4 or 14-5
Baking Oven	16 x 19 x 12 inches	14 x 19 x 12 inches
Broiling Oven	16 x 19 x 8 inches	14 x 19 x 8 inches
Height to Cooking Top	34 inches	34 inches
Total Length with End Shelf	45 inches	39 inches
Total Length less End Shelf	43 inches	36 inches
Extreme Height	51 inches	51 inches
Floor Space Required	43 x 22 inches	37 x 22 inches

EXTRAS: AutomatiCook Heat Control, Cabinet Base, Utility Drawer. In ordering specify whether right or left oven is desired and if for artificial or natural gas.

STEWART

From Fuller & Warren Company's 1927 catalogue, this is the twentieth-century version of P.P. Stewart's famous cooking range. Courtesy, Rensselaer County Historical Society

federal government Urban Renewal Program. In 1966 the New York State Legislature created the Troy Urban Renewal Agency which, over a period of ten years, demolished central business district stores, the Troy Theater, and Troy Union Railroad Station. A plan had been devised to build a huge downtown Uncle Sam Mall covering twenty-four acres and costing ninety-six million dollars. A preferred developer was named, but that com-

pany backed out in 1975. Meanwhile much of the northern section of the central business district of Troy was demolished, leaving what came to be called "the great hole." An offer to build a much diminished one-story mall was made in 1976 and rejected because of the problem of scale. Finally, Carl Grimm of Troy erected the smaller Uncle Sam Atrium with the assistance of a $1,500,000 U.S. Urban Development Action Grant which covered the building of a public central courtyard or atrium.

The central business district of Troy, aided by a facade program and new developers who are taking advantage of a variety of government programs, currently shows clear signs of revival. Major companies like New York Telephone and the John Hancock Insurance Company, as well as a Holiday Inn, new banks, shops, restaurants, and offices, are appearing almost daily.

Meanwhile Cohoes' central business district, which did not undergo the trauma of urban renewal as its industrial area did, has also received a facelifting. A sense of historic preservation, aided by tax incentives, appears to have succeeded in bringing out the quality of the built environment in the business district of Cohoes and the remaining old business district of Troy, and this latter-day renewal appears to be meeting with a much more favorable response from consumers.

During the Depression that began in 1929 and lasted for a decade, not one Gateway area bank failed. Banks were also sufficiently strong to allow mortgagees to postpone payments, thus preventing many foreclosures. In fact, although there were wage cuts and the work week was shortened to spread work to more persons, unemployment was held at less than 5 percent during this economically difficult period. At present a change in the banking laws has resulted in both the absorption of old local banking institutions into large regional banks and an explosion in the number of banking institutions in the area.

The twentieth century has not been the heyday of industry in the Gateway area, nor is the area likely to regain the position of industrial prominence it occupied in the mid-nineteenth century. Nevertheless, there has been significant industrial activity during this period and it appears that the area may well be beginning what is sometimes referred to as the "Second Industrial Revolution" in high technology industries.

One of the most remarkable remains of Troy's early iron industry is both the factory and machinery of Portec

Inc., located immediately west of the Troy approach to the Menands bridge. In 1903 the old Albany Rolling and Slitting mill was taken over by the Continuous Rail Joint Company, which in 1905 merged with the Weber Rail Joint Company and the Independent Supply Company of Chicago to form the Rail Joint Company of New York. Since the beginning of the century, the mill has turned out insulated joints used in railroad signal and safety systems, as well as for joining together track. In more recent years the Rail Joint Company has become part of Portec Inc., which continues to manufacture insulated joints in the old factory and even with some of the original machinery. The two rolling mills themselves are no longer powered by steam but by 1,000-horsepower motors.

In the mid-nineteenth century, James Horner acquired the Pompton Furnace in northern New Jersey. James

Ludlum joined the company as a salesman and in 1864 was taken into a partnership with Horner. Eleven years later the Pompton Steel and Iron Company was formed with Ludlum as president. In 1892 James Ludlum died and was succeeded in the presidency by William H. Ludlum. Six years later the firm became the Ludlum Steel and

Built on the site of the Troy Iron & Steel Company, the coke plant in south Troy manufactured gas for power and light and coke for fuel. This photograph was taken in 1937. Courtesy, Rensselaer County Historical Society

Right: Two out of five of the giant water turbines in the Mastodon Mill (Harmony Mill #3) remain to help tell the story of the great cotton mills of Cohoes. Photo by Jim Shaughnessy

Below: The big gun shop at the Watervliet Arsenal in the late 1960s manufactured 175mm cannons among other weapons. Courtesy, Watervliet Arsenal Museum, U.S. Army photograph

Far right: Although the Harmony Mills Company was liquidated in the early 1930s, smaller textile manufacturers continued to occupy the nineteenth-century buildings. Beaunit Manufacturing Company utilized these knitting machines in 1951. Today a variety of manufacturers and outlet stores are part of the Harmony Mills complex.

Spring Company. The company moved to a new plant just outside Watervliet in the town of Colonie in 1907.

By 1938 the Ludlum Steel Company had its main office and a manufacturing plant in Watervliet. It had another large plant at Dunkirk, New York, and interests in three other companies. That year a merger was consummated between Ludlum and Allegheny Steel Company, creating a new name, Allegheny Ludlum Steel Corporation. Following the merger and substantial growth, the new company became the world's largest producer of high alloy specialty steels, with principal emphasis on stainless, tool, and electrical steels. However in 1976 Allegheny Ludlum sold its Bar Products Division to yet another new corporation called Al Tech Specialty Steel Corporation. Al Tech operates the plants at Watervliet and Dunkirk with its headquarters at the Dunkirk plant. More recently, in 1981, Al Tech became a division of GATX Corporation, a major U.S. corporation headquartered in Chicago.

Besides the steel and iron industry, a major automobile company is present today in the area. The Ford Motor Company owes its presence in the Gateway to a camping trip of Henry Ford, Thomas A. Edison, Harvey Firestone, and John Burroughs. In 1919 they pitched a tent on Green Island overlooking the dam at the headwater of navigation on the Hudson. Ford saw in the dam a valu-

able source of hydraulic power and immediately purchased 150 acres from the Tibbetts estate. Work on the power station to take advantage of the falling water at the dam began in 1921 and was completed the following year. Its turbines were capable of developing 8,000 horsepower of electrical energy. The Ford plant construction also began in 1921 and was completed three years later. Since that time a wide variety of automobile parts have been manufactured at the Green Island plant. Before World War II a river-front shipping dock provided for the unloading of steel and assembled automobiles from Detroit which were distributed from the plant. For a time a small landing field allowed Henry Ford to swoop down in his tri-motor "Tin Goose" for occasional plant visits. Although the plant continues to produce replacement radiators, its future at this writing is uncertain.

Troy was still an important collar, cuff, and shirt manufacturing city well into the twentieth century. A 1923 survey by the Troy Chamber of Commerce indicated that approximately 10,000 women and men produced detachable collars and cuffs valued at approximately forty-three million dollars that year. Some of the companies that were manufacturing these products and shirts at that time included: Corliss, Coon and Company; Earl and Wilson; George P. Ide and Company; the James K. P. Pine Lion Factory; Van Zandt's; and Joseph Bowman and Sons. Cluett Peabody and Company, which had its origins in 1850, and has for many years marketed its products under the Arrow name, is the only major shirt company still located in the Gateway area. Though shirts are no longer manufactured here, the company maintains its Technical Service Headquarters subsidiary of the Sanforized Company in Troy. Regretfully, however, the firm recently moved the museum of collars, cuffs, and shirts from Troy to New York City. The old industry which made Troy the "collar city" is thus still alive, if barely. A firm that entered the detachable collar and cuff business as late as 1924, the Standard Manufacturing Co., Inc., is now located in the 100-year old James K.P. Lion of Troy factory in Lansingburgh where it now produces mens' and boys' outerwear jackets.

The old Harmony Mills are now called the Cohoes Industrial Terminal, Inc. and are occupied by companies including Barclay Home Products, Inc.; Swanknit, Inc.; and Troy Town Shirts. And so the textile industry lives on in special ways in the old company town.

One of the oldest industries in the Gateway, paper manufacturing, is still operating. The Mount Ida Paper

125

The Troy that never was. An artist's optimistic conception of Troy in the year 2016, drawn for the souvenir booklet of the Troy Centennial Celebration in 1916. Courtesy, Rensselaer County Historical Society

Mill operated up to 1962, but its closure signaled only a pause in the 300-year history of water power on the Poestenkill at Troy's Gorge. Having consolidated their operations in Green Island, the Manning Paper Company became a division of Hammermill Paper Company with a world-wide distributing system for their long-fibered manila stock. Another Gateway area paper manufacturer of equal note is the Mohawk Paper Mills, Inc. of Cohoes and Waterford, manufacturers of the highest quality stock.

Only one manufacturing operation, the Mohawk Paper Mills, survives on what in the nineteenth century was the King Power Canal in Waterford. Gilbert, Murdock and Creighton founded the Enterprise Paper Company on the

Matton shipyard on Van Schaick Island in Cohoes originally built canal boats and later, as in this 1966 launching, police boats, tugboats, and barges. This shipyard, the last in the Gateway, closed in the fall of 1982. Photo by Gene Baxter

canal in the early nineteenth century. In 1931 George O'Connor of Waterford took over the failing Frank Gilbert Company mills in both Cohoes and Waterford. The company is still owned and led by a member of the O'Connor family, Thomas D. O'Connor.

Even in its most depressed twentieth-century days, the Gateway's economy has actually proven more solid than it appeared. Besides industry, New York State government and education have contributed largely to the area's viability. But now a new factor has been added that promises an even brighter future. It is the visionary contribution of the late George M. Low, the fourteenth president of Rensselaer Polytechnic Institute. Low had introduced both

incubator companies and the Rensselaer Technology Park as new components in the area's growth pattern.

Rensselaer Polytechnic Institute in the last decade has grown to become one of the leading technological universities in this country, in fact, in the world. The quality of the faculty has become an irresistible attraction to new high technology industries. And, of course, other Gateway area institutions of higher education, especially Hudson Valley Community College, have contributed to this attractive ambience. At present many new corporations or new subsidiaries of older companies, with names as old and famous as Bolt, Beranek and Newman, Inc. and as new and exciting as Bioreactor Technology, Inc., have set-

This was Cluett, Peabody & Co. and the collar shop district in Troy in the 1920s. Courtesy, Rensselaer County Historical Society

tled in the incubator space on the Rensselaer campus.

Two companies, National Semiconductor and Pac-AmOr Bearings, have built or are building plants at the Rensselaer Technology Park, south of Troy on the highlands overlooking the Hudson, and RPI has constructed multi-tenant facilities. In all, seven corporations have settled in the newly formed park making everything from cathode ray tubes to multi-player, cross-country board and card games. The park is expected to fill up gradually as the century ends, bringing new industries which are geared to keeping the U.S. at the forefront of progress. Besides these assets, Rensselaer Polytechnic Institute, in partnership with the State of New York, is currently building a huge Center for Industrial Innovation where campus research will aid corporations eager to stay at the cutting edge of world industrial development.

Over a decade ago when the Rensselaer County Historical Society formed a committee on preservation, it was decided to focus on industries and industrial properties. The

committee soon broke off from the parent organization to become the Hudson-Mohawk Industrial Gateway. Among its goals was the encouragement of continued operation of historic industries and preservation of historic industrial buildings and sites through adaptive reuse.

The early successes of the Gateway organization led to the establishment of the area as an urban cultural park, a concept that emphasizes special built areas as important cultural resources to be emphasized and preserved much as parklands are preserved. The Hudson-Mohawk Urban Cultural Park was established by the State Legislature in 1979, the first in New York State. Since that time a total of thirteen urban cultural parks, from lower New York City to the Niagara Frontier, have been established and the Gateway has been designated as the park that focuses on industry and labor. Recently on completion of a mandated management study plan, the area park was renamed Riverspark and a timetable set that will have the park completed in 1996. The continuing efforts of the Gateway area and Riverspark promise to make the region much more attractive to both new high-tech industry and to people who come to see sites associated with America's Industrial Revolution, giving the Gateway area both an additional purpose and an additional prominence. It is estimated that when the park is completed, 250,000 persons will visit the Hudson-Mohawk Gateway each year.

Leslie's

WATER POWER NUMBER

A WATER-WHEEL OF THE OLD SCHOOL.

A water-wheel sixty feet in diameter and of 1200 horse-power built at Troy, N. Y., in 1838 by Henry Burden, founder of the Burden Iron Works. Up to 1890 it supplied all the motive power for an enormous plant. It represents the type of power now nearly obsolete in large plants

Right: United Shirt and Collar Company of Lansingburgh produced this tin advertising sign circa 1900. The company's block-long building on Second Avenue is now occupied by Standard Manufacturing Company. Courtesy, Thomas Phelan

Previous page: Henry Burden's giant waterwheel was featured on the cover of Leslie's on February 20, 1913. Built in 1838 to run Burden's iron works, the wheel continued to symbolize the industrial might of the Gateway region long after it was obsolete. Courtesy, Rensselaer County Historical Society

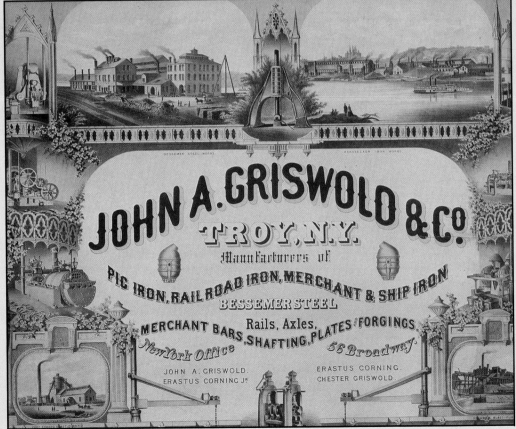

Above left: Ludlow Valve Manufacturing Company began in 1861 in Lansingburgh, moved to Waterford for several years, and then returned to Lansingburgh until 1896 when it took over the rail mill of the old Troy Iron and Steel Company on the banks of the Poestenkill. Courtesy, Thomas Phelan

Above right: The now-famous image of Uncle Sam originated with this 1917 U.S. Army recruiting poster by illustrator James Montgomery Flagg. Courtesy, Rensselaer County Historical Society

Left: This advertising lithograph was produced for John A. Griswold & Co. circa 1870. The Bessemer works in South Troy, established in 1865, were the first of their kind in the U.S. Located on the banks of the Hudson River near the Poestenkill, the Rensselaer Iron Works eventually became the Troy Iron & Steel Company. Courtesy, Rensselaer County Historical Society

Above: Poestenkill Gorge is depicted in this early-nineteenth-century lithograph made from a painting by T. Milbert. Benjamin Marshall developed the gorge in 1840 when he constructed a dam and 600-foot tunnel at the top of the upper falls to power his cotton mill. Courtesy, Rensselaer County Historical Society

Facing page: Troy was still a small port city in 1820, as seen in this engraving based on a watercolor by William Guy Wall. Water from the hills to the left was being used to run mills, but the Erie Canal was not yet completed, and the only bridges across the river were in Lansingburgh to the north. Courtesy, Rensselaer County Historical Society

Right: Major General John Ellis Wool was presented with this gold sword in 1848 for his service in the Mexican War. Photo by Greg Troop

Facing page: The Cohoes Music Hall, restored to its Victorian splendor in the early 1970s, provides a unique setting for a variety of theatrical and musical performances. Courtesy, Mendel, Mesick, Cohen, Waite, Hall Architects

Below: Margaret Olivia Slocum of Syracuse graduated from the Troy Female Seminary in 1847 and married New York financier Russell Sage in 1869. Following her husband's death, Mrs. Sage generously endowed many charities and founded Russell Sage College and the second campus of Emma Willard School.

Above: Troy was already beginning to outgrow the narrow strip of flat land along the Hudson River in 1848 when this lithograph was made. Directly above the people in the foreground are St. Paul's Episcopal Church and the newly completed First Baptist Church. Courtesy, Rensselaer County Historical Society

Right: This was the architect's rendering of William H. Frear & Co. department store. William Frear opened his grand "Troy Cash Bazaar" in 1897 and continued here until 1941. Courtesy, Rensselaer County Historical Society

Left: Proctor's Theater in Troy, now unused, provided entertainment for the Gateway for over sixty years. Opened in 1914 as a vaudeville theater, it switched to movies in the 1930s.

Facing page, top: This is the central tower of Harmony Mill #3 in Cohoes with a statue of Thomas Gardner, one of the mill's founders. Constructed between 1866 and 1872, the building was the largest cotton mill in the country with 1,600 operatives and 2,600 looms. Photo by Robert Chase

Bottom left: This townhouse, on Third Street in downtown Troy, was built for a merchant in the 1830s. Efforts of individual property owners have been responsible for much of the restoration and preservation of historic structures in the Gateway.

Bottom right: The T.J. Eddy House on Third Street in Waterford, built in the early nineteenth century, displays the high-stepped gables characteristic of many houses of that period.

Above: The Rice Building, at First and River streets in Troy, was constructed in 1871. Photo by Robert Chase

Right: The Anna M. Plum Memorial Hall, on the Russell Sage College campus, was designed by Troy architect Marcus Cummings for the Troy Female Seminary in the early 1890s. Photo by Robert Chase

Left: St. Mark's Church in Green Island is now a community center.

Below left: Vail House on First Street in Troy is now part of Russell Sage College. Courtesy, Rensselaer County Historical Society

Below right: St. Paul's Episcopal Church in Troy was remodeled in the 1890s with windows and furnishings designed by Tiffany and Holzer. Photo by Robert Chase

Top: This trolley car was built in 1905 by the Jones Trolley Car Company of Watervliet. Jones streetcars were once used all over the world. This one is on display at the trolley museum in Kenne-bunkport, Maine. Photo by G. Steven Draper

Bottom: A barge and a tugboat were moored at the Troy river-front in 1981 near the newly com-pleted Green Island Bridge which replaced the bridge that collapsed during high water in the spring of 1977. Photo by G. Steven Draper

Facing page, top: The annual arts festival at Riverfront Park in Troy is sponsored by the Rensselaer County Council for the Arts.

Below left: A variety of improve-ment programs in the downtown areas of Gateway communities have led to significant restoration and renovation of storefronts and residences.

Below right: Nineteenth-century townhouses line the streets of downtown Troy near the commer-cial district. Photo by G. Steven Draper

Left: This view from Mount Ida in South Troy looking across the old iron and steel district toward Albany was taken at sunset in 1983. Photo by G. Steven Draper

Right: A ladle car, once used for transporting molten iron, is one of the few reminders of the great Burden Iron Works and Republic Steel in South Troy. Photo by G. Steven Draper

Above: Seasonal splendor of the Cohoes Falls of the Mohawk River was captured in the early 1980s. A dam built across the river above the falls to utilize water power led to the development of Cohoes as an important textile manufacturing center. A hydro-electric plant still uses the power of the great falls. Photo by G. Steven Draper

Left: The Wynantskill Gorge in South Troy, used for water power since the seventeenth century, reached its peak of development in the late nineteenth century. Photo by G. Steven Draper

This is the architect's rendering of the Troy Savings Bank on Second Street designed by George B. Post and completed in 1875. The Music Hall, located on the upper level, is nationally renowned for its fine acoustics. It is home of the Troy Music Hall Association and Troy Chromatics which provide concerts of popular and classical music. Courtesy, Troy Savings Bank

PARTNERS IN PROGRESS

If there is a single determining factor in the development of the Hudson-Mohawk Gateway area, it has to be water. Not the water of the prehistoric Lake Albany which covered the area about 20,000 years ago (although that left its contribution in iron-molder's sand), but the water that has flowed and bubbled down out of the glacial remnant hills to the two scenic rivers—the Hudson and the Mohawk—pausing on its way to turn mill wheels.

It is the water of the rivers themselves which has carried the boats of trade into and out of the area.

The land now occupied by Troy and Watervliet, being at the head of navigation on the Hudson, was a natural place for explorers and settlers to break their journeys. Because they found tillable land, they soon needed grist-mills, and the streams tumbling down from the hill country provided the power.

The settlers also used the rivers to transport the crops of their fields to the markets down the river and to bring back needed goods.

Second to the abundant water—and contingent upon it—is technology, a factor that today outreaches water in its importance. This started with the development of machinery and the installation of mills along the waterways.

This, in turn, brought more people into the area and, with them, more providers of the services people need. Banking came early to the Gateway area because the wealthy mill owners saw a way to help their employees and themselves in the business of money handling. Prominent among the industries were the cotton and iron mills, and their natural offspring: shirt, collar, and stove making.

Schools and colleges followed—the earliest and most important being Emma Willard School and Rensselaer Polytechnic Institute in Troy. Many of the future engineers who learned their life's skills at RPI remained in the area to work in existing businesses and often to start their own new ones. Today the Gateway area is synonymous with the term "high tech."

With education and industry, culture couldn't be far behind.

Troy had a wide variety of theaters in its early days—businesses that no longer exist—and both Troy and Cohoes built elaborate music halls in the later nineteenth century. Those halls are in use today; Troy's has never closed and the Cohoes hall reopened after renovation ten years ago.

The Gateway cities were known too for the contributions made by their ethnic "pockets" of Frenchmen, Irishmen, Italians, Armenians, Ukranians, Germans, Danes, and others, most of whom came to the area to work in one or another of the industries.

Much of the manufacturing has moved elsewhere or has changed in character. Most of the theaters have closed and been torn down or remodeled. Banks still flourish and education has assumed increased importance in the area. In the Hudson-Mohawk Gateway the computer has replaced the mill wheel.

The organizations whose stories are detailed on the following pages have chosen to support this important literary and civic project. They illustrate the variety of ways in which individuals and their businesses have contributed to the growth and development of the Hudson-Mohawk Industrial Gateway. The civic involvement of the region's business, learning institutions, and local government, in partnership with its citizens, has made the Gateway an exceptional place to live and work.

HUDSON-MOHAWK INDUSTRIAL GATEWAY

The ironworks, the textile mills, and the detachable-collar factories that were built near the confluence of the Mohawk and Hudson rivers are almost as real today to many people as they ever were—even though most were closed long ago.

For that, residents of the New York State communities of Troy, Watervliet, Cohoes, Green Island, and Waterford can thank the Hudson-Mohawk Industrial Gateway. For over ten years this organization has, through lectures, tours, and other programs, shown why the area is a birthplace of America's Industrial Revolution. Local resi-

Once headquarters for the vast ironworks developed by Henry Burden, the former Burden office building is now owned by the Hudson-Mohawk Industrial Gateway.

dents have learned to take pride in their history.

The combination of water—the courses of the Mohawk, the Poestenkill, and the Wynantskill cascading into the still-navigable Hudson—and ingenuity—that of industrial giants like Henry Burden and David Johnston—created a near-perfect situation for nineteenth-century industrial development.

Organized to spearhead the revitalization of the area using the old industries and industrial buildings as asset, the Gateway grew out of the work of the Preservation Committee of the Rensselaer County Historical Society. It was chartered in 1972 by the Regents of the University of the State of New York as a nonprofit educational corporation with the responsibilities of public education and the development of tourism.

Although an early aim of the Gateway—the reconstruction of Henry Burden's sixty-foot overshot waterwheel—has not yet been accomplished, the organization is rehabilitating the office building of the Burden Iron Company, has proposed adaptive reuses for a number of Troy firehouses that were to be abandoned, and has been instru-

mental in the preservation and reuse of the Cluett Peabody Bleachery complex on historic Peebles Island. In addition, the organization has provided advice and technical assistance to the owners of several local historic properties and brought developers into the area.

Lobbying by the Gateway has been instrumental in the facade-rehabilitation programs in both Troy's and Cohoes' downtowns, and the group was a force in the formation of the Hudson-Mohawk Urban Cultural Park in 1977. The first in the state, it has served as a model for a proposed statewide system of such parks. The Burden office building, which will one day be the headquarters of the Gateway, will house a theme attraction for the UCP.

Probably the area in which the Hudson-Mohawk Industrial Gateway has been most evident to residents of the communities is in its tours. Although many facets of its program appeal to tourists visiting the region, others—tours by bus and boat—answer the questions of local people. The trip up or down the Waterford Flight of Locks in the New York State Barge Canal System, for instance, is a drawing card for many. And the walking tour of the Burden Upper Works site has had appeal for hardier visitors. In addition to federal and state grants, the Hudson-Mohawk Industrial Gateway is supported by membership dues, funds from the New York State Council on the Arts, and private contributions.

The Hudson-Mohawk Industrial Gateway area is at the confluence of the Hudson and Mohawk rivers, where DeWitt Clinton's ditch, the Erie Canal, met the navigable Hudson. These barges are tied up at the Watervliet "cut" awaiting the spring opening of the canal.

GREATER TROY CHAMBER OF COMMERCE

The Troy Chamber of Commerce was organized on January 31, 1900, with 330 members. Ten dollars purchased a year's membership in the fledgling organization, which rented rooms in the new Ilium Building at the corner of Fulton and Fourth streets.

W.F. Gurley was the chamber's first president; Arthur M. Wright was its first managing secretary, overseeing the day-to-day operations of the body.

The early 1900s were years of interest and growth in Troy. The Commercial Travelers' Association sponsored mercantile expositions in the city in 1899, 1901, and 1904—drawing to public notice "what Troy has to offer," according to an issue of *The Reporter* published in 1908. "The Chamber of Commerce," the writer stated, "was just the medium that was needed to give concrete expression to what was 'in the air' because it was representative of all the commercial and civic interests of the city."

In its early years the association was engaged in a variety of projects. It was taking the public pulse in the matter of a Community Chest; lending its support to the fight against a ship canal from the Great Lakes into the St. Lawrence River, which would likely harm the Erie Barge Canal; compiling a list of city property available for construction, and surveying the industrial advantages of the city in an effort to attract new business; supporting street-paving projects, and working to improve bus transportation to the outlying areas; and considering the annexation of areas contiguous to the city.

The chamber had put several feathers in its cap by 1925. It had secured the erection of a million-dollar hotel (The Hendrick Hudson), which has been renovated to meet the need for commercial office space in downtown Troy; restored the Rensselaer Hotel (formerly the Hotel Troy and now the Monument Square Apartments); effected the abolition of tolls on the Congress Street Bridge; extended the park and playground system in Troy; and lobbied successfully for a federal waterpower bill that assured Green Island of the Ford plant, which then employed 1,500 workers.

In 1954 the organization became the Greater Troy Chamber of Commerce—encompassing Troy and Rensselaer County, as well as the nearby communities of Watervliet, Green Island, Cohoes, and Waterford.

The chamber has drawn up a "Design for Action in the Eighties," with five departments set up within the body comprising Membership Development and Services, Governmental Affairs, Business and Trade Promotion, Communications and Public Relations, and Economic Development and Research. Functions of these divisions are carried out by the more than 650 members.

The organization is involved with numerous civic and cultural groups, such as the Troy Livability Campaign and the Hudson-Mohawk Urban Cultural Park Commission, which promote the historical and livable aspects of the greater Troy area. More than $120 million in new construction and renovations since the early 1980s has made Troy one of the success stories in the Northeast. The chamber will continue to play an important role in the future of the area.

MOORADIAN'S

From roots planted in 1923 as a butcher shop, Mooradian's has grown into a retail furniture company comprised of three stores—each in a separate city in the Hudson-Mohawk Gateway area.

Mihran Mooradian, who had come to the United States at the age of seventeen from a part of Turkey that was once Armenia, founded the small butcher shop at the corner of Nineteenth Street and Third Avenue in Watervliet, New York. In 1931 he expanded his holdings by opening an appliance store next door, taking over the premises of a florist's shop. The new enterprise—called Modern Home Appliances—carried large appliances such as stoves and refrigerators, as well as smaller conveniences.

A year later the entrepreneur opened a similar operation, across the Hudson River, in Troy. First located on Fifth Avenue, the store subsequently moved in 1941 and 1945 to River Street on Franklin Square—where the business was extended to include a full line of furniture. During this period Mooradian purchased the building that housed the Watervliet store, the larger quarters allowing the incorporation of furniture merchandising.

Mihran Mooradian died in 1948, leaving the operation in the hands of his two older sons, Richard and Edward; the third son, Myron, was still in school at that time. Shortly after the latter's graduation from college and entrance into the business in 1966, the three brothers instituted a third store on Remsen Street in Cohoes.

Foreseeing the proverbial writing on the wall, as urban-renewal construction became imminent, the Mooradian brothers in 1972 purchased a former shirt factory on River Street (on the bank of the Hudson River) in Troy. The seven-story Jacobsen Building was remodeled to serve both as store and warehouse when they had to vacate the Franklin Square building, with the wrecker's ball moving up in their wake. The opening at the

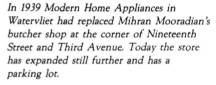

In 1939 Modern Home Appliances in Watervliet had replaced Mihran Mooradian's butcher shop at the corner of Nineteenth Street and Third Avenue. Today the store has expanded still further and has a parking lot.

new address took place in the spring of 1973.

The dimensions of the Watervliet store were doubled in 1975, with a new facade added three years later, and its size was increased still more in 1979. The Cohoes store was given a face lifting in 1978, in conjunction with the city's reurbanization program. Further renovations added parking areas to both facilities.

Commemorating the company's fiftieth anniversary in the business of selling first appliances, and then furniture to the residents of the Gateway area, all three stores held an open house for their customers on May 3, 1981, and offered special purchases throughout the remainder of the year.

Richard Mooradian is in charge of the Troy store, Edward of the expanded Watervliet operation, and Myron directs the establishment in Cohoes.

The thriving family business with three retail stores, a warehouse, and its own fleet of delivery trucks has come a long way since its beginnings as a little butcher shop over a half-century ago.

Today Myron, Richard, and Edward Mooradian (left to right) operate the furniture and appliance business founded by their father in 1931. Started in Watervliet, the firm also has stores in Troy and Cohoes.

GEIER & BLUHM, INC.

Two young European instrument makers formed a friendship in London in 1902 that, in a sense, lasts to this day in the firm that bears their names—Geier & Bluhm, Inc., of Troy—which produced a part of the instrument packages used by NASA on the moon during the Apollo 12 mission.

James Geier was born and trained in Switzerland; Joseph Bluhm was a native of Hungary, where he was apprenticed as an instrument maker in Budapest at the age of thirteen, and later worked in Germany before immigrating to England in 1902. They met at a London night school, which they attended in order to learn the English language, and three years later decided to seek their fortunes in the United States. After arriving in New York City, the men continued to Troy (where Geier had an uncle) and found employment with the Hanna Manufacturing Company, a maker of surveying instruments.

In the spring of 1907 the enterprise of Geier & Bluhm was established by the young entrepreneurs. However, early financial difficulties prompted Bluhm to work in New York City, sending money back to his partner in Troy, until their business was financially stable. During this period they also studied for citizenship of the United States, which they earned in 1910.

Incorporated in 1922, with Geier as president and Bluhm as vice-president, the company from its beginning until the 1930s made surveying instruments—with Bluhm holding a number of patents on the devices manufactured. The rights to the fabrication of the firm's line were then sold to the Bostrom Brady Manufacturing Company of Atlanta, Georgia, while Geier & Bluhm received the distributorship of Bostrom Brady instruments in the Troy area. The energies of the organization subsequently turned to manufacturing spirit levels, still its

principal product.

During World War II the corporation provided inclinometers to the United States Army and Navy, and cloud-height measuring instruments to the U.S. Weather Bureau.

Following James Geier's death in 1946, his partner assumed the presidency. Harold F. Oster was brought in as manager, succeeding Bluhm upon his retirement in 1965. Bluhm, however, continued to come to work each day, and upon his eighty-eighth birthday in 1971 was still timing his work and trying to improve his performance; he died two years later. The firm was by then under the direction of Oster's wife, Marion, who was named president after his death in 1968. Today their sons, Russell and David—who are also Joseph Bluhm's great-grandsons—serve as president and vice-president, respectively.

The founders originated their business in a small shop on Ferry Street in Troy; they subsequently moved to 670 River Street, and after World War I bought that property. In 1956 the firm relocated to its present address at 594 River Street, where it continues to be one of the foremost manufacturers of circular spirit levels in the country.

While its participation in the Apollo 12 mission is a source of pride to Geier & Bluhm, Inc., the firm regards with equal pride the work it has been able to do for the military, automotive, aerospace, scientific, construction, and textile industries.

JOHN L. THOMPSON, SONS & COMPANY, INC.

John L. Thompson, for whom the firm was named, became an apprentice in his brother-in-law's apothecary shop in 1818. In 1828 he acquired the firm, which exists today as John L. Thompson, Sons & Company, Inc.

When Dr. Samuel Gale, Jr., assumed his ailing father's medical practice in Troy in 1797, he also opened an apothecary shop that has evolved into John L. Thompson, Sons & Company, Inc., the oldest drug-wholesaling firm in the United States still at its original location.

As the Hudson River was a more important travel route than the roads at the turn of the century, a doctor in a prominent river port (where goods were delivered) was a key figure. Consequently, Dr. Gale was regarded as a source of drug supply by physicians less fortunately situated. He was joined in operating the shop in 1805 by his brother, William, and five years later married Betsy Thompson of Amenia—whose brother, John L. Thompson, became apprenticed to the company in 1818. The business flourished, necessitating larger quarters by 1820. Although the original building was replaced, on the same site at 161 River Street, the subsequent

Ellis Howes Robison, chairman of the board, treasurer, and chief executive officer.

structure is still in use.

The Thompson name was added to the enterprise in 1821, when Dr. Gale and his brother-in-law formed a partnership; it became known under that nomenclature upon the physician's retirement seven years later, at which time he sold his interest in the business to his associate. The sole proprietor then further expanded the growing operation's facilities.

In 1841 David Cowee, who had entered the company as a clerk, became a partner and the firm was renamed John L. Thompson & Company; its present title was adopted when John I. and William A. Thompson joined their father in business in 1851. That same year another building was purchased, and a warehouse erected on the riverbank below River Street.

Cowee's son, James F., was admitted into the partnership in 1867. It was also during this period that the company's products took a new direction—away from drugs and into heavy chemicals, which were much used by the factories in the

Hudson and Mohawk valleys.

After the deaths of John I. and William A. Thompson in 1901 and 1903, respectively, the business was incorporated with James Cowee as president. William A. Thompson's son, William Leland (who had come into the firm in 1893) was made treasurer; becoming president upon Cowee's death, he held the position until his retirement in 1954.

Entering the organization in 1927 as general manager, Ellis H. Robison succeeded Thompson as president and became sole owner. The corporation today is still owned by his family. He is chairman of the board, treasurer, and chief executive officer; James A. Robison, who joined the operation in 1959 as sales manager, continues to hold that position as well as serving as president and general manager; Elissa Robison Prout is secretary; and Richard G. Robison, associated since 1954, is vice-president, assistant treasurer, and sundries buyer.

This brick building, constructed in 1829 at 161 River Street in Troy, is still the company's home. Photo circa 1860

NORTON COMPANY/COATED ABRASIVE DIVISION

While Norton Company's Coated Abrasive Division in Watervliet had its beginnings in a rented loft above a Brooklyn bakery, and a paper mill in Troy, it has become world renowned for its products.

Herman Behr and Company was originated in 1872 by a young German immigrant of that name, who initially fabricated "pouncing" paper—a product used in making felt hats. In the neighboring community of Troy, Manning Paper Company had been founded in 1846 to produce manila fiber-rope paper, which was used for wrapping electric cable and for flour bags. The founder's son, John A. Manning, unsuccessfully tried to sell his paper to makers of sandpaper; undaunted, he decided in 1912 to diversify by manufacturing the product. Erecting its first building on the present site in Watervliet that year, Manning Sandpaper Company in 1919 became Manning Abrasive Company.

Both firms had become giants in the sandpaper industry by 1928, at which time they merged—creating a firm nearly double the size of the nearest competitor. Three years later Behr-Manning Company, which retained that name until 1968, was acquired by the Norton Company, based in Worcester, Massachusetts. Pike Manufacturing Company (since 1832 a producer of sharpening stones) had also recently joined Norton, whose acquisitions made it the largest abrasive producer in the world.

Over the years the coated abrasive industry has changed extensively. Today over 100 varieties of sandpaper are made to meet specialized customer needs. Major industrial markets include metalworking, woodworking, automotive manufacturing and refinishing, as well as the familiar hardware and consumer do-it-yourself segments.

A merger in 1928 (around the time of the top photo) created the Behr-Manning Company, the forerunner to the Coated Abrasive Division of the Norton Company in Watervliet (above).

Several important product developments have occurred within the industry, pioneered through the research and development efforts of the Norton Company. In 1972 the Norzon® product line was introduced, incorporating a new generation of long-lasting abrasive grain containing zirconium (a constituent of the gemstone zircon). The result was an industrial grade product that lasted up to three times as long as the older generation of aluminum oxide products.

A further major commercial success followed in 1975, when the Coated Abrasive Division developed a process for stabilizing synthetic fabrics so they could be used for backings for coated abrasives. These "polyester" backings proved superior to woven cotton fabrics, which had been the major cloth backing in use up to that point.

The most recent generation of new products developed by the

company incorporates additional new technology. A new line of high-performance products was introduced in 1981 under the System-E trade name and reflects the use of still another generation of backings that are yielding better-performing products. In addition, a plastic film-backed abrasive was designed to meet the ultraprecise finishing requirements in the optical and electronics markets.

While Norton Company is a worldwide marketer of coated abrasives, the Watervliet facility has become the center for the firm's research and development efforts in this field.

FREIHOFER'S

The origin of the Freihofer Baking Company goes back to Philadelphia in 1884, when Charles F. Freihofer, himself born in New Jersey to a German immigrant, started a bakery.

He ran it alone for six years, at which time he went into partnership with his brother, William. In 1913 company folk history has it that Charles, stopping off in Troy on his way to Montreal to examine a new bread oven, questioned the station conductor about the "Collar City." Learning that Troy industry employed many women, Charles decided to start a bakery to provide fresh bread for working women. He returned to Philadelphia and sent his three sons, Charles C., Edwin, and Frank, "up north" to Troy.

The growth of the company began upon its arrival in the capital district in 1913. One year after the opening of the Troy bakery, a plant in Schenectady was opened, followed by an Albany plant in 1915. In 1918 a cake bakery was purchased and Freihofer's began offering sweet baked goods as well as bread products to turn-of-the-century customers.

Freihofer's home delivery service was an integral part of capital district life from the early 1900s through the 1960s. The familiar sound of the Freihofer horse and wagon could be heard at 3 a.m. as the routeman made his first round of deliveries. He returned in the early morning to take orders for the next day or to sell products right from his delivery vehicle.

Flyers were left each week for homemakers to choose which special items to order. Called "Freihofer's Bakery News," the colored flyers included special cakes, pictures, and taste-tempting descriptions of products, and sometimes had special offers for cookie jars, casseroles, or platters.

Pans of bread were slid into the ovens by hand in the 1920s, as opposed to the automated methods used in the new Freihofer bread plant in Albany. Today 3,000 loaves of bread can be baked at one time, more than 11,000 in an hour.

World War II not only saw an exodus of Freihofer routemen and bakers to the armed services, but also a shortage in bakery ingredients and difficulties in equipment repair and maintenance. The postwar years brought the demise of the horse and wagon as well as a tremendous effort by the company to shift from home service to the wholesale bakery business. Production, accounting, and route delivery modernization went hand in hand with wholesale preparations.

However, it took until the early 1970s to completely phase out the home service operation. The company vowed no routeman would be laid off with the coming of wholesale business. A route was only discontinued when a routeman retired, and on January 22, 1972, Freihofer's made its last home delivery in the area where it had made its first—Troy.

It was during this time of

transition that the firm began to expand the area it serviced. Some twelve years before its last home delivery, Freihofer's opened a distribution center in New Paltz. Another center was later opened in Glens Falls. In 1971, still one year before the firm ceased home delivery, a Verona branch was opened to serve Syracuse, Utica, and Oswego. A later addition of a branch in Nelliston filled the distri-

Children would always gather when the Freihofer horse arrived in the neighborhood. The scene, on Seventh Avenue in Troy, depicts one of the firm's last deliveries by horse and wagon.

Connecticut, market, a metropolitan area with a population of more than one million. Within three months Freihofer's exceeded sales goals and developed a reputation among residents not unlike the one the company holds in its home territory.

Shortly after the Hartford expansion, Freihofer's opened a distribution center in Rockland County, New York. The seventieth anniversary in the capital district also marked Freihofer's first year in Rockland County, where sales figures show the burgeoning loyalty of yet another customer base.

To produce consistently delicious breads in the quantities necessary to serve the large number of Freihofer's customers requires modern computerized production and distribution systems, exacting training programs for all employees, and a fussy attitude about the ingredients that go into all Freihofer's products.

The firm's belief in quality goes back to 1913, when the first loaves of bread baked were pan bread and French bread. Freihofer's makes several dozen different white and variety breads, as well as the Sunbeam and Rite Diet lines, national brands baked locally by the company.

With Robert Freihofer as president, Freihofer's is now in its fourth generation of family ownership, making it one of the few remaining family-owned businesses in the nation and one of the largest family-owned bakeries of its kind. Freihofer's also enjoys a unique loyalty and affection from its customers, especially the families of the capital area.

bution gap between Schenectady and Syracuse.

Between 1971 and 1982 the company consolidated baking operations from Troy and Schenectady in a new state-of-the-art production plant on Prospect Road in Albany. White and variety breads, English muffins, and rolls are produced at this central location according to a schedule calculated to ensure maximum freshness from dock to supermarket shelf. Sweet goods and cookies are produced at

Today trucks have replaced the horse-drawn vehicles and deliveries range farther afield. Here a caravan of delivery trucks heads for Hartford, Connecticut.

separate facilities, with the cookie plant baking one million chocolate chip cookies and other varieties each day.

The increase in production capability allowed Freihofer's to take on its biggest challenge to date. In 1981 the firm entered the Hartford,

153

COHOES SAVINGS BANK

For more than 130 years Cohoes Savings Bank has been an integral part of the busy community of Cohoes. It was founded by local businesspeople to serve themselves and their neighbors—the community had no savings institution—and has always maintained its local character.

A mutual savings bank (one owned solely by its depositors) was chartered on April 11, 1851, under the name Cohoes Savings Institution. Its first president, elected in 1853, was Egbert Egberts, son of a Revolutionary War officer who had retired from business in 1852. Egberts and his partner, Timothy

Bailey, successfully introduced the power knitting frame in the area and had extensive manufacturing holdings in Cohoes.

Like Egberts, the other original trustees were men of prominence in both business and professional circles in the community.

The Cohoes Savings Institution opened for business on August 16, 1853, on Remsen Street, near Oneida. While its first-day deposits totaled $81 from three depositors, after four years its deposits were $29,248.78. During its first few years the stripling institution carried on its business through the Merchants Bank of Albany.

In 1951 Cohoes Savings Bank was remodeled, and the famous Lithgow murals, depicting the history of the immediate area, were unveiled. One panel can be seen at upper right. The lobby appears much the same today.

In 1859 the Bank of Cohoes was organized by Egberts to serve the business interests of the growing community. The savings bank made an arrangement, similar to those made with the Merchants Bank, with this organization to look after its operations.

The savings institution changed its business techniques in 1861 and

began to make investments, issuing its first mortgage. Loans to develop real estate helped the community to grow.

In 1882 the contract with the National Bank of Cohoes (formerly Bank of Cohoes) was terminated, and the savings institution began to keep all of its own accounts. Its assets in 1880 had exceeded $570,000, and its resources and surplus showed a steady increase.

Cohoes Savings Institution merged with Mechanics Savings Bank of Cohoes in July 1933, and the combined assets exceeded $10,190,000.

In August 1904 the lot at the corner of Remsen and Seneca streets was purchased and a building erected. This was enlarged in 1924 and remodeled in 1950-1951. It was at this time that the historical murals, for which the bank is famous locally, were painted by David Lithgow. These depict the Indian legends about the area and the Cohoes Cataract, the coming of the white men, the birth of industry, and the discovery on the Mohawk River of the Cohoes Mastodon.

In recent years Cohoes Savings Bank has opened four branch locations—one in Cohoes itself and others in Latham, Lansingburgh

Cohoes Savings Bank, located on Remsen Street, has been a part of the community for more than 130 years.

(Troy), and Clifton Park.

Its net worth, as listed in December 1984, was nearly sixteen million dollars, but president Walter Speidel, who himself rose through the ranks of banking to his present position, rates it as much greater because of the loyalty of the employees and the rest of the community. From a sound and successful past, Cohoes Savings Bank looks forward to an equally sound and successful future.

TELEDYNE GURLEY

The history of Teledyne Gurley, as succinctly stated on the firm's calendar, is the history of the technology of measuring.

The Troy enterprise, which until 1968 was known as W. & L.E. Gurley, had its beginnings in Ephraim Gurley's foundry in Gibbonsville, now Watervliet. William and Lewis E. Gurley, from whom the firm took its original name, were Ephraim's sons.

In 1845 William Gurley formed a partnership with Jonas Phelps to make mathematical and philosophical instruments. Lewis became a partner in 1851, and the following year the Gurleys bought out Phelps and the company became W. & L.E. Gurley.

Lewis, who succeeded his brother as president, was followed first by his son, William Frank Gurley, and then by William's son-in-law, Paul Cook, as head of the firm. One of Lewis' daughters married Edgar Hayes Betts, a manufacturer of collars and shirts, who later became president of both the shirt firm and the Gurley enterprise.

After Betts' death in 1951,

leadership of the company left the family for some years, before it passed back into the hands of Robert Gurley Betts, grandson of Lewis Gurley. Aside from these leaders, probably the firm's best-known employee was Edward W. Arms, who designed the first fully automated dividing engine in America, the first mountain transit, and made the first aluminum transit.

In the firm's early years, it developed and manufactured surveying instruments, hydrological instruments, standard weights and measures, paper-testing instruments, and meteorological instruments.

During the World War II era, W. & L.E. Gurley perfected methods for producing complex patterns on glass and other materials. This technology, known as optographics, is employed in producing high-resolution targets, reticles, scales, step wedges, and code discs. During the Korean War the company produced as many as 20,000 reticles each month for tank range finders.

The combination of optographics with mechanical and electronic techniques led to the development of electro-optical encoders, which translate rotary or linear motion into electronic signals. These have become the most significant part of the firm's business.

In 1968 the enterprise became part of Teledyne, a major high-technology, multiproduct corporation, and its name was changed to Teledyne Gurley. The Gurley Building, at the corner of Fulton Street and Fifth Avenue in Troy, was completed in 1862 after the great fire which destroyed much of the city.

Teledyne Gurley's encoders, which achieve accuracies to a few millionths of an inch, are employed in space vehicles, military aircraft map-

Teledyne Gurley's electro-optical encoders are used in a wide variety of precision applications.

ping cameras, shipboard navigation systems, machine controls, robots, and medical diagnostic instruments. As a natural extension of its encoder business, the firm produces packaged digital-readout systems to improve the productivity of machine tools. The digital-readout system combines an encoder with a display console to provide an easily read digital indication of a machine's worktable position.

In addition, Teledyne Gurley continues to produce hydrological instruments for measuring the velocity of water flow, and paper-testing instruments for determining porosity, stiffness, and other properties of paper and similar materials.

Teledyne Gurley looks forward to maintaining its leadership role in the precision instruments field.

The Gurley Building, constructed in 1862, is a national historic landmark. It still houses the firm, known since 1968 as Teledyne Gurley.

NORSTAR BANK OF UPSTATE NY

In the summer of 1984 Norstar Bank of Upstate NY came into being. Formerly known as State Bank of Albany, the institution adopted the name, according to president Frank Odell, to "provide a closer association in the public mind" between the bank itself and the parent company, Norstar Bancorp, a holding company with assets of $5.3 billion.

State Bank of Albany can trace its roots in Troy back to 1801 and in Albany back to 1803. When The National City Bank of Troy became a part of State Bank in 1959, it was a merger of the oldest and largest banks in the two upstate cities. The addition of National City's deposits of $60 million and assets of $65 million increased State Bank's deposits to $370 million and its assets to more than $400 million, making it the third-largest bank in New York State outside of New York City.

The National City Bank of Troy, granted its national charter in 1905, was formed by the merger of Central National Bank and Mutual National Bank. In January 1930 United National Bank merged with The National City Bank, making the resulting institution the oldest in the city. The United National Bank, established in 1865, had assumed the business of Farmers Bank—founded in 1801—and the Bank of Troy—incorporated in 1811.

The National City Bank of Troy acquired the transactions of Troy Prudential Association in 1947, thereby expanding its personal-loan business. The Manufacturers Bank of Cohoes, founded in 1872, was merged with The National City Bank of Troy in 1948. The organization absorbed Ticonderoga National Bank of Ticonderoga and Citizens National Bank of Port Henry into the system in 1954.

Two years previously the expanding Troy banking institution had opened its Latham office at 775 New Loudon Road. In 1957 this office was moved to the new Latham Corners Shopping Center, and was relocated again in 1982 to a new structure south of the Latham Traffic Circle.

In 1948, eleven years before the Albany-Troy merger, National Bank of Watervliet became the fourth branch in the State Bank system. This institution, which was founded in 1862 as the Bank of West Troy, became the National Bank of West Troy in 1865, and National Bank of Watervliet in 1905. Other branches in the Gateway area include those in Menands, established in 1948; and Lansingburgh, established in 1974.

Norstar Bancorp was formed in 1972 by State Bank of Albany and Liberty National Bank to serve the eastern and western areas of New York State.

Shortly before the announcement of the upstate name change, the holding company made known its intention to restore an Albany landmark, the old Union Station, as its corporate offices.

Built to house The National City Bank of Troy, this pillared structure at Third and State streets in Troy is the home of a Norstar Bank branch.

The National Bank of Watervliet merged with State Bank of Albany in 1948. The building shown here was torn down in 1969, when the present Congress Street Bridge was built.

The Manufacturers Bank of Cohoes, founded in 1872, merged with The National City Bank of Troy in 1948.

HUDSON VALLEY COMMUNITY COLLEGE

At the forefront of new educational needs and emerging technologies, Hudson Valley Community College has grown dramatically during its thirty years of serving students, businesses, and the Hudson-Mohawk area communities.

Founded in October 1953 as the Hudson Valley Technical Institute, the college began as a veterans' vocational school—sponsored by Rensselaer County—with eighty-eight students in the former Earl and Wilson Shirt Company Building, at Broadway Street and Seventh Avenue in downtown Troy. As graduates of the school acquired marketable skills and readily found employment in companies in the Hudson-Mohawk area, its reputation spread and enrollment increased.

In 1959 the name was changed to Hudson Valley Community College. In 1961 a new campus with five buildings opened on 165 acres at 80 Vandenburgh Avenue. As part of the State University of New York, the college endeavored to make higher education accessible to more people. Its scope has expanded to encompass industrial and engineering technologies, business, health sciences, liberal arts, and community services, housed in twelve buildings. With 336 faculty members and forty-four degree programs, enrollment has reached 8,500 students who represent every county in the state, several northeastern states, and twenty-seven foreign countries. Twenty percent of that increase has occurred during the past four years; at the 1984 commencement the 25,000th student received an HVCC degree.

In order to prepare students for new industrial technologies, instruction has focused on such innovations as computer graphics for design and manufacturing, laser measuring devices, and digital

In 1959 the Hudson Valley Technical Institute became Hudson Valley Community College. It also acquired the site of its new campus on 165 acres at 80 Vandenburgh Avenue.

control equipment for sophisticated manufacturing. The institution, which helped organize the Capital District High Technology Council, cooperates closely with industries to develop specialized training courses—such as the automotive-technologies program that now teaches employees of national automobile manufacturers. Many private firms plus state government are users of these services.

The college's educational philosophy calls for using the community as a laboratory, with on-site learning occurring in many programs and over 250 community advisers sharing their talents. Many of its graduates will live and work in the area, with many continuing their studies at outstanding four-year colleges. Consistent with its goal of total community service, HVCC's Placement Office actively aids workers displaced from restructuring industries through continuing education or the Educational Opportunity Center's retraining programs.

One of HVCC's goals is to teach technical people to be aware of and

Hudson Valley Community College has grown dramatically during its thirty years of serving students in Rensselaer County and surrounding communities, and remains at the forefront of new educational needs and emerging technologies.

sensitive to the societal impacts of technology and its relationship with the arts. The Arts and Technology Colloquium has produced superb learning experiences on ancient Egypt and the classical and medieval eras—drawing eminent scholars across the United States as participants.

When the college recently converted a seminary complex into its headquarters, art gallery, and conference center, it acquired archaeological remains of the Burden Waterwheel—a symbol of Troy's industrial past. Conversely, one can say that Hudson Valley Community College will be a source of energy for industries of the future.

STANDARD MANUFACTURING CO., INC.

The year 1984 marked two anniversaries for Standard Manufacturing Co., Inc., of Troy—the 60th for the firm itself and the 100th for the building that houses it.

George H. Arakelian started a small company to make detachable shirt collars and cuffs—one of Troy's specialties—in 1924 in a shop at 382 River Street, at the corner of Federal Street. He was assisted by his son, Armen G., who worked with his father after school at first, and later on a full-time basis. Another son, John G., joined the business in 1929.

They worked together until 1941. It was during this period of time that the senior Arakelian secured a patent for his efforts on a buttonhole machine.

During World War II collars and cuffs were replaced by flying jackets, made for the Army, and the firm's path was set. Jackets have been the principal product ever since.

The first postwar jackets made by Standard Manufacturing were 100 percent cotton poplin, zipper-front, water-repellent golf jackets made in limited colors. At first this was the company's only product. As Standard developed, gradually other styles and product lines evolved and now includes a full line of outerwear that is sold worldwide.

Standard's customer base had changed with the times. Initially retail department stores and chain stores were its only customers. Today the firm sells to the sporting goods industry and also the imprinted sportswear industry. Many of its garments are imprinted with the names of schools, colleges, teams, and places of employment. A recent development is Standard's entry into the field of premium-type jackets along with uniforms and career apparel.

The "Sportsmaster" label, Standard's brand name, is sewn in several million garments produced annually. These jackets are worn by men, women, boys, and girls throughout the country for all seasons and a variety of activities.

In the course of its long history the company has moved several times. In 1970 Standard moved to its present location, the historic J.K.P. Pine factory, a block-long factory structure in Lansingburgh.

Standard Manufacturing Co., Inc., has seen many technical changes in sixty years; however, it is its fine complement of people that make it one of the leading outerwear manufacturers in the country.

Standard Manufacturing Co., Inc., moved to its present location, the historic J.K.P. Pine factory in Lansingburgh, in 1970.

BLUE CROSS OF NORTHEASTERN NEW YORK

In 1929 at Baylor University in Texas, Justin Ford Kimball devised a prepaid health program in which members paid a monthly sum to the University Hospital and in turn received health care as the need arose. During the Depression many Americans were unable to pay hospital bills, and Kimball's plan was eagerly emulated across the nation. By 1935 eleven plans existed and six more were under development. That same year a group of concerned citizens in Albany advanced a similar program for financing health care locally.

Conceived as a nonprofit community venture providing access to health care for members in the immediate Albany area, the Associated Hospital Service of the Capital District was established in July 1936. With $10,000 for start-up costs contributed by area hospitals, the Plan began serving Albany, Schenectady, and Rensselaer counties from a tiny office on State Street in Albany. By year's end there were 5,000 members enrolled and thirty-three claims had been paid. Ten more counties were added the following year to comprise the thirteen-county area now served by Blue Cross of Northeastern New York. Two years later the Plan officially adopted the Blue Cross emblem.

The American Hospital Association in 1938 formed the Council of Hospital Service Plans, forerunner of today's Blue Cross and Blue Shield Association, and interest was growing in similar plans to cover the cost of physician care. In 1946 a nonprofit Blue Shield Plan was instituted under the administration of Albany Blue Cross, which had grown to serve 300,000 subscribers.

Growth by the Plan has been almost constant. In 1956 coverage

Since 1971 Blue Cross of Northeastern New York has been headquartered in this building in Slingerlands.

for military dependents began under the CHAMPUS Program. Administration of the New York State Employees Health Insurance Program started in 1957, federal employees chose Blue Cross in 1960, and administration of Medicare began in 1965. Such dramatic expansion required that the Plan move, first from the Rice Building at 135 Washington Avenue in Albany to 1215 Western Avenue in 1966, and finally to the present facility on New Scotland Road in Slingerlands in 1971.

As the 1960s drew to a close, a new prescription-drug program was unveiled and development of major medical, dental, and other programs began. A health-maintenance organization, initiated by Albany Blue Cross in the 1960s, coalesced as the Capital Area Community Health Plan by 1976. An alcoholism program introduced in 1978 was a state first and a national pioneer.

Leadership of the Albany Blue Cross Plan began with Edward R. Evans, the first chief executive; he held that position from 1936 to 1955. He was succeeded upon his retirement by Ralph Hammersley, Jr., who served until his retirement in 1976. At that time Dr. Clifton C. Thorne was made president; Chester E. Burrell, who joined the Plan as executive vice-president in 1981, was named president following Dr. Thorne's death in 1982.

Dramatic gains by the Plan, in poor as well as prosperous times, have confirmed the validity of the original Blue Cross concept. By 1984 the Plan enrolled more than 850,000 subscribers, representing nearly three-quarters of its thirteen-county population.

MARINE MIDLAND BANK, N.A.

This tiny office, with its maple paneling, is where the financing for the USS Monitor was arranged. A painting of the famous Civil War battle between the first ironclad ships, the USS Monitor and the Merrimack, now hangs over the mantle. The room was preserved when the old Security Trust Company was demolished and the Manufacturers National Bank building rose in its place in 1922.

The offices of Security Trust Company and Security Safe Deposit Company, once the premises of Troy City Bank, were razed, along with building at right, to make way for the Fourth and Grand streets office of Manufacturers National Bank in 1923. It is now part of Marine Midland Bank, N.A.

The banking giant that is Marine Midland Bank, N.A., the nation's thirteenth largest, can trace its history through many branches of its statewide "family," but its principal line in the capital district goes back to the founding of Manufacturers Bank of Troy, which first opened its doors at 13 First Street in 1852.

The rapidly growing young institution soon needed larger quarters, and four years later moved to a three-story brick structure at King and River streets, where it became a major financial player in Troy's industrial success. It added "National" to its title in 1865, when it received its national bank charter.

It has remained mindful of its continuing role as a partner in the economic growth of Troy and Rensselaer County.

When it merged with two other area financial institutions, Security Trust Company and Safe Deposit Company in 1921, and the 64-year-old Peoples Bank of Lansingburgh two years later, it built an imposing new headquarters building on Franklin Square, at Fourth and Grand streets.

Although the old building housing the Security Trust Company on the site was demolished to make way for the new structure, one significant portion was preserved and incorporated into the new building: the historic Monitor Room, where plans were made for financing the *Monitor,* the ironclad Civil War vessel.

In 1929 Manufacturers National joined with fifteen other financial institutions in New York State to form the largest organization of its kind in the country—the Marine Midland Corporation. The merger included national and state banks and trust institutions, yet each member of the association maintained its own identity. Other banks joined the corporation in succeeding decades. Manufacturers,

which became Marine Midland Eastern, N.A., and later, Marine Midland—Capital Region, acquired the Troy Trust Company in 1941.

To deliver banking services to an expanded thirteen-county area, from Catskill to Plattsburgh, Marine Midland-Capital Region moved its operation center to Wolf Road in Colonie in 1971. Five years later it and the other nine regional banks became one statewide bank in what was at that time the largest merger in U.S. banking history.

A few recent highlights: In 1979, as part of the bank's fiftieth-anniversary celebration, branch displays of historic artifacts included a piece of the original metal plate of the *Monitor,* minutes of the first directors' meeting and statements of condition of the original bank founded in 1859 at Lansingburg, as well as currency of the same year issued by the National Bank of Cohoes; also in 1979 Marine sponsored the Heritage Trail marathon, a 26-mile qualifying event in the Empire State Games originating in Troy and traversing several urban cultural park communities along the Hudson; and in 1981 Marine joined the city in celebrating the 214th anniversary of the birth of Troy's "Uncle Sam" Wilson by mounting a large exhibit on Uncle Sam as cartoonists have depicted him through the years. The Rensselaer County Historical Society now houses the exhibit, which is available to interested area groups.

Today as part of Marine's Midstate Region, the eight offices in Gateway communities—six in Troy and one each in Cohoes and Green Island—offer the same personal service of years past, enhanced by state-of-the-art electronic capabilities that link them with the bank's other offices in its statewide, national, and international system.

ROSS VALVE MANUFACTURING COMPANY, INC.

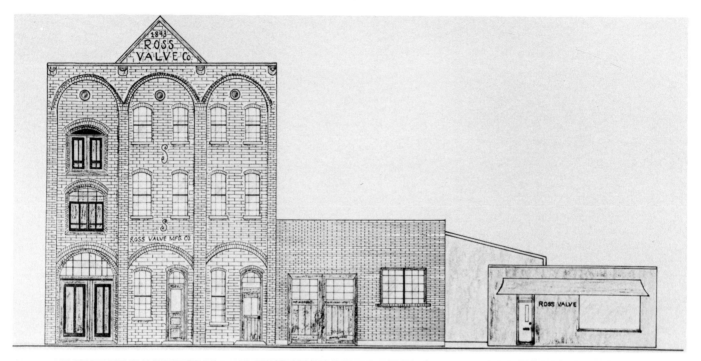

An architect's rendering of the handsome historic building on Oakwood Avenue, Troy, which Ross Valve Manufacturing Company, Inc., has occupied since 1893.

Since its inception in the late nineteenth century, the Ross Valve Manufacturing Company has produced hydraulic specialty valves to supply communities and industries with fresh water for people and processes.

The oldest automatic-valve maker in the United States, the firm grew out of the efforts of George Ross—who migrated to Troy from Scotland in 1851. A skilled cabinetmaker, he crafted furniture and patterns for the Delaware and Hudson Railroad. In 1879 he obtained a patent on a "fluid pressure regulator," a simple, direct-acting, spring-loaded valve. The Ross Valve Company was formed later that year, a family manufacturing enterprise that incorporated in 1917.

The following year the firm obtained another patent, for a "fluid balanced type" cutoff, the direct predecessor of today's valve designs. Used to control or reduce pressure in street mains and pipelines, and to regulate flow of water between reservoirs, the units were made of cast iron with bronze internal components. So rugged is their construction that many of the valves sold before 1900 are still in operation.

The business moved into a handsome three-story brick building on Oakwood Avenue in 1893, and still occupies the historic structure—little changed in its facade except for the addition of new offices. The present corporation was formed in 1917, and is now headed by fourth-generation members of the Ross family; two great-great-grandsons of the founder are employed by the firm.

In the early 1900s over 800 Ross valves were installed to control New York City's water supply, and all such units in the borough of Manhattan were made at the Troy plant. The contract for the devices from Ross to operate the gates of the Panama Canal was the largest single order for specialty valves up to that time, and they are still in operation. Other notable products have included reciprocating water engines, used to drive the bellows of church organs in the nineteenth century, and hydraulic booster pumps. Municipalities ranging from Teheran, Iran, to suburbs in Washington, D.C., use valves, which are historic in design but fitted with modern microprocessor controls to meet today's needs.

Ross Valve stresses quality and craftsmanship. The company's managers are directly involved in the production process, and encourage participation of everyone in the work force in meeting high-quality standards and suggesting improvements.

More streamlined manufacturing methods and careful environmental controls are priorities in this basic manufacturing industry.

THE TIMES RECORD

Since 1896 residents of the Hudson-Mohawk Gateway area have read the news daily from *The Times Record.* On April 4 of that year *The Troy Daily Record,* forerunner of *The Times Record* and its younger sister, *The Sunday Record,* made its debut, devoted, as its editorial read, "to the moral, material and political interests of the community."

One of the three principal newspapers in the Tri-Cities, *The Times Record* is the only one of the three located within the Gateway boundaries. Its management has not lost track of the community's interests and, through the paper's editorial policies, has been instrumental in many community improvements.

The introduction of high-technology firms into Troy and nearby North Greenbush has been supported and encouraged in the paper's editorial columns, as has the development of the Center for Industrial Innovation and the Urban Cultural Park—the first of several in New York State.

The Times Record's support was one of the factors that brought the popular Grafton Lakes State Park into being. And the newspaper stepped in to "bridge the gap" between Troy and Green Island, fighting for construction of a replacement when the old bridge collapsed into the Hudson River.

In a period when afternoon newspapers are struggling to survive, *The Times Record* maintains its place as the largest such publication in northeastern New York.

Although Harry S. Ludlow is considered the founder of the *Record,* J.K.P. Pine was the company's first president. The paper's first editor was Francis Joslin, and its original payroll listed twenty-seven employees, including the carrier

boys. Because all the early earnings were used for expansion, it was twenty years before stockholders received any dividends.

The Evening Record joined its morning sibling in 1899, and in April 1909 the headquarters of the two newspapers moved from an overflowing plant on River Street to the part of its present building at the corner of Fifth Avenue and Broadway. Private homes, a church, and a tavern all gave way as the company expanded.

The pattern of expansion and growth continued with the purchase of *The Troy Times* in 1935. The latest evidence of that growth is the $8.5-million expansion recently announced. This expression of confidence in the area will include erection of a three-story addition to accommodate a new, high-speed Goss offset color press. With the

Home of The Times Record *and* The Sunday Record.

new equipment the *Record* will acquire the capability of expanding into commercial printing.

The Times Record remained locally owned from its beginning until October 1972, when it became a part of the Ohio-based Horvitz newspaper group. The morning paper was discontinued in 1973, and *The Sunday Record* became a reality in 1974.

The old Linotypes have been superceded by computerized typesetting, the makeup has changed with the times, and the staff now numbers many times twenty-seven, but the dedication of the founders to the community is still a prime motivating factor at *The Times Record.*

163

TROY SAVINGS BANK

The third-oldest savings bank in New York State, and the fifth such institution in the state to offer life insurance, Troy Savings Bank has served the city for more than 160 years.

In the spring of 1823 eleven prominent Troy businessmen, including innkeeper Platt Titus, met at the latter's establishment on First Street and drew up a petition to the state legislature asking leave to establish a mutual savings bank "for the purpose of receiving on deposit such sums of money as might be offered by tradesmen, mechanics, laborers, minors (under legal age), servants, and others," and investing that money to the advantage of its depositors.

The legislature passed the act of incorporation on April 23, and named nine of the eleven incorporators and ten other prominent residents as managers (trustees) for the new venture. These appointed directors were permitted at that time to make arrangements with either of Troy's two commercial banks, the Farmers' Bank or the Bank of Troy, to receive deposits from the new organization. The institution opened for business the last Saturday evening of August 1823; deposits were put into Farmers' Bank every Monday.

After six years of meeting at Platt Titus' Troy House, the managers hired an attorney, Jacob L. Lane, to receive the deposits and moved their meetings to his office.

Several of the original and many of the later managers were also associated with other banks in the

Innkeeper Platt Titus, whose hostelry was on First Street near the junction with River Street, was one of the nineteen founders of Troy Savings Bank. The board of managers signed the papers of incorporation at his inn in April 1823.

growing city. All were prominent in business and civic circles, and most remained board members of the savings bank until poor health or death occasioned their removal.

The bank grew, weathered the financial problems of 1837, became a landlord, and invested in City of Troy bonds. In 1844 land was purchased on First Street, just south of Troy House, as the site on which to construct a new building.

By the early 1870s the institution's growth necessitated more space;

consequently, a larger structure was erected at the corner of Second and State streets. George B. Post was chosen as architect. The managers held their April 1875 board meeting in the new building, and an inaugural concert was presented on April 19, 1875, in the soon-to-be-famous Music Hall above the bank.

The organization—having survived the vicissitudes of the late nineteenth century and the 1930s—underwent further remodeling of its physical plant in 1950, and is consistently updating its services for customers. Branches have been opened in East Greenbush, Whitehall, Clifton Park, Glens Falls, South Troy, and Watervliet.

Troy Savings Bank has grown from its grassroots beginning to ride the cutting edge of new technology. Its story is one in which the more things change the more they remain the same, because, in contrast to the bank's tremendous growth of over 160 years, the grassroots tradition remains intact. It is a bank that helps the people and communities it serves. Today Troy Savings Bank is headed by Herbert J. Fadeley, Jr., chairman of the board and chief executive officer, and J. Barker Houle, president. Its list of trustees reads like a list of "who's who" in the Capital District business community.

Prior to its 1950 remodeling, Troy Savings Bank utilized only the south side of the main level for its own business. The rest of the space was rented out to other businesses and organizations.

GENERAL ELECTRIC
Silicone Products Division

Silicones are chemical combinations of organic and inorganic substances that provide most of the advantages of both with few of the limitations of either, thus adding greatly to the quality of life today.

Although often used incorrectly, the term "silicone" actually refers to polymers and copolymers based on silicon-oxygen chains. The specific molecular structure of each silicone determines its form—which may be a fluid, a rubber, or a hard resin. Because they remain stable in heat up to 400 degrees and cold of minus 100 degrees, their uses are legion.

General Electric research chemists at the Schenectady Research Laboratory began experimenting with silicone development in the 1930s; however, it was not until Dr. Eugene G. Rochow invented what is known as the "direct process" of manufacturing these useful compounds that they became commercially practical.

Under the guidance of Dr. A.L. Marshall, company scientists were working in the field of methyl and methyl-phenal silicone polymers—

which were destined for an important role in the industry.

Other such General Electric pioneers include Dr. W.F. Gilliam, who worked closely with Rochow; Dr. Winton I. Patnode, whose work earned the first basic patents in silicone fluids; M.C. Agens, who obtained the first basic patent for silicone rubber; and J.G.E. Wright, developer of bouncing putty—which served to bring silicones to worldwide notice.

The scientists' work proceeded rapidly, but not so rapidly that it outran the onset of World War II. Before the man on the street could buy silicones in every second or third purchase (as he might today), tight security was laid down on all industrial laboratories.

The first silicones for the war effort were produced in the General Electric Research Laboratory in Schenectady, and in 1942 the first silicone materials were made there for commercial use in another of the firm's plants.

The corporation began construction on its Silicone Products Division at Waterford in 1945,

General Electric's Silicone Products facility occupies a large tract—once fertile farmland—along routes 4 and 32, north of Waterford in Saratoga County.

opening the facility two years later. Since 1947 GE has invested heavily in the Waterford plant and its other facilities for the silicone industry.

Under its industrial silicone products the company lists a variety of sealants; resin adhesive for materials that do not bond readily; a sealant-adhesive for gasketing; a selection of compounds, gels, and varnishes for insulating and protecting; a variety of products for fabricating and reproducing parts used in automotive, aerospace, and health-care technologies; and a group of greases, resins, and fluids for the purpose of lubricating and protecting. There is a smaller category of products used in construction work, as well as consumer lines of household and automotive silicones.

The cosmetic industry also makes good use of silicones—in such products as hair conditioners, antiperspirants, and eye makeup.

DESEVE ECONOMICS ASSOCIATES, INC.

DeSeve Economics Associates, Inc., is a firm of professional economists and policy-design specialists serving clients in government, business, and the legal profession. Collar City native Charles deSeve established the company in Troy in 1976. In 1983 another office opened in Washington, D.C.

Based on a pledge to deliver individualized services to each client, deSeve Economics is more than a source of economic and computer analysis. Innovative opportunities and creative alternatives to assist decision makers are the first priority of project managers and staff.

Customer services are available to research and policy development studies, including tax and revenue analysis, debt-structure studies, computer-model development and simulation, corporate-planning assistance, economic-impact analysis, development-venture specialists, and litigation economics.

The firm maintains a network of micro- and mini-computers with computer graphics and mass storage capabilities to meet the specialized requirements of clients.

Wherever economic issues, trends, or analyses are discussed—in Congress, state legislatures, municipal government, the boardroom, or the courtroom—deSeve Economics has developed the technical expertise and credibility to communicate in a clear voice the answers to questions asked by decision makers in today's complex and challenging economic environment.

Its commitment to excellence and its staff resources uniquely qualify deSeve Economics Associates to assume a role of leadership in economic analysis and partnership with today's decision makers.

A commitment to enhancing Troy's historic architecture and to the economic viability of downtown

has led to an active role of deSeve Economics' president Charles deSeve in major downtown development ventures. In 1983 the McCarthy Building was renovated with attention to historic detail, and its prime river-front location was highlighted. The structure had been built in 1904 to replace a former McCarthy Building, which burned to the ground. It was erected in nine months, and was equipped with one of the first sprinkler systems in the country. By the fall of 1984 the Keenan Building, constructed in the early 1880s, showed another successful combination of the convenience of modern commercial space with a historic building's space and beauty.

The Keenan Building, long a landmark in downtown Troy, has been remodeled and restored to its original character. This is the second of the deSeve restoration projects to be completed.

Additional projects involving the mid-nineteenth-century Market Block Complex and others serve to further demonstrate the successful interplay of economic feasibility and pride in the city's historic architecture.

Downtown Troy's Market Block complex, one of the deSeve development projects on the drawing board, will look like this when restoration is complete. The buildings are at the junction of Third and River streets.

LEVONIAN BROTHERS, INC.

The firm of Levonian Brothers, Inc., has—in the words of the managing directors—"not just coped with change," but has "created change" since its founding in 1947.

Started in a modest frame building on River Street in Troy with four employees, the operation now occupies nearly 60,000 square feet of space—still on River Street—and employs seventy-five people.

The original directors, brothers Elia Y. and Levon Y. Levonian, and their nephews, Elia M. and Levon M. Levonian, are no longer active, but the company is still family owned. Two other nephews, Gregory L. Nazarian and Ralph Darian, literally grew up in the business; they worked for their uncles during college vacations, became managing directors in 1957, then corporate officers in the 1970s. Nazarian is president, and Darian serves as corporate secretary and director of sales.

At first the enterprise was engaged only in meat distribution, serving principally the small independent markets of the area. During the 1950s and 1960s the independent outlets were gradually disappearing and the stores were becoming larger, prompting the organization's entry into the manufacturing end of the meat business in the early 1970s. Since a change was called for, the directors decided to establish an identity with their own products.

Uncooked corned beef, still one of the firm's best-known and most prestigious products, was the first item produced. Gradually the line was expanded to include cooked corned beef, roast beef, and pastrami, then ham and bologna. The additions of several smokehouses to the plant subsequently enabled Levonian Brothers to incorporate hams and smoked pork

The first home of Levonian Brothers, Inc., was this frame building on Troy's River Street, at the same location as the present plant. This 1947 photo shows one of the founders, the late Levon Y. Levonian (center), with two unidentified friends.

loins in its production.

While the business enlarged its original quarters in 1961, ten years later a million-dollar expansion program was begun. Completed in January 1973, the new building was designed by Henry A. Lurie and Associates, Design Engineers, of Cincinnati, Ohio, and built by Waldbillig Construction Company of Albany.

In 1982 the neighboring structure (erected originally by a chicken-processing concern) was purchased and converted into the company's distribution center, leaving the

newer building for the offices and manufacturing operation.

Levonian Brothers, Inc., has always tried to provide the best in both quality and service to its customers. The firm is equally considerate of the people it employs, those who have helped bring the success it has today. Since 1959 the employees have been unionized, and relations between union and management have always been very amicable. A company newsletter highlights special achievements—such as enthusiastic support of projects like the United Way—and explains corporate policies.

A fleet of refrigerated trucks and tractor trailers takes Levonian products regularly to New York, New England, New Jersey, and Pennsylvania.

In 1973 Levonian Brothers occupied this new facility, which houses the offices and manufacturing operations since the acquisition of the neighboring structure in 1982 for a distribution center.

D.A. FAZIOLI & SON, INC.

Donald A. Fazioli, president of D.A. Fazioli & Son, Inc., takes pride in the fact that he and his son and daughter still do business with the children and grandchildren of his father's early customers—including the first patron, acquired in 1929.

Dominick A. Fazioli, founder of the firm, was born in 1879 in Italy, and came to the United States as a boy of eight. He moved to Troy in 1895, and worked for a while for the Malleable Iron Works in Watervliet. In 1901 Fazioli opened a confectionary store on Union Street, and in 1929 he established the company that still bears his name.

The venture at that time dealt mainly with real estate, selling insurance only as a sideline. When Donald Fazioli joined the firm in 1947—after military service during World War II and then graduation from college—he took over the insurance end of the business, leaving the real estate operation to his father.

With the senior Fazioli's death, the company turned entirely to insurance. Donald's son, David A. Fazioli, worked in New York City after graduation from Manhattan College, then joined the family firm in 1975. He is a Chartered Property Casualty Underwriter (CPCU).

In 1980 Donald's daughter, Rita Fazioli Testo, a graduate of State University College at Cortland, joined the organization.

The agency has recently expanded by purchasing two other local agencies. The George H. Karl Agency in Averill Park, New York, was purchased in 1976, and the William H. Smith and William D. O'Connell agencies were purchased in 1984. All entities now operate under the Fazioli name.

The Faziolis operate their Troy agencies from a brownstone building, which was constructed after the tragic fire of 1862, on Troy's Fifth Avenue. The facility was renovated in the 1920s by a dealer in Oriental rugs; included in the renovation was a galvanized iron front—in the form of an Oriental prayer rug. Donald Fazioli purchased the building in 1980, and has decorated the office with reproductions of fire marks and fire apparatus. The Averill Park branch operates from a building that was converted from a Ford tractor dealership.

Dominick A. Fazioli, who immigrated to the United States from Italy as a child, founded the Troy firm of D.A. Fazioli & Son in 1929.

The family concern has been represented in state and national organizations. Dominick was president of the Troy Insurance Agents' Association, and both his son and grandson have since held that office.

In 1969 Donald Fazioli was president of the New York State Association of Insurance Agents, and from 1971 to 1974 served as a director of the national association. Since 1971 he has been on the board of directors of the New York Property Insurance Underwriters' Association, an organization that writes fire insurance for those who cannot obtain it through regular channels. He is one of three public members of this board, having been reappointed each time his term has expired.

Donald Fazioli has also served on many civic committees, and both he and David have been members of agents' advisory boards for the firms they serve. They have represented most of their clients for more than thirty years.

Donald A. Fazioli (left), with daughter Rita Fazioli Testo and son David A. Fazioli, who assist him in the operation of the family firm in Troy and Averill Park.

RUSSELL SAGE COLLEGE

The Troy campus of Russell Sage College, on First and Second streets, is only a short distance from the city's vital downtown business area.

"A new institution which should be of assistance to all women who support themselves. . . ." A phrase, perhaps, from a women's organization of the 1970s? No, the words belong to Margaret Olivia Slocum Sage, the founder of Russell Sage College, and they were first used almost seventy years ago to describe the goal of the new school.

Another phrase is also apropos here—"ahead of one's time"—for it applies perfectly to Mrs. Sage. After the death of her financier-husband in 1902, she became the premier female philanthropist in the United States, establishing the Russell Sage Foundation to improve the country's social and living conditions. In its early years the foundation accomplished a great deal in the area of public health: rebuilding hospitals; adding nurse training to college curricula; initiating projects to fight tuberculosis, infant mortality, and blindness; and expanding medical school programs.

In the course of her work, Mrs. Sage also rebuilt the Emma Willard School, the oldest American preparatory school for women and Mrs. Sage's alma mater. Yet it was not until she was eighty-eight years old that Mrs. Sage made her greatest contribution to education. With Eliza Kellas, Emma Willard's principal, she created a curriculum that offered female students a new concept in American education—

preparation for important careers. The idea was to serve as the guiding philosophy for Russell Sage College, which first opened its doors in 1916.

The college grew steadily during its first four years, and by the time of its first graduation in 1920 the school's academic program was solidly established. Seven years later the New York Board of Regents granted a new and separate charter for the college.

Over the past half-century enrollments have climbed, and two coeducational Albany divisions have been established—the Sage Evening Division (1949) and the Junior College of Albany (1957).

Today Russell Sage offers the most complete and diversified private educational opportunity in the tri-city area, providing associate, bachelor's, and master's degree programs in a variety of majors in the liberal arts, more than fifteen professional programs, and interdisciplinary majors.

The Troy campus, on First and Second streets, is only a short distance from the city's vital downtown business area, and the college is proud of its urban setting, which allows students to be true

community participants. The college's early policy of preserving its historic buildings and erecting new structures only when absolutely needed has continued faithfully to the present day. One important new project has been the $3-million Robinson Athletic Center, constructed to meet the pressing physical needs of both the school and the community.

The college has prepared more than 15,000 alumni for positions of distinction in business and industry, the professions, government, and the arts. Now in its seventh decade, Russell Sage, under the direction of president William F. Kahl, has fulfilled the promise of its founder to prepare women for careers in the professional and business worlds. And with its active role in Troy's metropolitan community, embodying the concept that preparation for life is a college's prime concern, Russell Sage appears once again to be ahead of its time.

PIONEER SAVINGS BANK

Like many other important institutions in the Hudson-Mohawk Gateway area, Pioneer Savings Bank developed from modest beginnings. Now approaching its centennial, the bank was founded as a building-loan association in March 1889.

Troy at that time had no bank where a resident could make small deposits, so it was difficult for the average wage earner to acquire enough money to build or buy a home of his own. The printers at the *Troy Daily Press* were thus prompted to seek the advice of their publisher, Henry O'Reilly Tucker, in the matter of starting a suitable cooperative.

Impressed by their ambition and sincerity, Tucker "with rare liberality and as an expression of good will to his workmen, engaged at his own expense the services of a lecturer and organizer, who labored here for some time perfecting the preliminaries." What was probably just as helpful to the savings association was the fact that Tucker "opened the columns of his paper to the movement," gaining support of large and small investors in Troy and surrounding communities.

In its initial articles, the association's purpose was clearly stated: "making loans to stockholders whereby they may be enabled to purchase real estate, to build or provide dwelling houses, to remove encumbrances there from and to accumulate a fund to be returned to the members who do not obtain advances." The organization prospered and was able to survive a financial panic in 1893-1894.

Until 1964 the directors met every Tuesday; they now meet monthly, but still on that weekday. Tuesday played another important part in the bank's early days. It was the only day of the week when the thrifty members made their deposits

of a minimum twenty-five cents. In 1914 money was received on Monday evenings as well, and in 1916 the institution opened daily for transactions.

Originally quartered in a structure on River Street near what is now Riverfront Park, the association—after twenty-seven years and three moves—purchased its first building at 30 Second Street. In May 1950 it moved to its present facility at 21 Second Street.

On July 1, 1972, the Pioneer Building-Loan and Savings Association became Pioneer Savings Bank under the leadership of Allen L. Gillett, who has since been succeeded by Edward H. Nash as president.

The first branch office, in nearby Latham, was opened in June 1958 in temporary quarters; it moved to permanent space six months later. The Watervliet office was established in 1972, when the savings association became a savings bank, and a fourth office was subsequently opened in Rotterdam.

It has been a source of satisfaction to trustees, officers, and staff that Pioneer Savings Bank, through many years and many changes, remains in the forefront of mortgage-issuing institutions in the area—true to the aims of its founders.

The main office of Pioneer Savings Bank is at 21 Second Street in Troy. Pioneer Building-Loan and Savings Association, as the bank was then known, purchased the building in 1950.

ALLIED AUTOMOTIVE BENDIX FRICTION MATERIALS DIVISION

The Allied Automotive Bendix Friction Materials Division traces its growth from the Asbestos Spinning and Weaving Corporation—a company formed in Waterford, New York, in the early 1900s that used water-powered looms to manufacture conventional woven and stitched brake linings.

One of the principals, Edward Slade, invented an asbestos paper-backed brake lining, and in 1924 founded the Slade Products Corporation in Watervliet to manufacture the product. Four years later the firm moved to Green Island and became Slade Asbestos. Vincent Bendix, a large stockholder, was instrumental in the election of Furber Marshall as president in 1929, when the name changed to Marshall Asbestos. The company became a wholly owned subsidiary of the Bendix Corporation in 1933, and part of Allied in 1983.

Under the direction of William C. King, group vice-president, NA/LA Friction Materials, the group and division are headquartered in Latham, and have research, engineering, and manufacturing

facilities in Green Island that currently employ 700 people; an additional 500 persons work at a second plant in Cleveland, Tennessee.

After experiments with rubber and pulverized coal-based linings, Bendix engineers had developed full-molded linings by 1939. Through manufacturing its own synthetic resins, the firm could accurately control the characteristics of its products, making possible major advances in technology and quality control. Ongoing research and development programs at Friction Materials Division laboratories allowed the company to enter the industrial resins field in 1953, producing specialized resins and adhesives used in a wide range of applications.

In 1971 the division introduced a new type of semimetallic brake pads for passenger cars and trucks that is now standard equipment on over 50 percent of all cars and light trucks made by American manufacturers, and is ideally suited for heavy-duty vehicles such as buses, fire trucks, and concrete haulers. Another

innovation, Cerametalix®, is made from a combination of powdered metals and ceramics, and was originally developed for military aircraft brakes. Designed for machinery that demands high heat dissipation and long life, this material is also used in commercial aircraft brakes, heavy-duty clutches in over-the-road trucks, earth movers, tractors, and stationary hoists.

Friction Materials Division is today one of the world's leading manufacturers of automotive and aircraft brake linings, blocks, and pads.

Research and product innovations have brought Allied Automotive Bendix Friction Materials Division from the looms that wove brake linings early in this century to today's high-technology manufacturing methods, and will enable it to offer high-performance materials for the future.

Research, engineering, and manufacturing facilities are located at the Friction Materials Divison plant in the village of Green Island.

GARDEN WAY, INC.

The history of rotary tillers for home gardening and agriculture in America has been written in large measure at the Garden Way plant in Troy.

In the continuing search for better ways to prepare soil for planting, today's rotary tillers have evolved from horse-drawn machines made in Europe in the mid-nineteenth century. Weighing several tons and powered by steam engines, these contraptions cultivated the earth with a steampowered iron cylinder armed with curved iron spikes. Great improvements were made in 1910 when a Swiss inventor, Konrad von Meyenburg, patented a design with small, flexibly mounted cutting tools revolving behind two self-powered wheels that an operator could guide on foot.

These gasoline-powered tillers were imported to America beginning in 1930 by the Rototiller Company, founded by an American automotive pioneer named Cadwallader

Washburn Kelsey. Offered financial backing by George B. Cluett of Troy, Kelsey in 1937 moved the fledgling industry to the former Draper Cordage factory at 102nd Street and Ninth Avenue in the Lansingburgh section of the city.

The business continued to sell rear-tined tillers until Kelsey retired in 1957, after which it was sold and relocated. Chief engineer George Done and two partners purchased the spare-parts business, and reopened the factory in 1961. Using his twenty-six years of experience making tillers in Troy, Done brought out an improved, economical model, the "Trojan Horse," in 1962.

To augment sales through dealerships, the company began to develop a mail-order marketing approach to reach serious gardeners. Advertisements in magazines, newspapers, and seed catalogs drew inquiries from gardeners across the United States, and Garden Way has become

Garden Way, Inc., employs approximately 1,000 people in its Troy facilities.

one of the premier direct-mail marketing organizations as a result.

The tiller was renamed the Troy-Bilt® Roto Tiller, and the firm became Garden Way Manufacturing Company. It grew from producing fewer than 7,000 tillers in 1970 to almost 97,000 a decade later. Dean Leith, Jr., the first full-time sales and advertising manager, today serves as chairman of the board.

Garden Way tillers are high-quality products made by a skilled work force using advanced technologies, in historic traditions of craftsmanship. Customer service is an ongoing priority, including generous product guarantees, regular mailings on gardening, and the *Troy-Bilt Owner News.*

In addition to its manufacturing facility, Troy is also the site of the corporate headquarters and all marketing activities.

GRIMM ENTERPRISES

Max Grimm began to merchandise coal in and around Troy in 1884 to displace wood as the primary home heat source. Delivery was by horse-drawn wagons and the coal was carried up to second- and third-floor flats. Later, to fill in the slower summer months, he broadened the line with construction and builders' supplies. The business prospered.

By 1929 Carl Grimm had been apprenticed long enough to take over. That was the start of difficult times. By 1942, with the postwar construction boom on the horizon, an arrangement was made with General Building Supply Co. of New York City, a firm managed by James Farley of the Roosevelt Cabinet, for Grimm to represent General Building Supply Co. in the upstate area.

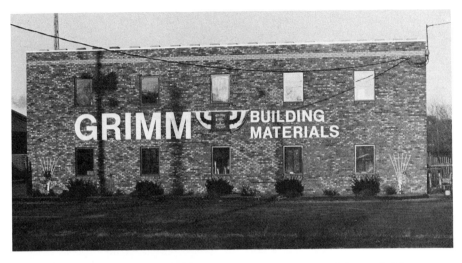

To ride the crest of the building wave, in 1946 the company expanded into construction, erecting the YMCA facility at Tahawas for the National Lead Co. This led to construction projects for General Motors, Gar Wood, Standard Brands, Caterpillar Tractor, and other national concerns, including the growing Rototiller Company, which was to become Garden Way.

In 1960 the Grimms took over the operation of Marvin-Neitzel Corp.,

The headquarters of Grimm Building Materials, Green Island, is in this new building near Troy Green Island Bridge. Carl Grimm is the second generation of the family to run the business. Peter and David Grimm comprise the third generation, with Todd, Charles, and Matthew coming along as members of the fourth.

It is always summer in the Uncle Sam Atrium, built by Grimm Enterprises. This is the view of the second level on the Fourth Street side. Stores surround the garden spot on both levels.

maker of uniforms, which had fallen into hard times. This proved to be a successful operation and now employs an expert staff of textile workers and ships garments to most states from its Troy factory.

About the same time Rototiller was reorganizing and the Grimms were interested in helping the company get into high gear. That became the Garden Way of today and one of Troy's active industries. Garden Way ships to all fifty states and many foreign countries from its Troy factory.

By 1977 the City of Troy was searching for a developer for the downtown area. The Grimm firm accepted the challenge and built the Uncle Sam Atrium as the focal point of a new downtown area.

Carl Grimm has been assisted in these endeavors by his two sons, Peter and David, and many others. The fourth generation of the family is apprenticing and will soon take over the business.

173

RENSSELAER POLYTECHNIC INSTITUTE

In its commitment to first-quality education concentrating on science and technology, Rensselaer Polytechnic Institute (RPI) has grown from the Rensselaer School that pioneered engineering education to an internationally renowned technological university.

Founded in 1824 by Stephen Van Rensselaer "for the purpose of instructing persons, who may choose to apply themselves, in the application of science to the common purposes of life," the school developed during the massive transformations of America's Industrial Revolution. Informed scientists were needed to teach the public about science, and imaginative civil engineers were needed to construct the Erie Canal, bridges, railroads, factories, cities, and other industrial works. Van Rensselaer's mission statement is still relevant, after 160 years of RPI's development, and is incorporated in the *Rensselaer 2000* plan for the twenty-first century.

Through the schools of Science, Engineering, Humanities and Social Sciences, Architecture, and Management, the Institute now offers more than 110 degree programs that enroll 6,500 highly talented students from sixty countries; a distinguished faculty teaches and conducts research now totaling approximately fifteen million dollars annually. RPI graduates are highly recruited by industry, and have made outstanding contributions in many fields of human endeavor.

As inventive scientists, engineers, authors, artists and technocrats, industrialists, entrepreneurs and managers, bishops and revolutionaries, Rensselaer graduates have contributed to building civilization from the nineteenth century to the present. Their accomplishments

The Ricketts Building on the campus at Rensselaer Polytechnic Institute.

range from design of the Ferris wheel, the Brooklyn Bridge, Japan's system of railroads, and the Panama Canal to the Verrazano-Narrows Bridge, the microprocessor, and the NASA space program's Apollo flights to the moon.

To implement the university's goal of expanding graduate programs and research, New York State and RPI are jointly constructing on the campus a $60-million George M. Low Center for Industrial Innovation that will include three rapidly growing research components: the Center for Manufacturing Productivity and Technology Transfer, which investigates robotics, new fiber-based composite materials, and other manufacturing-related topics; the Center for Interactive Computer Graphics, which uses state-of-the-art computer graphics equipment for a wide range of products; and the Center for Integrated Electronics, specializing in large-scale integration of circuits for computer chips.

Rensselaer 2000 pays special attention to RPI's multifaceted relationship with Troy and Capital District communities: economic contributions, activities in culture, the arts, sports and entertainment, joint programs with local schools, and many other involvements enhancing the quality of life in the Hudson-Mohawk area.

In addition, the institution is committed to attracting research and high-technology industries to the area—encouraging interaction among students, faculty members, and people from industry. Through its Incubator Program to foster growth of new high-technology companies, and through developing the Rensselaer Technology Park—an industrial park on 1,200 acres of university land in nearby North Greenbush—RPI is forging new links with industry. The utilization of its strength in critical technologies to restore America's once-peerless productivity and to maintain its academic excellence is the vision that inspires the direction that Rensselaer Polytechnic Institute has set for itself for the future.

LEAHY FUNERAL HOME

When Patrick Leahy started his livery business in South Troy in 1853, he probably had no thought of founding a tradition. But today his great-grandson still operates the business he began.

The Leahy Brothers Livery occupied the building at Third and Madison streets and supplied horses and vehicles for all occasions. Important among these were horse-drawn hearses and carriages for funerals—so important, in fact, that the Leahy livery even kept small white horses for children's funerals.

All of Patrick Leahy's twelve children took part in the business at some time. Dennis, Patrick, and Joseph, who succeeded their father, each had a special team of horses, which he alone drove. At first the horses were kept at the original building, part of which Patrick Leahy constructed, but they were later moved.

An unusual feature of that facility was the man-powered elevator used to lift carriages not in use to an upper storage level. William P. Leahy, remembers, as a small boy, seeing his father and uncles haul the elevator ropes.

It was in 1913 that the three Leahy brothers decided to change their rental vehicles to automotive power. They supplied the entourage for the first automotive funeral cortege in Troy, which went from St. Joseph's Church in the city's flat riverside area to St. Joseph's Cemetery in the hilly part of Troy. Much to the surprise of funeral goers, the vehicles made the hills without trouble.

This 1925 Meteor wood-body hearse was one of the area's first modern casket coaches. Ornate in design, it included hand carvings, brass accents, velvet drapes, and running lamps.

In 1929 William P. Leahy, Joseph's son, entered the business as a licensed funeral director. The business was then located on Fourth Street between Canal and Madison, about a block from its original location. In 1945 he purchased the home of Mayor Joseph Hogan, the site of the present funeral home, at 336 Third Street, between Canal and Madison. He notes that he was born within a block of the present location.

In the early 1950s, Leahy acquired the livery business from his father and uncle. In 1958 he was joined by his son, William C., also a funeral director. Shortly thereafter, the Leahys bought the Third Street Methodist Church, adjacent to their property, and built an addition and a parking area.

The elder Leahy is now retired, and both the livery and funeral businesses are operated by his son. The firm was incorporated in 1983.

The Leahys have buried mayors of Troy and presidents of colleges, and often supply vehicles for other area funeral directors. They have rented limousines to Presidents and movie stars, as well as to less illustrious clients. Theirs is one of the oldest funeral businesses in the tri-city area.

Within the past few years the Leahys have been approached by the major funeral homes in the Philippines and Belgium to be their representative here in America.

Both William P. and William C. Leahy have been very active in Troy's community affairs, and both have held memberships in local professional societies.

Today's funeral service needs are met by this 1984 Buick hearse. Traditionally ornate with drapes, lights, and chrome accents, it is one of the Hudson-Mohawk area's most modern casket coaches.

UNION NATIONAL BANK

Union National Bank, Troy's oldest commercial bank, had its beginnings on December 18, 1850, at a "meeting of persons favorable to forming a banking association," and received its name—Union Bank of Troy—a week later. Its first articles of association were written and adopted on New Year's Eve, and by January 15, 1851, its directors had chosen a building to house the new endeavor.

Continuing in the pattern of rapid action set by the directors, the Canal Commission designated the bank—even before its official opening—as one of the depositories of the Erie Canal tolls to be collected at West Troy (Watervliet).

Because the banking organization was in readiness before the building at 14 First Street—the bank's first real home—the directors opened for business on April 11, 1851, in a wholesale grocery store, at 349 River Street.

Eleven days later the new banking house opened its doors. The institution's capital at its opening was $30,000. One hundred years and two moves later, it had assets of more than sixteen million dollars.

Its original directors were Joel Mallary, John Kerr, William F. Sage, Thomas N. Lockwood, P.T. Heartt, Hiram B. Ingalls, L.A. Battershall, Jonathan W. Freeman, Lyman Bennett, Richardson H. Thurman, and David B. Cox.

At the outbreak of the Civil War, the directors voted to provide the bank's share of loan money to New York State to "equip and send to the field the volunteers authorized to be raised by the last legislature" and to take its share of the treasury notes assigned to Troy banks.

In April 1865 Union National became one of the first national banks in the country, electing officers under its new certificate of authority. Its name then became Union National Bank of Troy.

The institution moved from its First Street location in April 1888 to Fourth Street, occupying "one of the finest banking structures in upstate New York," according to a contemporary account.

In 1935 the bank announced plans for the construction of a new facility at 50 Fourth Street, which it still occupies today. The building opened in 1936, providing the most up-to-date banking facilities of its day.

When the bank observed its centennial in 1951, no big celebration was held, but a series of institutional advertisements in area newspapers provided a look at the bank's history and a forecast of its future. One of these read, in part, the "pioneer spirit still burns bright. We have no desire to make nebulous pledges of service. We prefer not to interrupt the routine of daily business with a centennial celebration."

The bank has taken pride in operating its credit policy for the benefit of the community as a whole, rather than for an elite group. It was a pioneer in the field of low-cost automobile and personal loans, and entered the first mortgage field long before FHA loans were originated. Union National also took an early lead in offering automated banking services for its consumer and business customers.

In the past thirty-three years the bank has expanded, and in 1972 its main office was moved from Troy to Albany, causing the name to be changed once more.

Today, in addition to the Albany and Troy offices, there are Union National Bank branches in Latham, Schaghticoke, Sycaway, Wynantskill, North Greenbush, Guilderland, and Westgate.

Still at its original location at 50 Fourth Street, the bank was remodeled in 1978, providing for more space and the addition of plants and artwork, giving the surroundings a more gracious look.

Congratulatory baskets of flowers line the walls at the opening of the new Union National Bank of Troy in 1936.

MANNING PAPER COMPANY

The history of Manning Paper Company began at the Mt. Ida Mill, at the Poestenkill Gorge in Troy, following the completion of Benjamin Marshall's hydraulic-power tunnel. William H. Manning, Gardiner Howland, and Calvin Williams leased a mill site with access to waterpower from the Marshall flume in 1846, and constructed a mill to produce Manila paper made from recycled hemp rope. Flour sacks, envelopes, and other hardware papers were among the first products.

In 1850 Williams sold his interest in the growing enterprise to William H. Manning and Reuben Peckham. Known as Manning, Peckham and Howland, and later Manning and Peckham, the business continued under several successive generations of men with those surnames. John A. Manning, who joined the firm after his father's death in 1855, expanded Troy's rope Manila paper business to one of the largest in the world. He founded Olympus Mill at 681 River Street in 1866, powered by water from the State dam, and a third in 1883 called Crystal Palace.

John A. Manning, Jr., who became president of the concern upon the death of his father in 1900, organized the John A. Manning Paper Company, Inc., to centralize the management and operation of the three properties.

Due to the lack of certainty about the future supply of power from the Federal Dam on the Hudson River, Manning moved the River Street Mills over to Green Island in 1915, on the site of the old Eaton & Gilbert Car Works at Clinton and George streets, its present location.

In 1912, before the move to Green Island, the Manning Sandpaper Company was formed. In 1918 the Sandpaper Company changed its name to Manning Abrasive

John A. Manning

This 1880 letterhead engraving shows the Mt. Ida Mill of the Manning and Peckham Paper Co. Courtesy, John M. Peckham

Company and moved to Watervliet. (In 1928 this venture became the Behr-Manning Corporation, presently a division of Norton Company.) The original Mount Ida Mill continued in operation until 1962.

The organization has continued its growth in Green Island as a renowned manufacturer of high-quality technical papers designed to meet specialized needs of numerous and diverse industrial users around the world. Cellulose-based papers made from virgin abaca hemp from the Philippines and Ecuador are still important high-strength, lightweight materials.

In 1970 the Hammermill Paper Company, with headquarters in Erie, Pennsylvania, acquired the Manning Paper Company. Hammermill is an acknowledged leader in the paper industry and has done much to improve the overall physical plant at Green Island.

The Manning Paper Company continues to use its experience and tradition of excellence to meet the fiber-products needs of the future. The firm presently employs approximately 150 hourly and 60 salaried people. New equipment and new processes are constantly being utilized to maintain its place as a leader in its field.

Manning Paper Company today.

GARRY KEARNS ARCHITECT, P.C.

The Troy firm of Garry Kearns Architect, P.C., is a young business in an old city, but one that has made its mark in the area.

Kearns, a native of Canada and a graduate of Rensselaer Polytechnic Institute, heads the firm; Troy native E. Stephen Finkle, also an RPI graduate, serves as vice-president.

One of the feathers in Kearns' cap is the design for the Olympic Broadcast Center that housed the telecasting of the 1980 Olympic Games at Lake Placid, New York. At the time of its completion the building was the most modern of its kind anywhere in the world. It was designed so that it could be converted into a municipal center after the games. A further connection with the events was Kearns' appointment in 1984 to the Olympic

Regional Development Authority.

The attractive Troy office of Home Savings Bank of upstate New York, another product of the firm's drawing boards, won a local beautification award, as did the conversion of an old brick firehouse (Hope 7) into a neighborhood community center. The Hope 7 project was also written up in *Urban Design* magazine.

The city's Grand Street Rehabilitation Project, reconstruction of the Hotel Troy into an apartment building, and the Conway Court housing center for senior citizens were other local Kearns designs.

Garry Kearns was the architect for the interior renovation of the Troy Publishing Company building, and also drafted the plans for the firm's multimillion-dollar addition for a new press—slated for occupancy in the fall of 1985. He additionally designed the Fitzgibbons Health Technologies Center at Hudson Valley Community College; the interior renovations to the Lansingburgh Fire Station; the Frear Park Ice Skating Facility; and the design of the Robison Swimming Pool for his alma mater.

In nearby Watervliet Kearns planned manufacturing modifications silos for Tek Hughes, and did an adaptive reuse analysis on several buildings for the Watervliet Senior Citizens. He has also done a variety of designs for the City of Mechanicville, including two fire stations, and recently completed design restorations for the Kenmore Hotel in Albany. In addition, he has executed commissions in Wisconsin, Florida, and Massachusetts.

Garry J. Kearns, president.

Before forming his own company, the founder worked for architects in Troy; Pittsfield, Massachusetts; and Milwaukee, Wisconsin. Finkle had extensive experience with Troy and Albany firms.

Kearns' corporate offices are located in a building unique even for a historical city such as Troy. The Farnam Institute at 545 Congress Street (near the legendary Poestenkill Gorge) was constructed in 1872, through the generosity of F.W. Farnam, to serve the Episcopal Church of the Ascension (across the street, and also built by a Farnam gift) as a parish house.

In adapting the building, purchased in 1974, the architecture firm has left the exterior unchanged. Inside, the neo-Gothic style of the structure remains obvious even though the area has been converted into offices and workrooms.

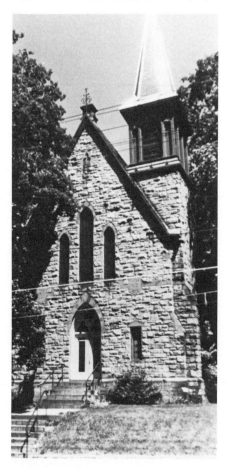

The Farnam Institute, built in 1872 as a parish house for the Episcopal Church of the Ascension, now houses the offices of Garry Kearns Architect, P.C.

FACTRON/SCHLUMBERGER

"When the chips are down, in the electronics industry, Factron shows why." This statement dramatizes the revolution in manufacturing generated by Factron's in-circuit test equipment for printed circuit boards, which has grown from concept to worldwide use since the early 1970s.

Evolving silicon-chip technology has impelled the expansion of Factron/Schlumberger since the firm's origination in 1971. Spinning off from an industrial-research enterprise founded as Faultfinders, Inc., the business has developed around enhancements of its in-circuit analysis precept. This technological breakthrough has been the single most significant factor in reducing the costs of printed circuit boards for numerous consumer and business products, from computers and telephones to video games.

Faultfinders introduced the first in-circuit test system in 1971, an analog device that supplanted time-consuming manual diagnoses of entire printed circuit boards or isolated components. Previously, manufacturers of complex boards experienced a 20 to 30 percent rejection rate, and required 10 to 15 minutes of a skilled technician's time to identify each defect—with about 2.8 per board, on average. Today's in-circuit testers locate all defects within 30 to 45 seconds, allowing producers to make 98 percent of the printed circuit boards usable.

The firm has continued to improve diagnostic instruments, introducing core memory in 1973 and the original short-circuit and continuity tester a year later; digital testing was incorporated in 1975, when the first computer-controlled unit began producing "intelligent repair tickets" for faulty parts. Increasing sophistication has been required to analyze quickly the

Factron's Series 30/333, one of several in-circuit test systems manufactured for major electronics corporations that produce printed circuit boards in large volume.

large-scale and very-large-scale integration designs that the industry now produces. Factron's more recent products include programmable mechanisms and overall test-area management systems; the company is also working in automation, robotics, and electronic-manufacturing controls.

The enormous cost savings resulting from Factron's innovations has induced all the major manufacturers of printed circuit boards to use this technology, including IBM, Digital, Wang, Western Electric, and Texas Instruments, among others throughout the United States, Europe, Japan, and Southeast Asia. In-circuit testing has now become a

$400-million business worldwide.

As a division of the SCHLUMBERGER group of companies, Factron/Schlumberger's work force has increased to over 500 employees. Its facilities have kept pace with the vigorous growth, expanding to a 215,000-square-foot ultramodern main plant on Old Niskayuna Road near Albany Airport. Its participative management style helps employees at all levels "buy in" to the organization through open-communication channels: rap sessions with the general manager, monthly meetings to recognize achievements, "Have Your Say" feedback sessions, and its in-house Factfinder publication.

This well-managed, profitable enterprise has initiated worldwide revolution in industry, and it shares the spirit of optimism that boosted the pioneering entrepreneurs of the Hudson-Mohawk area during the nineteenth century.

LEPERA & WARD, P.C.

In the nineteenth century accomplished architects created magnificent buildings and cities along the Hudson and Mohawk rivers in New York State. More than 100 years later the Troy architectural firm of Lepera & Ward has specialized in preserving the character of these priceless buildings while making them functional for the twentieth and twenty-first centuries.

Trained in architecture and engineering at Rensselaer Polytechnic Institute in Troy, the firm's principals—Vincent J. Lepera and John W. Ward—recognized even as students the potential posed by the area's historic structures. While still at RPI, Lepera formed the Troy Professional Assistance Program (TAP) to provide architectural services to people with homes and businesses in Troy's inner city. TAP is still thriving and is one of the oldest architectural and advocacy planning organizations in the country.

From this early work, Lepera & Ward understood the need to preserve and use the many historic structures that make up America's cities. The firm developed expertise in three areas crucial to the successful redevelopment of these older buildings: the design of new spaces sympathetic to existing details and structures; the cost-conscious construction management of a project; and the necessary experience in the preservation, protection, and reconstruction of exterior and interior building details.

Among the projects illustrating the principals' expertise in masonry work and exterior restoration is the on-site construction supervision provided on some of the area's finest buildings: the magnificent Gothic-style D&H Building in Albany, now the headquarters of the state university; Albany's City Hall, designed by noted architect H.H. Richardson; St. Peter's Episcopal Church in Albany; and "Lindenwald," the home of Martin Van Buren, a national landmark in Kinderhook, New York.

And among Lepera & Ward's largest projects is a group of over twenty buildings that is part of a widely acclaimed redevelopment effort in downtown Troy. The keystone of the multiuse project is the McCarthy Building, a six-story 1904 structure with a spectacular white terra-cotta Beaux Arts facade.

Originally constructed as a furniture showroom and warehouse, the building, which is on the National Register of Historic Places, was converted to house a medical facility, offices, retail space, and a restaurant. It is a widely recognized example of the firm's technical abilities, design skills, cost-conscious management, and sensitivity to a building's surroundings. It features a three-story atrium, ingenious stair tower, and the original, refitted birdcage elevator which now offers a spectacular view of the Hudson River through an award-winning window wall that opens the building's formerly solid brick-back facade to the Hudson River.

Lepera & Ward's other major projects also involved the sympathetic, cost-effective treatment of historic structures: the conversion of the Philip DeFreest house, a rare example of early Dutch architecture (circa 1740), now headquarters for Rensselaer Technology Park; the adaptation of storage buildings into affordable office space for new companies; the development of the Casparus Pruyn house, an 1830 residence, into a cultural center; the renovation of St. Mary's Church in Crescent, New York, reflecting the new liturgy of the Catholic Church; the adaptive reuse of a food-processing plant into a coal-utilization and research laboratory for the General Electric Company; and the renovation of many nineteenth-century residences.

Vincent J. Lepera, co-founder. Photo by Harvey M. Kaplan

John W. Ward, co-founder. Photo by Harvey M. Kaplan

COHOES MEMORIAL HOSPITAL

On Labor Day, September 5, 1898, a trolley car of the Troy City Railway, en route to Cohoes, was struck by the Troy-bound local of the Delaware & Hudson, traveling from Lake George. The locomotive collided into the open trolley's section, pushing it along the track and strewing wreckage and victims in its wake.

An old mill was taken over as an immediate treatment center and morgue, and the soon-to-be-opened Cohoes Memorial Hospital was opened to receive the injured—about twenty-five persons. Fifteen others were killed at the scene of the disaster.

The movement to establish a hospital in the community had begun some years earlier when a special act of the state legislature authorized Mayor John Garside to appoint a commission to purchase the John Scott property on Main Street. While lack of funds made equipping the medical facility a slow process, upon completion it was turned over to the City of Cohoes, which leased it to the Cohoes Hospital Association, a body formed in 1891. Members of the first board of directors were Isaiah Fellows, John Horricks, W.J. Johnson, John Scott, Hugh Graham, and Paul Andrae.

The institution's initial staff consisted of three surgeons, four physicians, five assistant physicians, and a house doctor. Once opened, the hospital soon began to expand. A new wing was added to the south of the structure, then a similar wing to the north. A brick-and-frame annex to the west of the Scott house that contained a second operating room was followed by an updated operating facility to the northwest of the central core.

By the 1950s it became evident that more additions would not solve the problems faced by the staff: A new hospital was needed. Therefore, a 27-acre site on Columbia Street was purchased by the board of directors, and fund drives were conducted in 1952 and 1958. The cornerstone for the $2-million facility was laid in September 1959, and the dedication took place on November 20, 1960.

Further growth prompted a program of renovation and expansion of the new institution, which was completed in 1974. Another annex to the property was the Mary and Alice Ford Nursing Home, an eighty-bed skilled-nursing facility that opened in May 1975.

Cohoes Memorial Hospital conducted its own School of Nursing from 1903 to 1938 and graduated 148 nurses.

Almost as old as the hospital itself is its auxiliary. This was organized in 1905, after president Harry C. Fruchting of the Cohoes Hospital Association called on the women of the city's churches to form such a body. Today, with a membership of about 220, the auxiliary is a vital part of the hospital and nursing home operation, as are the volunteers who donate over 25,000 hours of service each year.

These volunteers work very closely with the auxiliary in raising funds for much-needed equipment. In 1982 they received the first annual Kiwanis Outstanding Service Award as a tribute for their service to the hospital, nursing home, and community.

Cohoes Memorial Hospital, opened in 1898, used a former residence as its core with wings added on the sides.

The cornerstone for the new $2-million Cohoes Memorial Hospital was laid in September 1959.

KESTNER ENGINEERS, P.C.

Kestner Engineers, P.C., was established as an individual business on January 1, 1955, by Joseph A. Kestner, Jr., a 1936 civil-engineering graduate of Rensselaer Polytechnic Institute, to provide municipal engineering services for communities in the New York and New England areas.

In its first year of operation, the firm was retained by the Town of Brunswick to provide engineering services for extensive public water supply and sanitary sewerage facilities in the Sycaway area bordering Troy, along North and South Lake Avenue; it has served the town continuously ever since. During the mid-1960s the founder represented Brunswick in its negotiations to acquire the extensive City of Troy water supply facilities within the town. The negotiations included purchase of the city-owned Brunswick and Vanderheyden reservoirs on North Lake Avenue. These sites have been improved to provide residents with a public bathing beach and picnic and boating areas.

The company was awarded a contract in 1965 by the City of Cohoes to design an intercepting sewer system to eliminate thirty public raw-sewage discharges into

Joseph A. Kestner, Jr., seated on the left, is the founder and president of Kestner Engineers, P.C. Also seated is Mark L. Kestner, vice-president. Standing, from left, are Quentin T. Kestner, vice-president, and Anthony M. Kestner, business manager.

the Mohawk and Hudson rivers. The completed system connects with the Albany County Sewer District, Wastewater Treatment Plant. The interceptors utilized the paths provided by the abandoned Champlain Barge Canal and the city's extensive mid-eighteenth century canals and tunnels into which raw-sewage discharges were constructed over a 100-year period.

In 1967 Kestner Engineers was retained by the Town of Glenville in Schenectady County to engineer a fifty-mile municipal water system;

it continues to provide the town with engineering services required for water supply, wastewater treatment, and solid-waste disposal. That year as well, the firm completed a preliminary report for wastewater facilities for the Town of Sand Lake in Rensselaer County. Construction for the project began in 1978 and will be completed in 1985.

Sanitary sewers to serve the Pleasantdale section of the Town of Schaghticoke in Rensselaer County are presently under design and will be constructed during 1985. Kestner Engineers have also designed numerous public water supply, water treatment, and wastewater treatment facilities for other communities in the New York and New England areas.

During the 1970s three of Kestner's sons joined the firm, which was subsequently incorporated. Mark L. Kestner and Quentin T. Kestner are Rensselaer Polytechnic Institute graduates, licensed professional engineers, and vice-presidents of the organization. Anthony M. Kestner, a construction-engineering graduate of Arizona State University, is the business manager.

Located at One Kestner Lane in the Town of Brunswick, the corporation's office was one of the first suburban professional office buildings constructed in the area. The office facilities were doubled in size in 1974 to accommodate the increased engineering staff.

The company currently has a full-time group of twenty employees. Engineering services are provided for municipal water supply and treatment, sanitary sewerage, wastewater treatment, and solid-waste disposal. Services are also provided for the television inspection of pipelines and automatic sewage-flow measurement and sampling.

Kestner Engineers used the mid-nineteenth century power canals in Cohoes to carry the sanitary intercepting sewer system it designed for the city in the 1960s.

MOHAWK PAPER MILLS, INC.

As one of America's leading producers of premium uncoated cover, text, and specialty printing papers, Mohawk Paper Mills, Inc., sets standards of quality by weaving human craftsmanship—from over 100 years of papermaking—with new technologies.

Its history began with the Mohawk and Hudson Paper Company, established in 1872 at a former ax-handle factory on the Kings Canal in Waterford. Frank Gilbert, one of the paper mill's founders, purchased and renamed the enterprise the Frank Gilbert Paper Company shortly thereafter.

Nathaniel Sylvester's 1878 *History of Saratoga County* describes the operation as employing forty people who produced three tons of printing paper a day—using rags, wood, and straw as raw materials. The mill building was purchased in 1881 from Uri Gilbert, a prominent manufacturer of railroad cars.

In 1917 the firm constructed a second paper mill in Cohoes, just south of the junction of the Erie and Champlain canals, which manufactured groundwood, bond, mimeo, and even wallpaper. In 1931 it became Mohawk Paper Mills, Inc., under the ownership of George O'Connor. After struggling through the Depression the company gained momentum during World War II. Mohawk, under the leadership of Thomas D. O'Connor, George's son, had continued to grow by constantly improving the quality of its papers and equipment. Recently, a new paper machine and Lenox High Speed Sheeters have been added. Extensive wastewater-treatment

facilities were installed in recent years, which comply with federal and state guidelines on pollution control.

Papermaking at Mohawk starts with chemically bleached pulp—from North American hard and soft woods—which is agitated with water and filler chemicals in huge tile vats, called hydropulpers. Cellulose fibers are separated, cut to length, and frayed by beater knives; sizing, aniline dyes for color, and other ingredients are added; and the resulting slurry mixture is refined and fed into one of Mohawk's three gigantic fourdrinier paper machines.

Samples of each roll of paper undergo a series of tests, to assure that Mohawk's high standards of quality are met. The finished paper is monitored electronically, inspected, rolled or cut into sheets, and packaged for shipment.

Through the years Mohawk papers have played a part in many Fortune 500 company annual reports, countless fine limited-edition books and prints, and even Presidential Christmas cards from the White House.

The company employs over 300 people and produces more than one hundred million pounds of first-rate printing papers annually, in twelve grades with smooth or textured finishes. With fifty color options, Mohawk Paper Mills, Inc., sells more than 1,000 different paper products through a national network of distributors to meet the needs of designers, printers, and other consumers across the country.

Mohawk Paper Mills, Inc., Waterford Division.

The original Cohoes mill of the Frank Gilbert Paper Company—now the location of Mohawk's corporate headquarters.

STERLING DRUG INC.

A post-World War I auction of enemy alien-owned property brought one of Rensselaer County's largest employers to the Gateway area.

Sterling Drug Inc. had its beginnings in 1901 in Wheeling, West Virginia, in a little two-man, one-product enterprise called The Neuralgyline Company—founded by W.E. Weiss and A.H. Diebold, friends from their youth. By 1918 their operation had expanded considerably, and had taken the name Sterling Products Incorporated. Emboldened by the firm's success, its management decided to offer a sum equal to the entire earnings over eighteen years for the alien-owned stock in The Bayer Company and the large plant in Rensselaer, which would go to the highest bidder. The final purchase price of more than five million dollars came close to the organization's top figure.

The plant manufactured—among other things—a then-little-known commodity called aspirin. A separate Sterling subsidiary, The Bayer Company, was formed to market the product; at the same time Winthrop Chemical Company (which later became Winthrop Laboratories) was organized for the manufacture of the

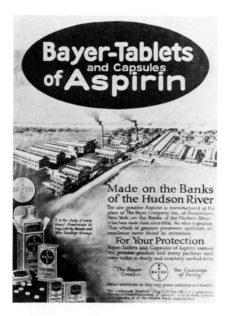

A Bayer aspirin advertisement which ran in the Sunday rotogravure section of The New York Times *on April 14, 1918.*

former firm's pharmaceuticals.

From then until World War II Sterling added many well-known products to its consumer line, including Phillips' Milk of Magnesia, Dr. Lyon's Tooth Powder, and Fletcher's Castoria. Its greatest contributions to the quality of American life were made in the

pharmaceutical developments at Winthrop. Among these were Luminal, the original phenobarbital; the first effective drugs in the treatment of syphilis; and Prontosil, the first of the sulfa drugs and the start of modern chemotherapy. Winthrop made other significant contributions in this era, notably in anesthesia. Through Novocain and Pontocaine the concept of spinal anesthesia was realized.

The corporation's research scientists developed Atabrine brand of chinacrin, which replaced quinine in the treatment of malaria. When World War II became a reality, scientists at Winthrop not only increased their efforts in the anti-malarial field but also sought domestic sources of materials to continue production of Atabrine should the Dutch East Indies, source of 90 percent of the world's quinine, fall into unfriendly hands. The firm had stockpiled about twenty million Atabrine tablets by the time of Pearl Harbor, and was producing more than a billion tablets annually when the Dutch East Indies fell to the Japanese in 1942. For this, and other accomplishments, Winthrop received the Army/Navy "E" Award four times during the war years.

In 1942 Sterling Products Incorporated became Sterling Drug Inc., and sixteen domestic subsidiaries were absorbed into the parent organization in the interest of greater operating efficiency.

Following World War II the company undertook a major program of plant construction and modernization, with a large part directed to expanded and overseas markets.

To coordinate the company's

The early manufacturing of Bayer aspirin tablets at the Rensselaer plant, circa 1920.

The Sterling-Winthrop Research Institute facility in Rensselaer.

Technicians at work in the "clean room" of the sterilization suite at the Product Development Center of the Sterling-Winthrop Research Institute.

research activities, the Sterling-Winthrop Research Institute was established in 1945, and in May 1950 its first building was completed and dedicated. Located on a 157-acre site in Rensselaer, the institute is Sterling's central research establishment. Opened with a staff of about 250 people, it today employs almost 900—more than half of whom are specialists with degrees in medicine, pharmacology, biology, chemistry, and other scientific disciplines.

Sterling has had many successes in the discovery and development of new products for the diagnosis, prevention, and treatment of disease. Among them were three breakthrough drugs discovered and developed at the institute: Talwin brand of pentazocine, which at its discovery was a totally new chemical compound for the relief of moderate to severe pain; Sulfamylon acetate cream, a lifesaving ointment used to reduce the risk of infection and mortality in severe burn cases; and Danocrine brand of danazol, a unique synthetic hormone initially approved for use in the treatment of the female disorder endometriosis. The institute also had responsibility for investigation of other important new compounds, including Marcaine long-lasting local anesthetic and, more recently, Amipaque brand of metrizamide for spinal radiography.

Other landmark contributions include NegGram brand of nalidixic acid, a urinary tract antibacterial, and Etrenol brand of hycanthone, an effective treatment for schistosomiasis (fresh-water snail fever) which afflicts millions in underdeveloped countries. Most recent drug discoveries in various stages of testing or approval include amrinone and milrinone for the treatment of patients with congestive heart failure, and Tornalate brand of bitolterol for the treatment of bronchial respiratory problems.

As a diversified pharmaceuticals company with worldwide operations, Sterling is involved in businesses that have as a common denominator the goal of improving the quality of life. In addition to the development, manufacturing, and marketing of prescription pharmaceuticals and proprietary medicines, the company makes and markets household and industrial cleaners and disinfectants, personal products, insecticides and rodenticides, and specialty chemicals and pigments. Winthrop-Breon Laboratories is Sterling's principal domestic pharmaceutical specialties marketing division, while major proprietary products are marketed by Glenbrook Laboratories. Those products include Phillips' Milk of Magnesia, Bayer aspirin, and Panadol, Cope, Midol Caplets, and Vanquish pain relievers. The Lehn & Fink Products Group markets such well-known products as Lysol brand disinfectants, Wet Ones moist towelettes, Minwax wood-finishing products, d-Con insecticides, and Ogilvie and Dorothy Gray personal care products.

Sterling's Gateway area manufacturing facilities include the Sterling Organics (U.S.) plant on Riverside Avenue in Rensselaer, which produces specialty chemicals and pharmaceutical intermediates for Sterling and for external customers, and a modern Pharmaceutical Group manufacturing plant in East Greenbush. At that plant, Sterling manufactures prescription and over-the-counter medicines in tablet form, including Panadol, Mejoral, and Cosprin analgesics and NegGram brand of nalidixic acid.

In total, the Sterling-Winthrop Research Institute, Sterling Organics, and the Pharmaceutical Group production plant employ approximately 1,500 persons in the Gateway area.

185

RYAN-BIGGS ASSOCIATES P.C.

The growth of industries in the Hudson-Mohawk area provides a central focus for the engineering practice of Ryan-Biggs Associates. The firm applies expert structural and civil engineering skills to a great diversity of projects, ranging from the analysis of important historic structures built during the Industrial Revolution to the design of buildings for the newest and most technologically advanced industries.

Ryan-Biggs Associates serves the engineering needs of industries, business and government, architects, developers and contractors, public-interest groups, and private individuals in the United States and around the world.

On April 1, 1973, J. Thomas Ryan founded the practice in the historic Rice Building in downtown Troy, and expanded there until 1978. That year David Biggs joined as a principal and the office was moved to the National State Bank building. David Seaman became a principal in 1979. The firm became Ryan-Biggs Associates P.C. in 1982.

Ryan-Biggs Associates P.C. was retained in 1978 to stabilize the historic Schoharie Creek Aqueduct, originally built in 1845. The firm earned numerous awards for the innovative repair techniques used, including a national award from the American Consulting Engineers Council.

The organization has grown steadily to a staff of twenty-six people in Troy, with an added office in Rutland, Vermont. It has demonstrated success in projects ranging from the design of a complex industrial facility, introducing state-of-the-art technologies, to small-scale technical investigations. Offering a variety of technical skills, Ryan-Biggs Associates maintains close coordination with clients' specialized needs to produce efficient, economically viable, and aesthetically sensitive designs.

Numerous awards underscore the corporation's reputation for excellence, including recognition from such professional organizations as the American Concrete Institute—Eastern New York Chapter, American Society of Civil Engineers, and the New York State Consulting Engineers Council.

In 1979 the firm received a National Award from the American

Consulting Engineers Council for its innovative approach to stabilizing the Schoharie Creek Aqueduct of the original Erie Canal. The 1841 aqueduct carried canal boats over the sometimes-turbulent creek, replacing a treacherous rope ferry. Its canal use ended about 1915 and several arches were demolished, with subsequent deterioration and erosion threatening to cause the remaining nine arches of the structure to collapse. The solution—implemented by the New York State Office of Parks, Recreation, and Historic Preservation—uses cables anchored to massive springs on shore that extend out to restrain the end of the aqueduct. This technique will allow the important transportation landmark to remain to help interpret the local canal heritage.

Another award-winning accomplishment has been the design of a Pepsi-Cola production and distribution plant with a complex materials-handling system. In both energy conservation and efficiencies of the flow of material, this installation is recognized as a major improvement on plant design; its features may be replicated throughout the country.

From gas-turbine plants designed for the Middle East and Japan to heat-recovery and noise-control systems for utilities in California and Alaska, Ryan-Biggs Associates P.C. maintains the Hudson-Mohawk area tradition of engineering innovation and excellence.

Inside the new 188,000-square-foot Pepsi Cola bottling facility in Latham. Ryan-Biggs Associates thoroughly researched a design that is recognized for engineering excellence.

PATRONS

The following individuals, companies, and organizations have made a valuable commitment to the quality of this publication. Windsor Publications and the Hudson-Mohawk Industrial Gateway gratefully acknowledge their participation in *The Hudson-Mohawk Gateway: An Illustrated History.*

Allied Automotive Bendix Friction Materials Division*
Blue Cross of Northeastern New York*
Clement Frame & Art Shop Inc.
Cohoes Memorial Hospital*
Cohoes Savings Bank*
deSeve Economics Associates, Inc.*
FACTRON/SCHLUMBERGER*
D.A. Fazioli & Son, Inc.*
Freihofer's*
Garden Way, Inc.*
Geier & Bluhm, Inc.*
General Electric
Silicone Products Division*
Greater Troy Chamber of Commerce*
Grimm Enterprises*
Wm. Hasslinger's Flowers
Hudson Valley Community College*
Garry Kearns Architect, P.C.*
Kestner Engineers, P.C.*
Leahy Funeral Home*
Lepera & Ward, P.C.*

Levonian Brothers, Inc.*
Manning Paper Company*
Marine Midland Bank, N.A.*
Mohawk Paper Mills, Inc.*
Mooradian's*
Norstar Bank of Upstate NY*
Norton Company/Coated Abrasive Division*
Pattison, Sampson, Ginsberg & Griffin, P.C.
Pioneer Savings Bank*
Rensselaer Polytechnic Institute*
Ross Valve Manufacturing Company, Inc.*
Russell Sage College*
Ryan-Biggs Associates P.C.*
Pamela Sawchuk Associates
Standard Manufacturing Co., Inc.*
Sterling Drug Inc.*
Teledyne Gurley*
John L. Thompson, Sons & Company*
The Times Record*
Troy Public Library
Troy Savings Bank*
Union National Bank*

*Partners in Progress of *The Hudson-Mohawk Gateway: An Illustrated History.* The histories of these companies and organizations appear in Chapter 11, beginning on page 145.

Smith's Restaurant in Cohoes continues its long and colorful history of providing good food and drink to area residents. The fifty-foot Victorian bar, purportedly from Tammany Hall in New York City, was purchased by owner "Big Mike" Smith in the 1930s. Photo by Robert Thayer

BIBLIOGRAPHY

The most important works used in the preparation of this book are cited here. Other sources include city directories, newspaper clippings, newspapers, maps and atlases, company documents, historic research papers done by the principal author's students, the files of the Rensselaer County Historical Society, and the files of the Hudson-Mohawk Industrial Gateway. Much of this material is available to the public in the municipal and college libraries of the area and in the archives of the organizations mentioned.

Adams, Samuel Hopkins, *Sunrise to Sunset*. New York: Random House, 1950.

Anderson, George Baker, *Landmarks of Rensselaer County, New York*. Syracuse: D. Mason & Co., 1897.

Broderick, Frances D., *The Burial Grounds of Lansingburgh, Rensselaer County, New York*. Published by the author, 1965.

Cohoes Centennial Committee, *Cohoes Centennial, 1870-1970*. Cohoes, 1970.

Crowl, John R. and Youngs, Kathryn A., *Harmony Mills Historic District*. Troy: The Hudson-Mohawk Industrial Gateway, 1978.

Fisher, Charles, *Social Organization and Change During the Early Horticultural Period in the Hudson River Valley*. Unpublished type script, 1982.

French, J.H., *Historical and Statistical Gazeteer of New York State*. Syracuse: R.P. Smith, 1860.

Funk, Robert E., *Recent Contributions to Hudson Valley Prehistory*. Albany: Memoir 22, New York State Museum.

Goddard, Abba A., ed. *The Trojan Sketch Book*. Troy: Young & Hart, 1846.

Hammersley, Sydney Ernest, *The History of Waterford, New York*. Published privately by the author, 1957.

Hayner, Rutherford, *Troy and Rensselaer County, New York*. 3 vols. New York & Chicago: Lewis Historical Publishing Co., Inc., 1925.

Holmes, Oliver W. and Rohrbach, Peter T., *Stagecoach East*. Washington, D.C.: Smithsonian Institution Press, 1983.

Hutchinson, Samuel, et al., *Green Island Heritage and the Bicentennial*. Green Island, 1976.

Kacharian, John C., *Watervliet Arsenal Yesterday, Today*. Watervliet: Watervliet Arsenal, 1984.

Kalm, Peter, *The America of 1750: Travels in North America*. 2 vols. New York: Dover Publications, 1966.

Lansingburgh Historical Society, The, *Lansingburgh, New York, 1771-1971*.

Souvenir Program, Troy, 1971.

Lord, Jane S., ed., *Lansingburgh, New York 1771-1971*. Troy: The Lansingburgh Historical Society, 1971.

Marcou, O'Leary and Associates, Inc. and Rensselaer Polytechnic Institute, *Historic Cohoes, New York, A Survey of Historic Resources*. Cohoes, 1971.

Masten, Arthur H., *The History of Cohoes, New York*. Albany: Joel Munsell, 1877.

McHugh, Jeanne, *Alexander Holley and the Makers of Steel*. Baltimore: The Johns Hopkins University Press, 1980.

Moore, H. Irving, *A Pictorial Reminiscence and Brief History of Lansingburgh, Rensselaer County, N.Y., Founded in 1770*. Published by the author, 1957.

Myer, James T., *History of the City of Watervliet, N.Y., 1630 to 1910*. Troy, 1910.

Parker, Amasor J., *Landmarks of Albany County, N.Y.* Syracuse: D. Mason and Co., 1897.

Parker, Joseph A., *Looking Back, A History of Troy and Rensselaer County 1925-1980*. Troy, 1982.

Pearson, Jonathan, *Early Records of the City and County of Albany and Colony of Rensselaerwyck*. Albany: The University of the State of New York, 1916.

_____. *Early Records of the City and County of Albany and Colony of Rensselaerwyck*. Albany: The University of the State of New York, 1918.

_____. *Early Records of the City and County of Albany and Colony of Rensselaerwyck*. Albany: The University of the State of New York, 1919.

_____. *Contributions for the Genealogies of the First Settlers of The Ancient County of Albany, 1630-1800*. Baltimore: Genealogical Publishing Co., Inc., 1976.

Proudfit, Margaret Burden, *Henry Burden, His Life and a History of His Inventions Compiled From the Public Press*. Troy: Pafraets Press, 1904.

Rezneck, Samuel, *Education for a Technological Society*. Troy: Rensselaer Polytechnic Institute, 1968.

_____. *Profiles Out of the Past of Troy, New York, Since 1789*. Troy: Chamber of Commerce, 1970.

Ritchie, William A., *The Archaeology of New York State*. Garden City, N.J.: The Natural History Press, 1969.

_____. *An Introduction to Hudson Valley Pre-History*. Albany: Bulletin No. 367, New York State Museum and Science Service, 1958.

Robertson, Constance, *The Unterrified*. New York: Henry Holt & Co., 1946.

Ross, James A., *A Martyr of Today, The Life of Robert Ross*. Boston: James H. Earle, 1894.

Sarnoff, Paul, *Russell Sage, The Money King*. New York: Ivan Obolensky, Inc., 1965.

Sylvester, Nathaniel Bartlett, *History of Rensselaer Co., New York*. Philadelphia: Everts & Peek, 1880.

Teachers of Troy Public Schools, *Our Community, Troy and Rensselaer County*. Troy: Troy School District, 1943.

Turbin, Carole, *Womans' Work and Womans' Rights: A Comparative Study of the Womans' Trade Union Movement and the Woman Suffrage Movement in the Mid-Nineteenth Century*. Ph.D. diss., New School for Social Research, 1978.

United States Bicentennial Commission of Cohoes, Inc., *Cohoes In '76*. Cohoes, 1976.

Vogel, Robert M., ed., *A Report of the Mohawk-Hudson Survey*. Washington, D.C.: Smithsonian Institution Press, 1973.

Waite, Diana S., *The Troy Light Company Gas Holder House*. Troy: Hudson-Mohawk Industrial Gateway, 1977.

Waite, Diana S. and John G., *Industrial Archaeology in Troy, Waterford, Cohoes, Green Island and Watervliet*. Troy: The Hudson-Mohawk Industrial Gateway, 1973, revised 1984.

Walkowitz, Daniel J., *Worker City, Company Town*. Urbana: University of Illinois Press, 1978.

Waterford Historical Museum and Cultural Center, Inc., The, *The Waterford Flight*. Waterford, 1965.

_____. *The White Homestead on Wheels*. Waterford, 1976.

Watervliet Arsenal, *Quarters One, A Place in History*. Watervliet, 1978.

_____. *A History of Watervliet Arsenal 1813-1968*. Watervliet, 1968, updated to 1982.

Weise, Arthur James, *History of the City of Troy*. Troy: William H. Young, 1876.

_____. *Troy's One Hundred Years*. Troy: Willam H. Young, 1891.

_____. *City of Troy and its Vicinity*. Troy: Edward Green, 1886.

_____. *The Firemen and Fire Departmens of Troy, N.Y.*. Albany: Weed-Parsons Printing Co., 1895.

Wertheimer, Barbara Mayer, *We Were There*. New York: Pantheon Books, 1977.

Woodworth, John, *Reminiscences of Troy: From Its Settlement In 1790 to 1807*. Albany: Munsell, 1860.

INDEX

189

HUDSON RIVER